Sainthood

Sainthood

Its Manifestations in World Religions

Edited by
Richard Kieckhefer
and
George D. Bond

UNIVERSITY OF CALIFORNIA PRESS
Berkeley • Los Angeles • London

University of California Press
Berkeley and Los Angeles, California

University of California Press, Ltd.
London, England

Library of Congress Cataloging in Publication Data

Sainthood: its manifestation in world religions / (compiled by)
Richard Kieckhefer and George D. Bond.
p. cm.
Includes index.
Contents: Imitators of Christ / Richard Kieckhefer -- Sainthood on the periphery / Robert L. Cohn -- Prophet and wali / Frederick M. Denny -- Indian developments / Charles S.J. White -- The arahant / George D. Bond -- The bodhisattva / Donald S. Lopez, Jr. -- The sage as saint / Rodney L. Taylor -- Afterword: toward a comparative study of sainthood.
ISBN 0-520-05154-8 (alk. paper)
1. Saints -- Comparative studies. I. Kieckhefer, Richard.
I. Bond, George Doherty, 1942-
BL488.S32 1988
291.6'1--dc19
88-6963
CIP

Printed in the United States of America

1 2 3 4 5 6 7 8 9

Contents

Preface

The notion of sainthood is problematic in two ways. First, for the scholar of religion there is the question whether the category of sainthood is useful outside of those Christian churches that have given specific content to this term. If one speaks of Muslim saints, Hindu saints, Buddhist saints, and so forth, is one stretching a Christian concept beyond its acceptable limits and risking the hazard of viewing these other traditions through Christian lenses? Even if meaning can be found for the term "saint" in all the world religions, is it essentially the *same* meaning, or can one retain the term only by using it in widely equivocal senses? Would it be better to retreat to a less specific, more generic term such as "holy person"? Historians and phenomenologists of religion have regarded sainthood as a category applicable to religions generally. Joachim Wach, in *Sociology of Religion*[1] viewed the saint as one of a number of "types of religious authority" who lead religious groups or around whom groups form; he treats types such as the founder, reformer, prophet, and magician. The particular kind of authority that the saint possesses is, roughly speaking, "inferior" to that of the founder and prophet because his or her impact on society is less. Conversely, like them but unlike the priest, the saint has charisma which depends on his or her person rather than on his or her office.

G. van der Leeuw, in *Religion in Essence and Manifestation: A Study in Phenomenology,*[2] treats the saint as one type of "The Sacred Man," a major division of "The Subject of Religion." In this division he analyzes the various modes in which power is manifested in human figures. Unlike such types as the king, medicine man, priest, and preacher, the saint is not classified as a "representative." For whereas the former represent power to the community and serve as official channels for its distribution, the saint is less a channel for power than a source of power. The saint is a figure whose very being exudes power. His or her potency is often manifested in miracles associated with his or her body or grave; the person of the saint is a relic. Indeed, "in the first place, a saint is either a corpse, or a part of one. The world has no use for living saints: they are dead persons, or still better: the potency of the dead."[3] The saint, for van der Leeuw, is thus preeminently an object of veneration or worship.

It is precisely this latter point that gives rise to the second problem of the notion of sainthood. For adherents of the various religious traditions a problem arises whenever notions such as sainthood appear: the tension between the saint's imitability and his or her utter distinctness from normal humanity. On the one hand, veneration of the saint tends to elevate him or her to a higher level of existence, to which most mortals cannot aspire. The saint performs miracles, receives visions, and generally has privileged contact with the supernatural order, by virtue of which he or she can serve as intermediary and intercessor. The imitation and the otherness stand in a certain tension: the more the saint's distinctive powers dominate and the more it seems that the saintly virtues themselves are rooted in or supported by a distinctive calling, the harder it becomes to take the saint as a model for imitation.

It was reflection on such problems that led to the formation of this book. The problems are fundamental, and discussion of them requires broad examination of sainthood in each of the traditions covered. Thus we have here not a series of articles on individual saints or specific aspects of sainthood but reasonably comprehensive essays on the phenomenon in each religion. While intending that these essays would be useful to students, we have sought to go beyond a mere textbook by ensuring that each essay would have an interpretative thrust that would be of interest to the specialist as well as the beginner.

What we have all found in our interaction with one another is that consideration of the second problem sketched earlier helps in solving the first. If there are individuals in each tradition who come to be both imitated and venerated, these individuals may by definition be regarded as the saints of each tradition. It is in this functional sense that the term is employed here. Perhaps it is necessary to add that only *religious* imitability and otherness qualify the saint as a saint; a folk hero such as Paul Bunyan or a political hero such as George Washington may share a similar tension, and it might be useful for the sake of comparison to include such figures in this compilation, but the bounds must be drawn somewhere, and it seems expedient to limit our attention to explicitly religious material.

The first two chapters deal with traditions that are closely linked historically but that take almost diametrically opposed positions on sainthood: although the concept is nowhere more significant and more fully developed than in Christianity, it is nowhere more problematic than in Judaism. Richard Kieckhefer's essay on Christian sainthood endeavors to take advantage of the fully articulated Christian notion of sanctity by providing a systematic overview of the topic first in its historical manifestation, then from a phenomenological perspective, and finally from the viewpoint of theology. In his historical overview Kieckhefer traces the notion of sainthood from the earliest veneration of the martyrs onward, through the many centuries in which the monasteries set the model for both Orthodox and Catholic sanctity, and into the era of the Reformation and Counter-Reformation, when the very concept of sainthood met challenge and refinement. Along the way Kieckhefer considers variations on the theme that were important in specific historical contexts: the holy bishop, the saintly monarch, the founder of a religious order, and so forth. The phenomenological section of the essay deals with the saints' imitable behavior (their asceticism, contemplation, and active service) and the inimitable gifts bestowed on them by God (their miracles and visions). Finally, the essay turns to some literary questions and to the theology of sainthood and its place in Christianity. The advantage of placing this material at the front of this compilation is that a fully and explicitly articulated concept of sainthood such as one finds in Christianity can be helpful as a starting point for exploring the possibilities inherent in sainthood generally. The danger to be guarded against is that Christian saintliness might furnish a Procrustean bed onto which the saints of other traditions may then be fitted.

Robert L. Cohn addresses forthrightly the first major question of this volume by showing why the very notion of sainthood is problematic for Judaism. For various reasons—basically a tendency to focus on the Jewish people as a whole rather than as individuals—official Judaism has discouraged the formation of anything resembling a cult of saints. Nonetheless parallel phenomena have arisen in Jewish history. Biblical figures and martyrs have been objects of such devotion, and tales of the early rabbis have encouraged their veneration long after their demise. Most important, various mystical movements have centered on saintly figures, of whom Shabbatai Zevi and the Baal Shem Tov are among the most notable. Ultimately, however, these holy individuals are far less significant for Judaism than the religious ideals that they embody: the ideal of scholarship incorporated in the *talmud ḥakham* (pupil of a sage), the notion of proper conduct exemplified by the *tsaddiq* (righteous person), and the goal of fervent prayer, discipline, or rapture suggested by the *ḥasid* (devout person). These ideals are in principle accessible to all. Just as the biblical heroes combine a shared humanity with a special divine calling, however, so too are there elements of inimitability in these ideas. Anyone may aspire to righteousness, but in certain mystical conceptions the *tsaddiq* is an exceptional individual called forth as one of the select few "foundations of the world." Anyone may become a follower of a *ḥasid* and share in the master's devotion, but the fullness of enthusiasm is expected only of the central figure. Thus although sainthood remains peripheral to Judaism, this tradition nonetheless presents instructive examples of the tension between imitability and otherness.

For Islam, as Frederick M. Denny shows, the problem appears in a different guise. The most clearly inimitable figures are the prophets, especially Muhammad; even their miracles are of a different kind from those of the saints. Saints do arise as a category distinct from that of prophets—*walīs,* a term designating the active relationship of friendship or patronage rather than any static quality. One central question for the student of Islam is why this latter class of figures should have arisen at all. Denny suggests that Muhammad, as the central prophetic figure for all of Islam, was an individual with general significance but that in addition to him the "little tradition" of Islam required local figures whose tombs could lend sacral value to specific places, and this is the function the saints performed. Focusing more on the cult of the saints (especially in Egypt) than on their legends or virtues, Denny nonetheless analyzes various roles or titles claimed by the saints, some of which they, like other Muslims, can earn for themselves (e.g., martyrdom, submission, devotion), whereas others must be bestowed by God (sinlessness, office of spiritual guide).

Charles White presents a diachronic view of sainthood in India in his chapter on the Hindu saint. Beginning with the protohistorical period and following through to the modern period, White traces the development and evolution of the notion of the saint as holy person in the Hindu tradition. Hinduism developed, White observes, not entirely but significantly in response to crises such as the rise of Buddhism and Jainism, the Muslim invasion, and colonialism. Saints arose in response to these crises and enabled Hinduism to adapt and to counteract the threats to its existence. This crisis reference role, however, was by no means the only one for the Hindu saint, and White provides a detailed survey of saintly figures from the earliest Ṛṣis to the modern Brahma-Kumaris, the maidens of Brahma.

In chapter 5 George Bond investigates the concept of the *arahant* in the Theravāda Buddhist texts. He asks whether the arahant, whom many Western writers have regarded as the equivalent of a saint, can justifiably be so regarded. Bond shows that the arahant serves as a paradigm for both imitation and veneration. To comprehend fully the arahant and the Theravāda notion of sainthood, however, one must see him in the context of the Theravāda worldview, symbolized by means of "linked foci" such as *saṃsara/nibbana,* mundane world/supramundane world, and ordinary person/arahant. The arahant represents what the ordinary person can become through the transformation effected by wisdom and perfection.

In the following chapter Donald Lopez traces the development of the second great saintly ideal in the Buddhist tradition, the Bodhisattva of the Mahāyāna. Exalted over the arahant, the Bodhisattva idea was developed by the Mahāyāna as a superior path to sanctification and individual perfection. Lopez examines the conception of the Bodhisattva in the Indian Mahāyāna writings, showing that this new form of Buddhist sainthood was distinguished by the emphasis on compassion and taking upon oneself the responsibility for liberating all beings. This chapter examines the Bodhisattva's path to Buddhahood with its many stages and levels or grounds. The Bodhisattvas pursue this path over countless lifetimes increasing their wisdom and perfecting their virtue. Lopez treats the stages of the path in detail and shows how the Bodhisattva's sanctification compares with the Western, and especially Christian, notion of sainthood.

To conclude the volume, Rodney Taylor examines the conception of the sage in the Confucian tradition and its compatibility with notions of sainthood. A dominant figure in the Chinese tradition, the sage appeared differently in different strata of the tradition. Confucius regarded only the ancient, ideal kings as sages, whereas the Neo-Confucians held sagehood up as a goal to be achieved by all. As Taylor describes the Confucian view, the Chinese sage shares many qualities in common with the Indian and Buddhist saints, thus representing what we might call the Oriental side of the consensus regarding saints and sainthood.

In a recent study of saints' cults Stephen Wilson has noted that "many features of the Christian cults of saints have analogies in other religious cultures." The central importance of martyrdom, burial sites, images, pilgrimage—these and other features can be found in the veneration of saints in many parts of the world. Wilson suggests that there would be value in a systematic comparison of the cults of saints, with full attention to the differences as well as the structural similarities from one culture to another.[4] What we have undertaken in this book is in a sense preliminary to the task that Wilson proposes. Rather than examining the ways in which people have venerated saints and sought to benefit from the power of these holy figures, we have looked at the ways in which different cultures have conceived sainthood itself. A systematic examination of saints' cults remains, then, an important further task to be undertaken.

NOTES

1. Joachim Wach, *Sociology of Religion* (Chicago: University of Chicago Press, 1944).
2. G. van der Leeuw, *Religion in Essence and Manifestation: A Study in Phenomenology* (New York: Harper & Row, 1963).
3. Ibid., p. 238.
4. Stephen Wilson, *Saints and Their Cults: Studies in Religious Sociology, Folklore and History* (Cambridge: Cambridge University Press, 1983), p. 41.

1
Imitators of Christ: Sainthood in the Christian Tradition

Richard Kieckhefer

Over the centuries Christianity has placed special emphasis on the role of the individual. To be sure, other religious traditions emphasize the importance of personal development in diverse ways and varying degrees. And Christianity does not typically neglect the communal element in religion: all of its major branches stress the importance of the Church as the natural context for religious life. But in numerous ways it is Christianity in particular that underscores the significance of individuals: through the unique role ascribed to its founder; by its doctrine of the soul, which attains salvation precisely as an individual, enjoying personal survival after death and standing alone before God at the particular judgment; and in the perennial fascination that Christians have with their spiritual and ecclesiastical leaders. The cult of the individual, commonly associated with the Renaissance, has deep roots in the Christian notion of personality. The West is often seen as placing strong and even exaggerated emphasis on the freedom, potential, and responsibility of the individual; as Michael Novak has pointed out, it is a distinctively Western conceit that within every woman there lurks a "real you" which can be brought to the fore only by the use of a particular hair rinse.[1] This outlook, in both its noble and questionable forms, ultimately owes much to Christian tradition.

Not surprisingly, then, Christians have long delighted in the lives and veneration of exceptionally holy individuals, or saints, and have exalted them to a position of great honor. Or rather, we should say that a great many Christians have done so—for the role of saints in Christian faith and cult is the subject of long-standing controversy. Whereas they hold an honored position in Orthodoxy, Roman Catholicism, and (with qualifications) Anglicanism, many Protestant denominations have held them in suspicion or disdain. Yet the notion of sainthood is far too deeply rooted in Christian culture to be wholly detached from it, and an understanding of what Christianity has meant and now means must take the saints into account.

The total number of saints in Christendom depends on how rigorously one defines the term; one standard reference, Butler's *The Lives of the Saints,* lists well over three thousand saints and *beati* without pretending to be nearly exhaustive. The number and diversity are great enough that any effort to survey the field will end in frustration. A brief essay cannot hope to catalogue all the varieties of saint, sketch all the virtues they are said to have mastered, or recount all the ways they functioned within their societies. Suffice to consider this multiform assembly from four perspectives: historical, phenomenological, literary, and theological. The following discussion will sketch at least a few of the things one might say about saints from each of these viewpoints.[2]

SAINTHOOD IN CHRISTIAN HISTORY

The history of Christian sainthood revolves around four main themes: (1) the development of ways to honor the saints; (2) the increasing control of their cult by the institutional Church; (3) recurrent opposition to their veneration; and (4) a theological and historical response to that opposition. Other themes might be proposed, but these four are central for understanding the history of sainthood.[3]

Even the use of the term "saint" as a token of special honor was a historical development that came about gradually. The word "saint" (Greek *hagios,* Latin *sanctus*) originally meant simply "holy person" and was used by Greek and Roman pagans for various classes of person: emperors, gods, deceased relatives, and so forth. When Christians adopted the term, they first used it in the plural, in referring collectively to the faithful on earth, those in heaven, the martyrs specifically, or the monks and clergy. When Paul addressed a letter to "the saints" at Philippi, he meant simply the Christian community there. The term later came to be used commonly in the singular but still with a broad variety of meanings: it could apply to a bishop, priest, abbess, virgin, emperor, martyr, or some other person, living or dead, worthy of honor and veneration. Eventually the Church developed technical meanings for the word, of which three are still current. First, in the broadest sense, a saint is a person who is leading or has led a life of heroic virtue. Second, a saint is a person who has gone to heaven, whether that fact is recognized or not; the Feast of All Saints is celebrated in honor of all members of this class. Third, in the narrowest sense, a saint is a person who, by virtue of the Church's judgment that he or she is in heaven (i.e., by reason of canonization), is the legitimate object of public cult. The first of these definitions is essentially moral, the second theological, and the third liturgical. The first two notions of sainthood have created no real difficulty, but the third has given rise to centuries of controversy. The history of sainthood in Christianity is largely a story of this debate: on the one hand, there has been clerical zeal to satisfy popular demand for objects of veneration; on the other, there has been resistance and harsh criticism directed against the cult of saints.

Veneration of exceptionally holy individuals arose during the Patristic Era (roughly A.D. 200–500). The earliest known case of such veneration comes from the middle of the second century, when St. Polycarp was martyred at Smyrna and his fellow Christians cherished his bones as "more precious to us than jewels, and finer than pure gold."[4] Every year on the anniversary of his martyrdom, the Christians at Smyrna gathered around his relics and paid him honor, at the same time fortifying themselves in the event of their own martyrdom. All the essential elements of the saints are either mentioned or suggested here: the treasuring of relics (usually the saint's bones), the commemoration of the feast day (typically the day of death, and thus of entry into heaven), and the eulogy that eventually served as the basis for a written biography.

Martyrs were the first persons set apart as distinctively holy, or as "saints" in a special sense, but in the course of time others enjoyed this honor: "confessors" who had suffered but not died for the faith, monks, holy bishops, and so forth. In particular during the fourth century, when Christianity became tolerated and then established as the official religion of the Roman Empire, and when martyrdom became virtually a thing of the past, the notion of sainthood was naturally expanded. While the fascination with martyrdom lingered, monks began to conceive themselves as "successors to the martyrs"; they did not give up their lives for Christ, but they did renounce the secular life of comfort. Monks thus became the new spiritual elite, and conceptions of holiness were molded largely in the monasteries.

At first there was no official canonization of saints. There was little question about the sanctity of a martyr; the Christian community could easily attest that a particular person had remained faithful to Christianity and undertaken a heroic death. Thus there was no need for an official inquiry and declaration. Even when the persecutions ceased, it remained customary for the populace to acclaim a person a saint—the voice of the people being taken for that of God. Only late in the Patristic Era did bishops (particularly in North Africa) begin to exercise systematic control over the cult of saints in an effort to prevent veneration of heretics or charlatans.

Whether regulated or not, veneration of saints provoked severe protest from certain influential men. In the fourth century Jerome had to take up literary cudgels against these critics, whose arguments assumed two main forms. First, they charged that the veneration accorded the saints smacked of idolatry both in form and in substance: in form because the kinds of ceremonies used for the saints were indistinguishable from those in pagan ritual; and in substance because the attention given to saints distracted from that due to God and transformed Christianity into a clumsily veiled polytheism. Jerome's response here was fundamentally an appeal to intention: those Christians who venerated saints did so with the salutary purpose of obtaining their support before God's throne, and they did not mean to blur the distinction between God and creatures. Second, the critics repudiated the underlying notion that one Christian could rise higher than another, particularly through ascetic practices. Harking back to Pauline motifs, and anticipating Luther's theory of justification, one of these critics maintained that any Christian who remained faithful to baptism would be immune from conquest by the devil, and all such persons—whether virginal, married, or widowed—would enjoy an equal reward in heaven. Jerome defended the exalted position of ascetics with a barrage of scriptural allusions and thereby upheld the viewpoint that dominated Christian spirituality for centuries to come.

Throughout the Middle Ages (about A.D. 500–1500) both the cult and the legends of saints grew increasingly elaborate. Miracles and wondrous stories of all kinds were ascribed to popular religious heroes. Extensive collections of saints' legends were compiled as a popular form of literature—ranging from the essentially regional collections of Gregory I and Gregory of Tours in the sixth century down to the classic encyclopedia of saints, the *Golden Legend,* assembled by Jacob of Voragaine in the thirteenth. Pilgrimages to the shrines of saints grew in significance from century to century, leading in the eleventh and following centuries to the rise of great shrines that attracted pilgrims from all over Europe. Canterbury and Santiago da Compostella were particularly renowned as the burial places of St. Thomas Becket and St. James, respectively. Systematic records were kept of miracles performed through the efficacy of the enshrined relics. For example, the following incident was noted at Canterbury:

> A woman with head pains and deafness went to Becket's shrine. As she stood in prayer, she felt a more than usual surge of pain, and within her head it seemed as if many twigs were being snapped into tiny bits. While she was thus afflicted, she called out to God, and He heard her. In the midst of her screaming, as if an interior infection had burst, a great deal of pus flowed from her ears, after which blood came out, and, after the blood, her hearing returned.[5]

Not all the miracles were quite so dramatic, but the sacred precincts of saints' shrines were places in which wondrous events of all sorts, curses as well as cures, might be expected. So potent were the relics of saints that a widespread demand for them arose; the relic trade became a lucrative commercial enterprise, complete with thefts, counterfeits, and potentially embarrassing duplications. (Two churches claimed the body of St. Luke, and at least ten displayed the head of John the Baptist.) The diversity of relics is typified by the collection held at Reading Abbey in the twelfth century; the abbey possessed 242 items altogether, including bones of Sts. Aethelmod and Branwalator; a rib and another bone from St. David; "some of St. Petroc, and some of the cloth in which his body was wound"; a fragment of the tomb of St. Edward the Confessor; bits of the Blessed Virgin's hair, her bed, and her belts; the hand of St. James; the head of St. Philip; and the head, jawbone, vestments, one rib, and some hair from St. Brigid. In theory the smallest fragment held as much power as an entire body. Possession of important relics could lend prestige to a church or monastery and could attract pilgrims, who brought donations. But although the cult had obvious political and economic aspects, it nonetheless remained an expression of sincere faith in the power of saints: the faithful on earth shared a conviction that those in heaven would intercede on behalf of supplicants who paid reverence to their earthly remains.

It was during the Middle Ages that canonization became centralized. During that period episcopal control became routine; at times the declaration of sainthood would be left to regional synods, so that the saint would be more readily recognized through a wider area than the diocese from which he or she came. The best way to secure a widespread cult, though, was to have the saint canonized by the pope; and beginning in the late tenth century it became common to solicit papal canonization. By the late twelfth century the pope was beginning to claim sole authority in these matters, as in many others. In the later Middle Ages it became increasingly common to distinguish between beatification and canonization. Having been beatified, a person would be referred to as "blessed" and could be venerated publicly only in certain locations; canonizations, which constituted the Church's final and authoritative declaration that the person was in heaven, was required for universal cult. Each stage would be preceded by detailed investigation and proof of miracles, which would serve as evidence that the candidate enjoyed a popular following and was exerting beneficial influence on people's faith. To this extent the voice of the people remained that of God.

During the Middle Ages opposition in principle to the cult of saints was by and large restricted to the heretics, such as the Waldensians and Lollards, who rejected the practice as an unwholesome excrescence on Christian piety mainly because it was nonbiblical. (Despite their principles, Lollards were known to salvage the ashes of their martyred coreligionists and preserve them as relics.) Much more widespread was doubt or skepticism about the authenticity of specific relics and legends. In the twelfth century Guibert of Nogent deplored the uncritical reverence that was widely given to patently false relics. Three centuries later Bernardino of Siena insisted that not all the cows of Lombardy could produce as much milk as was attributed to the Blessed Virgin. And the frequent assertions of saints' biographers that they obtained their information from trustworthy eyewitnesses suggests that they anticipated disbelief. Defenders of medieval practice responded to such skepticism in various ways; they might allude to the self-authenticating power of those relics that could work miracles, or they might argue that the faith of the believer was more important than the genuineness of the relic or the legend.

The most devastating attack on the entire cult of saints came in the sixteenth century with the Protestant Reformation. Martin Luther was reared in the heyday of extravagant veneration of saints, and in early life he participated enthusiastically. But he quickly lost faith in the saints' power to win grace for their devotees, and he applied his critical pen to the debunking of their cult. In 1520 he wrote an anonymous pamphlet parodying a relic collection of the archbishop of Mainz; he listed as items in this collection "a fine piece of the left horn of Moses, three flames from the bush of Moses on Mount Sinai, two feathers and an egg from the Holy Ghost, an entire corner of the banner with which Christ rose from Hell," and so forth. The pamphlet reads like a heavy-handed parody until one turns to the archbishop's own official catalogue and finds listed there such treasures as a clod of earth from the place where Christ gave the Lord's Prayer, a small piece of a cloak that Mary made for Jesus (and which had the marvelous power to grow as he did), two vats from Cana, one of Judas's silver pieces, and remains of manna from the desert.

In more serious moments Luther had four main objections to veneration of saints. First, like Jerome's adversaries in the fourth century, he insisted that the cult of saints was idolatrous and pagan in its origins and form. Second, in keeping with his own insistence that Christ acts directly upon the individual soul, he argued that saints cannot serve as mediators or intercessors any more than can priests or the Church in general. Third, in accordance with his teaching that grace is a wholly gratuitous gift, given all at once and without degrees, he concluded that saints have no more grace and dignity than any other Christian and that their virtuous works bring them no special merit. Finally, he protested that the stories of saints' lives as they had been passed down had been contaminated in wholesale fashion by legendary accretions. Yet despite these criticisms, it is important to bear in mind that Luther did not reject the idea of sainthood per se; indeed, he insisted that lives of the saints have an essential place in Christian spirituality:

> Next to Holy Scripture there certainly is no more useful book for Christians than that of the lives of the saints, especially when unadulterated and authentic. For in these stories, one is greatly pleased to find how they sincerely believed in God's Word, confessed it with their lips, praised it by their living, and honored and confirmed it by their suffering and dying. All this immeasurably comforts and strengthens those weak in the faith and increases the courage and confidence of those already strong far more than the teachings of Scripture alone, without any examples and stories of the saints. Although the Spirit performs His work abundantly within, it nonetheless helps very much to see or to hear the example of others without. Otherwise a weak heart always thinks: See, you are the only one who so believes and confesses, acts, and suffers.[6]

Still, the basic tendency within Lutheranism—and Protestantism generally—was to react against late medieval piety and downplay the role of saints in spiritual life.

Did the Protestant churches set forth their own saints, or the equivalent? The answer to that question depends largely on which definition one is using. Clearly there have been Protestant figures who were admired for their exceptional and even heroic virtue. The Reformers themselves hold an eminent position in the churches they founded and fostered, as do countless Protestant missionaries. In an extended sense one can perhaps speak of a "cult" and a hagiographic tradition for such figures as George Fox and John Wesley. The closest Protestant parallel to traditional sainthood, however, is the veneration of martyrs. In this respect Protestantism returned to the usage of the early Church. When two of Luther's fellow Protestants were executed in 1523 for their adherence to his Reformation, he unhesitatingly proclaimed them martyrs, and he composed a hymn in their honor that might be sung during religious services. In 1554 Jean Crespin published his *Book of Martyrs* in the French language in Calvin's town of Geneva. The town council, faithful to Protestant squeamishness on such matters, approved the book but insisted that the terms "saint" and "martyr" be expunged from it. The title of the first published edition was thus *A Collection of Many Persons Who Endured Death Steadfastly for the Name of Our Lord Jesus Christ.* When Crespin published the second edition he reverted to the shorter title; however, he took pains to explain that he was not trying to promote the cult of relics, the dissemination of fables, and other Catholic abuses but was merely seeking homage to God and consolation and instruction for the faithful. Included in his work were not only rank-and-file Protestant victims but political leaders such as William of Orange. Better known in the English-speaking world is John Foxe, who published the first English martyrology in 1563. Not only were the Protestant martyrs not accepted as such by Catholic authorities (the theologian Suarez dubbed the Anglican candidates "not true martyrs but miscreants who deserved their punishment"); even Protestants disputed among themselves whether a figure such as Michael Servetus, executed by Calvinists for his peculiar brand of heresy, qualified as martyrs.[7]

In Catholicism, however, devotion to saints remained firm throughout the Counter-Reformation and beyond. The subject received detailed attention in the documents of the Council of Trent. Essentially the standard Catholic rebuttal to the Protestant challenge included the following considerations: that the apparatus of the cult of saints is not idolatrous but rather a way of focusing attention on what the saints have accomplished and can accomplish and a means for arousing proper religious fervor among the devout; that whereas God alone may be "worshiped" as a supreme being, saints deserve that "veneration" which arises from appreciation of their virtues and their status; that the saints stand before God's throne as his special friends and thus can serve as efficacious intercessors more than can persons still on earth; and that although grace is indeed gratuitous it elicits a human response, and a person who answers God's call with heroic virtue deserves emulation and veneration because he or she has built upon that justification that comes with faith.

The importance that saints retained in the Catholic Church well into the present century is perhaps best suggested by the liturgical cycle that Counter-Reformation churchmen put into fixed order. Through the 1960s most days of the year were special feast days of saints. (Actually any day would be the feast of several, but only one would be commemorated liturgically.) A person following the mass in a missal would find that the prayers for the day were introduced by a short biography of the saint whose day it was, and as many as four of the prayers might refer explicitly to the deeds and virtues of this saint. During the 1960s various factors—ecumenism, ambiguous attitudes toward tradition, and sweeping liturgical reform, among others—brought a decline in the role of saints. Liturgical changes in 1969 included the deletion from the calendar of fifty-two saints whose very existence was questioned, while ninety-two others were allowed merely optional feasts. Although some recent saints were added, the net effect was to diminish attention given to the saints. The extent to which this trend has been and will be reversed, and the possibilities for new kinds of veneration, will become fully clear only in the course of time.

Critical hagiography, or scholarship regarding saints' lives, began during the Counter-Reformation in an effort to defuse the Protestant criticism of apocryphal legends. During the seventeenth century a group of Belgian Jesuits called the Bollandists (after John Bolland, an early member) began editing a definitive collection of the best sources for saints' lives. Their multivolume compilation, the *Acta Sanctorum,* is still in progress and represents one of the most monumental of all collective scholarly enterprises. Other compendia, such as Alban Butler's classic *Lives of the Saints,* originally written in the eighteenth century, showed the same impulse at work on a smaller scale. Faced first with critical tendencies of the Reformation and then with Enlightenment skepticism, Catholic apologists increasingly put distance between themselves and the more obviously apocryphal legends and sought to puzzle out whatever historical truth the lives of saints would yield. During the past century the lives of the saints have attracted scholars from numerous disciplines: political history, social history, ecclesiastical history, literary analysis, folklore research, theology, history of spirituality, and phenomenology of religion. Scholars with devotional interest in the saints have come to work alongside historians without religious conviction in a common effort to unfold the complex significance of the saints' lives.[8]

We have attended so far almost entirely to the evolution of sainthood in Western Christendom. Developments in the East from at least the sixth century onward have been related to those in the West, yet in important ways they are distinct. The central factor here is the relatively decentralized nature of Eastern Orthodoxy. Although there were patriarchs and metropolitans early on who attained special honor and powers, the East never allowed the degree of centralization that Rome secured in the West. The process of centralization did come about, albeit gradually and never with full success, in the Russian Church, which in the modern era represents by far the largest branch of Orthodoxy. Around the fourteenth century the metropolitan of Moscow, later called the patriarch, attained supreme jurisdiction in canonization of saints. Even then many unofficial canonizations were made by local bishops. When Peter the Great established the Holy Synod in the eighteenth century, all canonizations required authorization of this body and confirmation by the tsar. Since 1917, with the abolition of the Holy Synod, authority to canonize saints has reverted to the patriarch of Moscow in conjunction with the national synod. In short, the situation in Orthodoxy even at its most centralized parallels an *early* stage of development in the West: the juncture, during the early Middle Ages, when canonization was the responsibility either of local bishops or of regional synods.

The place of saints within Orthodoxy has always been central yet circumscribed. They are commemorated in the liturgy; indeed, in one vigil service the entire life of St. Mary of Egypt is supposed to be read. Orthodox churches are commonly replete with icons of saints, whose pictorial presence is important: it reminds the worshiper that the liturgy is an earthly version of paradise. Yet the cult of individual saints has seldom been as developed in Orthodoxy as in the Western Church.

Relics are at times venerated but seldom in shrines dedicated to favored patrons. Intercession of the saints is implored but more often in extended litanies than in prayers to single individuals. Saints in Orthodoxy as in the West represent the Church Triumphant—that portion of the Church that has attained glorification in heaven and can intercede on behalf of the earthly church. The particularities of specific saints, however, take second place to the general saintly collectivity.[9]

THE PHENOMENON OF SAINTHOOD

The martyrs, the first persons venerated as saints, manifested the highest ideal of the early Church: they maintained their faith in the face of extreme adversity. In an age when the very survival of the faith was being challenged, those whose heroism defied compromise and attracted converts naturally received special veneration.[10]

There had been instances of martyrdom in Jewish literature (2 Maccabees, the "Martyrdom of Isaiah," and so on). But these texts, which occur mostly in noncanonical works, do not betoken a cult of individual martyrs such as emerged in Christianity. Judaism tended to stress the sufferings of the nation rather than those of individuals. If there is a direct precedent for the ideal of martyrdom, it is to be found in the passion of Jesus rather than in pre-Christian sources. Indeed, from the second century onward it was a commonplace that the martyr imitates Christ and becomes assimilated to him; at the moment of martyrdom, it was believed, Christ appeared to the martyr, or even (as in the martyrology of Perpetua and Felicitas) entered into the martyr and undertook all suffering in his or her place. Like Christ, the martyr was expected to submit passively to execution but not to seek it actively. The most a zealous Christian might do was place himself or herself in circumstances that would lead to capture. In this case too the model was Christ, who exposed himself to conflict with the Temple authorities and foresaw the fate he thus courted.

The concept of martyrdom, developed in the Patristic Era, remained important in subsequent centuries. In the Middle Ages and Modern Era most martyrs have been killed in the course of missionary work (Boniface, the Japanese Jesuits, etc.); unlike the early martyrs, they suffered for extending the faith, not merely for holding it. Some have died because of conflict between Church and state (Thomas Becket, Thomas More) or in defense of their virtue (Maria Goretti). Yet the essential notion of martyrdom—the ideal of faithful imitation of Christ's suffering even in death—has remained constant. Christians have never lost their fascination with this ideal. But in most situations in which they have found themselves, it has not been realistic to expect this fate, and the notion of dying for Christ has often been relegated to the level of a romantic fantasy. Practical models for imitation have tended to focus more on holy life than on heroic death.

Under the influence of the monks—spiritual heirs to the ideal of martyrdom—there has been a strong tendency in Christian tradition to conceive the religious life as a process of purgation leading to contemplation. The purgative or ascetic element in holiness is a deliberate and systematic effort to rid oneself of vices and passions; once this is accomplished, one is free to turn one's soul toward higher spiritual objects and ultimately to attain union with God. As early as the Patristic Era, however, there was difference of opinion regarding the relative merits of the contemplative and active lives; some maintained that contemplation justified withdrawal from society, others insisted that active service to fellow human beings was the higher ideal. Thus alongside asceticism and contemplation, the element of action became vital to the Christian notion of sainthood. Most of the saints contrived in various ways to combine these three ideals, though they might emphasize one or another. Indeed, it became common to view action and contemplation as mutually supportive and to see asceticism as a requisite for both. Manifesting these ideals to an extraordinary degree, the saint attained special status in the eyes of God, whose favor was indicated by the special powers that the saint enjoyed. The holy man or woman was thus distinguished by miracles and visions, which were signs of God's grace working in him or her. In short, the essential components of Christian saintliness can be outlined as follows:

I. Moral elements
- A. Asceticism
- B. Contemplation
- C. Action

II. Extraordinary manifestations of power
- A. Miracles
- B. Visions

Considering that it was the monks who defined and elaborated these ideals, it is not surprising that asceticism quickly took on fundamental importance. It may be defined as the voluntary renunciation of inherently permissible deeds or objects, or the voluntary acceptance of suffering, for religious motives. The potential objects of renunciation are various. The saint often goes without food; indeed, systematic fasting has always been part of monastic life. St. Catherine of Siena, for example, began in her adolescence to live on bread and raw herbs alone, and later she gave up the bread. Saints have also dispensed with sleep. Early hermits in the desert are said to have taken seriously the New Testament command to pray without ceasing; to fulfill it they remained much or most of the night in vigil. It is standard for saints to renounce money and property. Numerous Christians through the centuries have been inspired to a life of poverty by Christ's injunction to the rich young man to sell what he had, give to the poor, and become a disciple. Francis of Assisi commanded his followers to despise money, and if they saw coins they were to treat them like dust under their feet. The saints also forfeited sexual relations. Indeed, celibacy is one of the earliest forms of asceticism in Christian tradition and the only one still consistently imposed upon or accepted by a large class of Christians, the Catholic priests. Again, the saints often renounced their own free wills, opting to place themselves wholly under obedience to their superiors. Benedict of Nursia, in his classic sixth-century rule for monks, repeatedly stressed abandonment of self-will; he allowed a monk to object meekly if his abbot commanded something impossible, but if the abbot persisted in his directive, the monk was to proceed and hope for the best. (One Irish monk even obeyed his abbot's command to drown his own child.) Finally, the saints often fled from human company or from worldly society. Anthony the Hermit shunned school for fear of the contaminating influence of his classmates and throughout his life kept withdrawing deeper into the desert to avoid unnecessary human contact. Orders of monks such as the Trappists have, with varying degrees of strictness, retired from ordinary society, and in many parts of the world this form of spirituality flourishes to this day.

Some of these examples of renunciation no doubt seem extravagant, perhaps even pathological. However one judges them, it is the essence of heroic sanctity to manifest ascetic and other virtues with uncompromising exuberance, and examples such as the foregoing could be drawn from the lives of the most popular canonized saints in any era. Theologically, the essential principle is that the ascetic abstains even from what is in principle permissible. One does not qualify as an ascetic merely by refraining from gluttony or promiscuity; one must go further and take upon oneself supererogatory norms. The effect of asceticism is thus to establish two levels of citizenship within Christian society: the bulk of Christians merely fulfill their moral obligation, but the spiritual elite take a further burden upon themselves. In traditional parlance it is said that "commands" are imposed upon all but "counsels" affect only those willing to accept them. Poverty, celibacy, and obedience to a superior are ways to attain special merit (and ultimately a higher place in heaven); they are not binding for all Christians. Moderate self-denial may be important for all as a means of discipline, but systematic asceticism is for the few.

Vigorous renunciation of pleasure may or may not lead to an actual feeling of pain. If pain does come, however, Christian tradition views patient suffering as meritorious. Numerous saints distinguished themselves for heroic acceptance of diseases that they recognized as sent by God. St. Fina lay for five years on an oak board (her version of a cross) until at last she was infested with vermin and rats; through it all she retained her patience. Suffering could furthermore be inflicted by demons: the classic example is St. Anthony the Hermit, who was beaten unconscious by demons in bestial form on one occasion and who wrestled with them frequently afterward. Apart from patient endurance of suffering inflicted by God or demons, the saints commonly assumed pain (or at least discomfort) at their own hands, usually by wearing hair shirts or by self-flagellation.

Asceticism is not merely voluntary renunciation or suffering but renunciation and suffering for specific motives. There have been secular ascetics, such as Lenin, who renounced their own comfort for reasons of political or psychological principle. While these cases furnish interesting points of comparison, they are not directly pertinent here. Specifically religious asceticism in the Christian tradition has typically been practiced for three motives. First, there is a kind of asceticism that makes it possible for a person to fulfill his or her active religious calling effectively: Christ enjoined his disciples to leave family and possessions behind so they could follow him and preach the gospel; saints in the Modern Era have often adopted lives of poverty so they could relate more effectively to the poor people they served. Second, asceticism has been thought of as enhancing one's present state of soul: it uproots vices, cultivates virtues, and helps in attaining a heightened awareness of God's presence in contemplation. Third, as a form of sacrificial offering to God, an act of asceticism earns reward in the afterlife. These motives are by no means mutually exclusive, and most ascetics would no doubt have subscribed to all three principles.

These religious motives do not exclude psychological and even pathological factors: obsessive-compulsive neurosis, depressive disparagement of self, sadomasochism, and the like. But the veneration that the saints received by people who had known them suggests that they functioned effectively in their societies, at least in most cases. Their behavior was encouraged by the tradition in which they were raised and in most instances probably owed more to the cultural assumptions of this tradition than to personal psychological dispositions.

As already mentioned, the ascetic and contemplative ideals have traditionally been linked—to the extent that the term "contemplative life" commonly designates the life of ascetic withdrawal from society for the sake of contemplating God. The word "contemplation" by itself traditionally designates a form of prayer: unlike meditation, which makes use of discursive thought and mental images (such as that of the Crucifixion), contemplation is a submitting of oneself to the spontaneous and intuitive action of God in one's soul. Because the heights of contemplative prayer are in principle ineffable, however, and because even less exalted levels of prayer are inward processes, the biographies of saints contain far less information about contemplation than about the ascetic preparation. Conceptions of contemplation are more often conveyed in treatises than in biographies.

One autobiographical treatise that conveys some notion of a saint's life of prayer is Teresa of Avila's *Life.* The pertinent sections of this work are devoted to an extended analogy between the stages of prayer and the watering of a garden:

> It seems to me that the garden can be watered in four ways: by taking water from a well, which costs us great labour; or by a water-wheel and buckets, when the water is drawn by a windlass (I have sometimes drawn it this way: it is less laborious than the other and gives more water); or by a stream or brook, which waters the ground much better, for it saturates it more thoroughly and there is less need to water it often, so that the gardener's labour is much less; or by heavy rain, when the Lord waters it with no labour of ours, a way incomparably better than any of those which have been described. . . . It has seemed to me in this way to explain something about the four degrees of prayer to which the Lord . . . has occasionally brought my soul.[11]

As Teresa passed from the first to the fourth degree of prayer, she found that it was less necessary for her to exert effort; increasingly the work was done by God, and the experience was more satisfying. The first degree is that of a beginner in systematic prayer, who is often beset with periods of spiritual dryness or frustration. In the second, which Teresa also calls the "prayer of quiet," the faculties of the soul pass into a state of recollection, and the will "allows itself to be imprisoned by God." That is, the will is directed wholly toward the supreme goodness that is God. It is common for contemplatives to reach this stage, but few go beyond it to the third and fourth levels, in which the soul is more thoroughly absorbed in God, at least for brief periods, after which it proceeds to ordinary activity in the world but with a new consciousness of God.

In her later *Interior Castle,* Teresa gives a more elaborate scheme of spiritual progress, which is less explicitly autobiographical but still based on personal experience. Here again there is development from laborious to spontaneous prayer, with the same shift from active effort to passive submission. Two elements of contemplation emerge more clearly in the second work: First, Teresa stresses the need for constant vigilance against worldly and carnal distractions, represented by poisonous reptiles: even in one of the highest stages "a few little lizards" can insinuate themselves. Second, she develops the motif of the spiritual betrothal and marriage: in the penultimate stage of development the soul enjoys a blissful union with its Beloved, followed by a painful separation; only afterward is it privileged with a permanent union or marriage with God, which pervades its entire daily life.[12]

Teresa's emphasis on experience of God within the soul is typical of Christian contemplatives; however, there are other models of mystical experience. Francis of Assisi and other "nature mystics" have stressed a consciousness of God's presence within nature; they have underscored the role of nature as a manifestation of God's creative power and as containing a wealth of symbols that point to spiritual realities. Yet this sort of nature mysticism is less pervasive in Christian spirituality and in saints' lives than the notion of inward prayer.

Like systematic asceticism, contemplative prayer has always been a calling for the few. The closest most Christians will come to contemplation is verbal prayer and meditation—in short, the lower forms of prayer. This conception of a spiritual elite owes much to the monastic setting in which ascetic and contemplative spirituality evolved. Only those who undertook strenuous renunciation and exercises, usually under an experienced spiritual guide, would reach the higher rungs of the spiritual ladder. The mysterious nature of the highest forms of prayer is indicated by the term "mysticism," which corresponds roughly to the term "contemplation": most of those figures in the Latin or Western tradition who are known as mystics would have called themselves contemplatives instead. In any case, they clearly constituted an elite.

The third element of Christian sanctity, active service, is different in this way: it requires no special or extraordinary qualifications—though, to be sure, a particular form of service may demand special talents or training. From the earliest centuries of Christianity charitable action has been valued highly. Christ performed numerous works of compassion and said that whoever aided the needy was in fact doing service to him. Early Christians provided aid to widows and orphans, the unemployed, the elderly and disabled. Even in the first century deacons were established for this task. By the middle of the third century Christians in Rome were sustaining more than fifteen hundred needy people, who were "fed by the grace and kindness of the Lord."

Even when the monastic movement emerged the demands of charity remained paramount: monastic writers often accentuated the need for service to fellow monks and to visitors, even if they did not encourage outreach to those beyond the monastery walls. Monks were expected to work in the fields, kitchens, scriptoria, or infirmaries of their monasteries. If guests came, a dutiful monk would welcome them, wash their feet, and serve them at dinner. Lives of holy monks told how they humbled themselves by caring for lepers; even before leaving his secular life, St. Martin is supposed to have shown such humility by ministering to his own slave. Almoners were delegated for routine charitable aid outside the monastery—but other monks who happened to be out "in the world" might have occasion for incidental works of charity, and the lives of monastic saints tell how they availed themselves of such opportunity. St. Germanus is said to have helped a group of workers carry a heavy burden, and Wandregiselus aided a poor man who was struggling to set an overturned wagon upright. In both East and West, despite their zeal for seclusion the monks became the most numerous and the most effective missionaries of the late Patristic Era and the Middle Ages, in large part because they were not tied to fixed locations. In this role they performed not only spiritual services—preaching, working conversions, and administering the sacraments—but also material ones. When St. Wilfrid arrived in Sussex, the pagans were suffering the effects of drought, so he taught them to supplement their food by fishing with nets.

Diocesan priests and bishops too had ample occasion for charity, particularly by counseling people and distributing alms. St. Germanus of Paris is supposed to have lavished such quantities of alms on the poor with his own hands that only the Lord could keep account of his beneficence; he drew both upon his episcopal property and upon donations from the people and the king. In the early thirteenth century, when the Franciscans, Dominicans, and other mendicant orders emerged, the activist thrust in Christianity received a powerful boost: unlike the theoretically cloistered monks, the mendicants were founded explicitly to work among the lay population, furnishing spiritual and corporal aid especially in the cities. The charitable work of the mendicants was primarily in the hands of men; the women's orders were for the most part cloistered. With the advent of the seventeenth century, female orders such as the Sisters of Charity gave wider scope for women to engage in nursing, teaching, and other forms of service.

Dedication to active service has often been coupled with a high degree of respect for the poor. While Judaism merely reproved selfishness and encouraged charity, the New Testament contained a clear streak of opposition to wealth per se and sympathy toward poverty that leaned toward exaltation of the poor. The parable of Lazarus and the rich man and the logion about fitting through the eye of a needle are the best-known texts. More scathing is James 5:1–6: "Come now, you rich, weep and howl for the miseries that are coming upon you." Later theologians and preachers were to warn the poor that they should not be arrogant, for (to take Matthew's version of the beatitude rather than Luke's) it is the poor *in spirit* who are blessed. But the saints' lives more commonly spoke a simpler message, that the poor enjoy special status as a blessed class. More than one saint of modern times has manifested this special reverence for the poor: stories are told about saints who were too busy with prayer or too exhausted from their labors to receive distinguished visitors but who opened their doors at once to poor people who came for aid. St. Gerald of Aurillac always supported the weak against the strong in his medieval society and presumably identified them respectively as the oppressed and the oppressors—though he did so in such a way that "the stronger were overcome without being hurt." Indeed, the poor were a source of salvation for the rich: the life of St. Eligius remarks that God could have made everyone rich, but instead he made some poor "so the rich might have means by which to redeem their sins."

The saints' willingness to make sacrifices for the needy links their action with a kind of asceticism. St. John Vianney was willing to lay bare his pantry for the poor, keeping nothing but a few potatoes to last a week. Likewise, he would literally give the clothes off his back, and when he met a barefoot man with bleeding feet, he surrendered his own shoes and socks. Similar stories are told of many others. The saints' voluntary adoption of a simple life has placed them on a level with the beneficiaries of their service and enabled them to relate to the poor without arousing feelings of inferiority. In at least some cases this assimilation to the life of those served has been an explicit policy, as with Mother Teresa of Calcutta.

When required, the saints have often prepared themselves for service by undergoing long training. Some have received medical education before ministering to the ill. One early instance of this is St. Samson of Constantinople, who founded a hospital for the poor in the fifth century; better-known examples are the medical missionaries of modern times. To prepare himself for missionary work among the Moslems, Blessed Raymond Lull spent nine years studying Arabic and other subjects.

The saints have not typically sought or advocated political solutions to the problems of the needy—and certainly they have not been inclined toward revolution. Many of them founded institutions or orders and spent considerable time administering their foundations; Joseph Cottolengo's Little House of Divine Providence developed into an elaborate complex with three large hospitals and special homes for people suffering various specific ailments and handicaps. What the saints emphasized, however, was not the need for bureaucracies but the need for direct day-to-day personal involvement in service to the needy. Critics of this approach argue that such efforts function as palliatives and deflect effort away from the radical political measures that would actually solve problems. Confronted with this argument, Mother Teresa of Calcutta has responded that what she and her sisters provide is different from the services of government agencies: they offer personal attention and love for individuals. And this conviction is typically shared by the saints.

Even when the saint was a ruler and theoretically had power to take more radical action, he usually restricted himself to symptomatic solutions. St. Louis IX was venerated for his justice and piety but endeared himself to hagiographers particularly by his service to the Church and the poor. He erected hospitals and personally tended the sick; he provided meals for more than a hundred beggars each day. It is perhaps understandable that a medieval ruler, lacking in modern techniques of economic manipulation, took no steps in the direction of a welfare state. More worthy of note is the nineteenth-century saint who served as confessor to the queen of Spain but refrained from involving himself in affairs of state, even on behalf of the poor.

One of the most controversial questions in the Christian notion of saintliness—though again a subject dealt with more in treatises than in saints' lives—is the relative merit of action and contemplation. Traditionally the active life has been associated with Martha, who rendered culinary services to Christ, and the contemplative with Mary, who chose "the better part" by staying at his side and conversing with him. There was difference of opinion on this matter even among the desert fathers. Some figures have ranked the contemplative life above the active: Blessed Richard Rolle argued that the contemplative life is as much superior to the active as uncreated goodness (God) is to created good. Others, particularly in modern times, have inclined toward the opposite opinion. In the words of the head of a Protestant seminary: "When I think of a saint today, I think of a person who is willing to spend his whole life in a struggle for justice." Most Christian writers, however, have exalted a mixture of the two ideals. Augustine recognized contemplation as a foretaste of the beatific vision, inherently desirable and theoretically preferable to action—but he also recognized that the Church needed the services of precisely those people who tended toward the contemplative life. Thus he proposed a "mixed life" of alternating action and contemplation as the best accommodation of theoretical ideals to practical necessities. Most of the saints contrived in some way to fuse action and contemplation, as well as asceticism, in some amalgam.[13]

The elements of sanctity discussed so far are modes of behavior that a person adopts in an effort to become holy. Miracles and visions do not fall into the same category. They may at times be seen as devices by which God induces a person to seek holiness; more often they are taken as signs of a sanctity already attained. In any case, they are God's deeds rather than the saints'—not only in the sense that grace is required for their fulfillment but in the fuller sense—that they are totally and directly contingent on God's will and power. The most the saint can do is pray for a miracle or provide an occasion for God's action. To be sure, this point is sometimes lost in popular dissemination; however, it is frequently emphasized explicitly.[14]

Most of the miracles in saints' lives, as in the Bible, fall into three broad categories: healings, nature miracles, and prophecies. Of these classes the most significant numerically were healings—again as in the Bible, or at least the New Testament. This type accounts for almost all the saints' posthumous miracles, recounted at length in canonization inquiries and frequently at the ends of biographies (though bodily incorruptibility and the miraculous "odor of sanctity" were also important posthumous proofs of holiness). Diseases could be cured in various ways: St. Molua breathed on a dumb girl and enabled her to talk; leprosy was often cured by a kiss or by application of saliva. Although Gerald of Aurillac refused out of modesty to perform miracles, the sick would steal the water he had used to wash his hands and use it to effect cures; one lame boy, for example, had someone procure this water from Gerald's servants, and when it was sprinkled on his leg, the lameness was immediately healed. When necessary saints could at times resuscitate people who had died; thus when Catherine of Siena's mother died without receiving the sacraments, the saint vowed that she would not move from where she was until her mother returned to life, and shortly the miracle transpired.

Closely related to miracles of physical healing are the exorcisms that figure large in the lives of certain saints. One of the most striking examples of exorcism is in Sulpicius Severus' classic life of Martin of Tours. On entering a certain house Martin stopped at the door and commanded a demon to depart; instead, the demon took possession of the cook, who began to bite and scratch those around him. Martin thrust his fingers into the cook's mouth and said, "if you have any power, bite these"—but the cook drew away, "as if he had taken a white-hot iron in his throat." The mouth of the cook being blocked, the demon "was expelled in a discharge from the bowels, leaving behind a track of filth."

The saints' nature miracles manifested their power over all four of the traditional elements but particularly water and fire. The saints demonstrated mastery over water in numerous ways: they survived underwater for several hours or even days; frequently they made bodies of water dry up; their garments, or books they had left outdoors, remained dry in spite of rain; they drove vehicles across the water or knelt down on it to say their prayers; one saint, walking across a river with a heavy statue of the Virgin, left footprints in the water. The saints were equally ingenious in their manipulation of fire: many of them produced flames from their fingers and faces; St. Comgall heated a house by breathing on icicles, while St. Brachius used snow for the same purpose; others slowed the course of the sun or draped their clothes on sunbeams.

Likewise within the category of nature miracles falls the production or multiplication of food. Numerous saints multiplied loaves of bread. When the supply of flour was desperately low because of drought, St. John Vianncy had a kitchen worker add yeast to what little flour remained, and as she kneaded it, it increased to the point of satisfying the community's needs. When Francis of Assisi was ill, he cured himself with wine that he produced from water. His contemporary biographer adds: "And truly he is a saint whom creatures obey in this way [cf. Matt. 8:27] and at whose nod the elements change themselves to other uses."

Miracles could involve animate as well as inanimate nature. Francis's extraordinary dealings with animals are well known. Less famous is the story of how Germanus of Paris went to the rescue of a woman whose lands were being devastated by bears: he made the sign of the cross, causing the bears to fight with each other; one of them strangled the other, and then the survivor accidentally impaled himself on a fencepost. More common are the tales of animals that brought food to saints or ministered to them in other ways.

The saints were able to prophesy all sorts of future events, significant and insignificant: many predicted their own deaths; Godric forecast the precise number of visitors coming to him; Dunstan read it as an ill omen when King Aethelred the Unready polluted his baptismal font; Columba, whose biography is roughly one third taken up with "prophetic revelations," correctly prophesied that one man's son would be dead and buried within a week, while another's would live to see his grandsons. Frequently the "prophecy" did not entail foreknowledge but, rather, an ability to discern secret thoughts, especially sins. Other saints' prophecies were warnings about what would happen to contemporary rulers if they failed to do God's will; perhaps the most famous example is Bridget of Sweden's forecast that Pope Urban VI would die unless he remained in Rome—a prophecy that was fulfilled within months of his departure for Avignon.

Not only such prophecies but other forms of miracle could constitute curses rather than blessings. There was precedent for miraculous curses in the New Testament (the cursing of the fig tree) and particularly in the Apocrypha (where the child Jesus struck unruly playmates dead when they vexed him). One life of St. Patrick tells that when he arrived in Ireland, he found no fish in two waters, so he cursed them and they remained barren thereafter. And when thieves stole fruits and vegetables from his monastery, Comgall had God blind them so that they wandered about in the garden until they recognized their guilt.

For most of Christian history maturity and old age have been objects of great reverence, and saints' biographers have delighted in telling how their subjects were precociously mature. Thus many of the saints' miracles illustrated extraordinary development soon after birth or even in the womb: the motif of the *puer senex,* or aged child, is a favorite hagiographical theme. There were saints who cried out from the womb, stood upright at birth, jumped to the baptismal font and dipped themselves in the water, learned the basics of writing in three days, were born with monastic tonsures, or toddled off to monasteries as soon as they learned to walk. One life of St. Nicholas tells that from his origins he fasted by suckling only once on Wednesdays and Fridays.

Christians have long differed regarding the significance of miracles. The synoptic gospels show a certain ambivalence toward them and insist that they must not be rated more highly than moral qualities. The Church has emphasized repeatedly that even demons can work wonders; and Thomas Aquinas maintained that in demonstrating his power God can employ any person he wants as an instrument, so miracles are no proof of holiness. Yet the viewpoint of the sixth-century poet Fortunatus that a saint's prominence may be gauged by the number of his miracles has commonly prevailed among the laity and is an underlying assumption of many writings by clerics. Augustine maintained in his early years that miracles had been needed in the time of the apostles to win conversions but that they were no longer necessary; if habitual, they could dull people's sensitivities to the marvelous and distract from the true marvels to be found within the soul and in the Church. In his later years, however, he witnessed enough miracles personally to change his mind. He still emphasized that God's extraordinary deeds should not distract from his ordinary wonders: the slow multiplication of wheat by natural growth is just as marvelous a sign of God's generosity as the miraculous multiplication of loaves. Yet he was willing to recognize miracles, especially for their apologetic value, and he used them to impress educated pagans. The view that ultimately prevailed among clerics was that represented by Gregory I, who told a great many miracle stories but insisted that virtue is more important than miracles and that converting a sinner is a greater accomplishment than raising a dead man. Indeed, he conceived miracles largely as rewards for virtue—a point that he illustrated by the story of Honoratus. This saint's youthful abstinence was tested when his parents took him to the mountains, where fish was unavailable and he had nothing to eat but meat. He bore their laughter and revilement patiently. When a servant went to a stream for water, however, a fish slipped in that was large enough for Honoratus, thus vindicating him, forestalling further derision, and rewarding his patience.

If miracles have been extensions of saints' active lives, visions may be seen as extraordinary analogues to contemplation. Both in contemplation and in visions the saint's attention is called away from terrestrial and toward spiritual realities. The main difference is that visions have specific visual and auditory content that can be retold. Thus, Blessed Julian of Norwich had particularly vivid visions of the Crucifixion which she described in a classic mystical treatise. Catherine of Siena had numerous visions, including her "mystical marriage" to Christ. Many saints have been granted visions of scenes from the life of Christ from the nativity onward. Saints have often had visions of other saints, and in modern times the apparitions of the Blessed Virgin to St. Bernadette Soubirous and others have received particularly widespread attention. Not infrequently saints have received locutions, either by themselves or along with visions; thus Francis of Assisi heard Christ speak from a crucifix in a dilapidated chapel telling him to rebuild his church. Saints' passage to heaven with angelic accompaniment has often been visible to others, and after death saints have commonly appeared to give exhortation or to announce that they want shrines erected for their relics.

Sometimes the visions occur during sleep, perhaps the best-known instance being Jerome's dream in which Christ castigated him for his love of pagan classics. When St. Willibrord was conceived, his mother had a prophetic dream revealing the greatness of her offspring: in it the moon fell into her mouth and caused her entire body to glow. More often the vision takes place during a rapture, during which the saint usually becomes stiff and unmovable, may remain unharmed by fire or pinpricks, and may levitate. (The term "rapture" is not used uniformly in the literature but usually refers to a state of inattentiveness or even insensitivity to the physical world—a condition that can accompany either a vision or the higher stages of contemplation.)

Quite often visions were responsible for a saint's conversion to a life of religious dedication. One example, which again manifests the theme of the *puer senex,* is that of St. Ansgar. When his mother died, his father sent the five-year-old Ansgar off to school, where he began to imitate the foolish and childish manners of his fellow pupils. During the night he had a vision of the Virgin, his own mother, and others—but he could not run to them because he was mired in a "slippery place." The Virgin told him that to share their company he would have to set aside all vanity and childish jests and recognize the seriousness of life. Immediately he was transformed and devoted himself so much to profitable occupations such as reading and meditation that his companions (presumably also about five years old) were amazed.

The saints have typically been as cautious about visions as about miracles. Even the heretics could claim to have visions, presumably bestowed by the devil. Teresa of Avila was constantly attentive to the possibility that her own visions might be diabolically inspired; one of her contemporaries, who had enjoyed considerable renown for sanctity, had at last confessed to long-standing allegiance with hell. Teresa proposed tests of a vision's authenticity, based mainly on the effect they had on one's character. But virtue in itself could be a safeguard against delusion: when the Devil tried to deceive one of the desert hermits by disguising himself as an archangel, the hermit modestly replied, "Look to it that you were not sent to some other, for I am not worthy that an angel should be sent to me." Although the saints were keenly aware of demonic delusion, however, they seem to have paid little attention to the effects that disease or prolonged fasts and vigils might have on their perceptions. Yet whatever notions might have prevailed regarding the causes of visions, neither visions nor miracles have officially been recognized as equal to virtue or as infallible proofs of holiness. In the words of St. John of the Cross, "all visions, revelations and feelings coming from Heaven, and any thoughts that may proceed from these, are of less worth than the least act of humility."

EXCURSUS: REGIONAL CHARACTERISTICS

In setting forth the phenomenon of sanctity we have so far prescinded from any differences between one region and another and have assumed that sainthood is essentially identical throughout Christendom. To a great extent this procedure is historically justifiable. First, it was monks who laid down the basic norms for holiness throughout the Christian world, and in every land they set a monastic imprint on the ideal of saintly life. It is thus no accident that the lives of saints from diverse lands reveal similar if not identical patterns of conduct. Second, different regions were in some measure dependent on one another for their notions of saintliness; they borrowed from and often rivaled one another. The biography of Anthony the Hermit quickly reached the West in a Latin translation, and for centuries it inspired emulation; when Gregory I penned his biographies of Italian ascetics in the sixth century, he explicitly intended to show that the West had saints as good as those of the East. Thus again it is not surprising that motifs from one context crop up elsewhere. Third, when veneration of saints came under central ecclesiastical control, there was powerful incentive for uniformity. The best example of this process can be seen in the Western Church around the thirteenth century, when canonization of saints was reserved to the papal curia and churchmen from all over Western Europe exerted themselves to prove that their prospective saints met Roman norms.

In spite of all these factors, however, there was inevitable diversity, and the establishment of a common pattern is to that extent an exercise in phenomenological abstraction. Different parts of Christendom emphasized different components of the saintly life and underscored different themes in their theology of sainthood. At times the differences were in nuance, but at times the regional variations were pronounced. It is clearly impossible to detail here the distinctive hagiography of each possible culture: Coptic, late Roman, Merovingian, Carolingian, Anglo-Saxon, and so forth. Suffice it to say two cultures had more or less distinctive forms of hagiography as examples of the kind of diversity that could occur: the Byzantine and the early medieval Irish.

Byzantine Christianity—that Greek-speaking cultural world that from the fourth through the fifteenth century claimed Byzantium (or Constantinople) as its political and spiritual capital—holds a central position in Christian history. Far from being a backwater, it was the motherland from which the West derived much of its theology, art, and hagiography. As the centuries passed, however, the rift between the Greek and Latin worlds became greater, and as Moslems claimed formerly Byzantine territory the Christian East diminished in size and power. Defining the cultural identity of the far-flung and long-lasting Byzantine world might seem impossible, but one can at least pose the question that is relevant here: Was there a distinctively Byzantine hagiography? Grand generalizations come easily. Thus Lynn White has suggested a clear-cut distinction:

> The Greeks believed that sin was intellectual blindness, and that salvation was found in illumination, orthodoxy—that is, clear thinking. The Latins, on the other hand, felt that sin was moral evil, and that salvation was to be found in right conduct. Eastern theology has been voluntarist. The Greek saint contemplates; the Western saint acts.[15]

But if anything, the Eastern monasticism of St. Basil was more activist than the Western monasticism of St. Benedict—more deeply involved, for example, in charity and education. And it is by no means clear that a hierarch such as John the Almsgiver—the patriarch of Constantinople who earned his epithet by lavish generosity, even to a huckster who came begging three times in three different suits of clothes to disguise his identity—was a thinker rather than an activist. Perhaps he was an exception to the general rule, but the exceptions can be multiplied enough to call the rule itself into question. Again, one might suggest that the Eastern Church was subject more than the Western Church to political domination and that for this reason members of the imperial family gained recognition as saints. Certainly the East has its share of imperial and royal saints, but so does the West, and it is not clear that the balance is so different as to suggest a divergence in principle.

If Byzantium had a distinctive form of hagiography, it is perhaps best defined in terms of certain values that were held in higher esteem there than in the West, or held more consistently in high esteem. Although it would be misleading to suggest that Byzantine saints were speculative and therefore not practical, it is true that one finds greater emphasis in Byzantine hagiography on the saints' intellectual gifts. One classic case is Constantine (or Cyril), the ninth-century missionary to the Slavs who taught for some time in the imperial school at Constantinople. In his youth he had a dream in which, of all the girls of the city, he chose Sophia (or Wisdom) as his bride. Much of his biography details his debates with heretics and pagans, all of whom succumb to his wisdom and learning. After the youthful saint delivered an unanswerable rhetorical blow to one heretical opponent, his aged adversary "fell silent, ashamed." The saint's biographer even refers to him quite routinely as "the Philosopher." Perhaps one can see a modern survival of this piety of wisdom in the eighteenth-century monk Nicodemos the Hagiorite, whose claim to spiritual authority on Mount Athos was linked to an absorbing interest in scholarship and a significant output of scholarly works. Certainly the West has had its scholar-saints, and the East (particularly Russia) has had "holy fools" who gained veneration for their lack of intellectual accomplishment. The culture in and around Byzantium proper, however, was marked by an unabashed sophistication that was relatively rare in the early medieval West.

Another feature that typifies Byzantine hagiography more than Western is what one might call a liturgical mysticism. Theodore of Sykeon's face was radiant when he served the divine liturgy, and when he began chanting "Holy things to the holy" before communion, the consecrated bread "made the motions of one that skipped for joy by rising high above the paten and coming down with a little thump on to the paten." It is not surprising to find such motifs in a culture that took great delight in liturgical splendor. Yet if these themes are more pronounced in Byzantium than in the West, the difference remains essentially one of degree rather than of principle. Scarcely anything in Byzantine hagiography is without some parallel in the West, and vice versa.[16]

Far more sharply distinct are the lives of Irish saints from the early Middle Ages. Reading them one is plunged into a magic world of mystery and wonder but with rather little sense of moral attainment. More than other saints, the Irish held sway over the elements of nature, particularly water and fire. It was Irish saints especially who could generate flames from their fingertips or survive immersion in water. Patrick could also melt snow by making the sign of the cross over it. Indeed, it has been plausibly argued that these saints took over many of the folkloric functions of pre-Christian Celtic nature deities. Likewise, Irish saints more than others were prone to cursing their enemies. When a druid reviled Christianity in St. Patrick's presence, the offender "was raised into the air and forthwith again cast down, and his brains were scattered on the stone, and he was broken in pieces, and died," provoking great fear in his heathen companions. And when a certain tyrant refused to sell grain to St. Comgall and his monks, the saint foretold that mice would devour the withheld provisions. Doubtless there were moral values behind the saints' conduct, but those values often had little to do with Christianity. A local chieftain who wanted a male heir was disappointed when his wife bore him a girl, so he took the child to St. Abban, who obligingly baptized her and in the process turned her into a boy. If the Irish saints' lives accord poorly with gospel norms, what they do provide in rich abundance is entertainment. The best example perhaps is the *Navigation of St. Brendan,* an adventure story based on pre-Christian literary precedent in which the saint and his companions encounter a whale that proffers its back for their temporary repose, birds that produce music by flapping their wings, and other marvels. The work is loosely Christianized; the whale offers itself, for example, every year on Holy Saturday and thus symbolizes the whale of Jonah, a standard Old Testament type of Christ's tomb. Yet the themes that dominate in this enchanted world are essentially Celtic in inspiration rather than meaningfully Christian.[17]

These two examples represent opposite ends of a spectrum. Byzantium, a long-venerated center of Christian culture, displayed sophistication and self-conscious absorption in Christian tradition. Though politically isolated at the eastern end of the Christian world, it remained an effective center of spiritual and literary culture for centuries. Ireland, newly converted in the fifth century, was at the other end of Christendom; while it too possessed in some ways a high level of culture, its own cultural contributions were both refreshingly and exasperatingly naive and pervaded with the values of a barbarian society. Much depended, no doubt, on what these Christian people found in the culture of their ancestors. If the Irish borrowed folklore and adventure, the Greeks inherited a dedication to "philosophy" and a high respect for ritual mysteries. Examination of other cultures and their hagiography would no doubt yield similar results, modified by ecclesiastical and other developments in the various realms of Christendom.

THE LITERATURE OF SAINTHOOD

It might seem hopeless to sketch the literary characteristics of saints' written lives, or vitae, because these documents present endless variation. How could one make general statements applicable to a third-century martyrology, a collection of hermits' sayings from the fifth century, the account of an early medieval Irish monk's sea voyage, the official canonization biography for a thirteenth-century scholar-turned-bishop, and the autobiography of the founder of a sixteenth-century religious order? Yet all of these works feed into the broad tradition of Christian writings about saints' lives. One might limit oneself to hagiography proper: to fully developed accounts of the lives, virtues, miracles, and holy deaths of individuals whose holiness displayed the power of God. But even at that one would be left with a motley collection of texts showing regional and temporal variation. Thus all one can do is cite trends that occur often in the vitae, not with the intention of defining and describing the genre in detail but in hopes of helping the reader to identify and understand these trends whenever they do occur in the sources.

The form of the vita can perhaps best be discerned if we limit our study to the documents written between the fourth and the thirteenth centuries—what one might call the classical period of hagiography. In the Greek-speaking East the most important specimen at the outset of this period was Athanasius' life of Anthony the Hermit, a work quickly translated into Latin and widely disseminated in the West. The Western vita that more than any other dominated the course of development was Sulpicius Severus' life of Martin of Tours. These and other works influenced by them are marked by certain "family resemblances," if not common traits.[18]

The precedent for saints' vitae, as for Christian culture generally, was twofold. First there was the model of life set forth in the Gospels. Not only do the vitae show the saints as imitators of Christ's virtues and miracles; even the paratactic structure of many vitae, their clear division into discrete episodes, is reminiscent of the Gospels' concatenation of pericopes. The Gospels center on the death of Christ: he foretells his dying and goes deliberately toward it; he consoles and instructs his disciples just before the event; his passion is recounted in detail; and after death he is exalted in glory. Echoes of this theme occur frequently in the saints' vitae. The saints too predict their demise, gather disciples about their deathbeds for comfort and instruction, and after death are seen gloriously rising toward heaven. Whether the authors of these vitae were conscious of the influence or not, their Christian culture would inevitably condition them to see life's termination as the culminating display of life's merit.

The second set of models, the biographies of classical antiquity, pulled hagiographers in a rather different direction. Hagiographers were often quite conscious of their dependence on classical writers, especially Suetonius. In a pattern very unlike that of the Gospels, Suetonius typically gives a chronological survey of his subject's life up to the high point of that subject's career, then proceeds to thematic discussion of his accomplishments and personality. Sulpicius Severus follows essentially this pattern in his life of Martin of Tours, discussing first the course of his subject's early life up to his appointment as bishop, then his public life as bishop (especially his work against paganism), and finally his private and ascetic life. Yet Sulpicius and his followers saw themselves as heirs not only to classical biography but to broader currents of ancient history: just as writers such as Sallust recounted the deeds of great pagans to inspire emulation, so the hagiographer sought to cultivate the great Christian heroes as models for imitation.

Certain features of the vitae might have been inspired either by the Gospels or by pagan biographies. Miracle stories, for example, were common fare in certain forms of classical biography, such as the life of the philosopher Apollonius of Tyana, as well as in "aretalogies," or records of the miracles attested at pagan shrines through invocation of the gods.

Drawing, then, upon both the Christian and pagan precedents, the hagiographer would typically put together a vita that in one way or another combined miracle stories and illustrations of the saint's virtue with the essential episodes in his or her curriculum vitae. The precise nature of the composite—the way the biographer built upon available models—would inevitably vary according to the facts of the saint's life and according to the special interest of the biographer. An author concerned with the threat of heresy might focus on the saint's refutation of heretics, while a writer who needed to demonstrate in the face of skepticism that his subject really was a saint might take pains to include an impressive array of miracles.

During the high Middle Ages, particularly in the thirteenth century, the literary character of vitae underwent some modification, for various reasons. First, the authors had commonly been exposed directly or indirectly to the systematizing elements in scholastic learning. Second, the vitae written at this time for recently deceased saints were addressed in the first instance to a bureaucracy: they were documents compiled for submission to Rome, as proof of sanctity for a person whose canonization was under consideration. Third, and related to this second factor, there was increasing emphasis on the saint's moral virtues; as Thomas Aquinas and others observed, miracles performed during a person's lifetime could be feigned—indeed, they might be the work of the devil—so the only miracles that weighed heavily in assessing saintliness were those posthumous miracles that simultaneously attested the presence of an existing cult and manifested God's approval for that cult. Under these influences vitae often took the form of more or less schematic treatises, first setting forth examples for each of the saint's virtues and then cataloguing the miracles worked at his or her tomb. Because canonization was reserved at this time for a central authority, at least in Western Christendom, local variations became submerged and the form of the vita became more standard than it had previously been.

The classical background of hagiography led to some ambivalence in the matter of style. Some biographers, supported by Isidore of Seville's dictum that "when we speak of great things we should do so in grand style," risked the accusation of presumption and followed classical models of eloquence. They might excuse themselves by pleading that this eloquence came not from their own art or talent but from the prompting of the Holy Spirit, it being necessary to appeal to readers through style as well as content. Their approach was traditionally known as *sermo grandis,* as opposed to the more common *sermo humilis,* or "lowly style" of authors such as Sulpicius Severus. Proponents of the latter, however, found it no less problematic than the former. Was their subject matter not worthy of a noble and refined manner of writing? Yes, they sometimes admitted, but they were unfortunately not capable of a finer style, and thus they could only do their best. Others suggested that saints' lives, like Scripture itself, could best be phrased simply out of consideration for the uneducated audience they had to reach. Still others argued that *sermo grandis* smacked too much of rhetorical exaggeration, and that *sermo humilis* was more fitting for the simple truth of a saint's life. Perhaps the expressed preference for lowly style was at times a way of apologizing for and at the same time diverting attention from one's literary limitations. Yet classical models were readily at hand, and if monks had not genuinely preferred the simpler and more ascetic style, they could easily have cultivated the alternative.[19]

Development of character in the vitae, even more than in other medieval literary genres, is through assimilation to types. The saint emerges less as an individual with idiosyncratic emotions, views, and habits than as a representative "holy monk," "martyr," "saintly bishop," or "Christian monarch." The stereotyping can be either implicit or explicit. Sulpicius Severus represented Martin of Tours as converting from military service to pacifism, then confronting the emperor with the words "I am a soldier of Christ, and thus I cannot fight." This verbal blow clearly recalled the exchanges that martyrs had had with the Roman authorities. In effect, Sulpicius was assimilating Martin into the category of martyrs. In later centuries it was not uncommon for hagiographers to state in so many words that a saint was another Anthony, another Moses, or the embodiment of some other ideal. Behind this tendency was the notion that this ideal alone was worth highlighting. Occasionally an author might go so far as to say that "in the communion of saints all things are common": those who share in the essence of sanctity share in the same essence, and thus there are no significant differences among them. The ultimate theological ground for this tendency is the idea that the saint is a saint because she or he reembodies the holiness of Christ. It is only as an *alter Christus* that anyone can attain sainthood. And it is only those features of a person's life that display this exemplarity that need to be set forth in the vita.

The same inattention to particulars can be seen in the way the vitae deal with space and time. As one author has suggested, most vitae are set beyond space and time and recreate "an ideal world where such categories are dominated and seen from a kind of abstract point of view."[20] This is true in the sense that the hagiographers are often careless about indicating precisely when and where events occurred. Places are important only insofar as they are vital for a saint's cult; the place of burial has the clearest significance for this reason. Some Irish saints' lives, confounding one saint with another who lived as much as three centuries later, will cavalierly surmount the resulting chronological discrepancies by claiming that their subjects lived for three hundred or more years. But more important than this indifference to the temporal and spatial grid is the hagiographers' unconcern about historical circumstances. Saints confront mythical emperors whose empires are immemorial; they confront pagans whose idolatry differs little from that of Moloch; they serve as bishops over flocks that graze on timeless hillsides. If a saint needed to protect ecclesiastical privileges or properties against some monarch, the political subtleties are lost in a conflict between the man of God and the tyrant. Historical details would serve only to bind the saint to a particular culture and circumstance with relative norms and a mixture of justice and injustice on each side of every controversy. Complexity of this sort was not at all what the hagiographers sought. They strove to portray the ideals of Christian life and to represent those ideals as embodied in human figures untainted by the contaminating realities of historical humanity.

The further one moves beyond the classical period of Christian hagiography, the more exceptions one finds to these generalizations. But this is only to say that Christians—even those devoted to the saints—become less interested in devising forms of literature adapted to represent the saints as saints. The Bollandists brought all the skills of critical scholarship to bear on the problems of hagiography, but with the result of dissolving the very stuff they analyzed: their careful work with the vitae led to profound distrust in these documents and a preference for the hard facts of posthumous cult as a measure of saintliness. Biographies of saints continue to be written, but if they differ at all from purely secular biographies it is essentially in their tone and their reluctance to examine their subjects too rigorously. One cannot speak of a modern alternative to classical hagiography—a modern literary genre suited to explore the saintliness of a saint—unless perhaps one wishes to consider such avowedly fictional works as Kazantzakis' *Francis of Assisi.* The age of formal hagiography has long since passed.[21]

THE THEOLOGICAL DIMENSION

In a study of sainthood one cannot distinguish rigorously between the theological side of things and other dimensions: theological questions arise in any survey of the history of sainthood, and they intrude in any phenomenological discussion, as we have already seen. The relationship of active and contemplative lives is central to the phenomenology of Christian sainthood, but it is in itself a theological problem. Counter-Reformation response to the Protestant challenge is part of the history of sainthood, yet again the arguments adduced are theological. In these and other ways we have already covered theological ground. What remains to be examined is the conception of sainthood in the writings of recent theologians. Having seen what various writers from the Christian past had to say about saints and saintliness, let us turn to the effort of modern theologians to work out an understanding of this topic.

Unfortunately, few theologians have attended to the matter thoroughly and systematically. General studies on "spirituality" (the modern counterpart to ascetic-mystical theology) abound, but few writers have devoted much attention to the special problem of heroic or saintly virtue. Certain technical questions that once aroused controversy (such as whether canonizations are infallible) no longer attract interest. Even in traditions in which sainthood has been important, systematic inquiry about saints has never been part of the standard theological curriculum. There is thus no set of well-defined problems to summarize or corpus of established works to survey. Nonetheless the field has not been altogether neglected. Modern theologians have made some effort to answer the central question: What role does the ideal of saintliness and the cult of saints play in the life of the Church? The work done in this area, even if sparse, amply repays examination.

In a brief but important essay entitled "The Church of the Saints," Karl Rahner asks why the Church sets forth canonized saints. Most fundamentally, he replies that the Church "must praise the grace which has had powerful effects, which has conquered, which has become real and manifest to us." If the Church is to be a "sign raised up for the nations" (Isaiah 11:12), its holiness cannot be a purely hidden reality, an incidental counterthrust to the uglier elements in the Church, or an abstract possibility or challenge. Instead, one must recognize this holiness as a concrete reality, a victorious power, "the *pneuma* which is poured out." The official proclamation that certain individuals have attained sainthood is the Church's way of declaring the efficacy of God's grace in these her members. In addition, the saints are vital for their exemplary role. One might suggest that it is enough to follow Christ as the exemplar of Christian living, but the canonized saints are exalted by the Church as models for ever changing historical circumstances: "They are the imitators and the creative models of the holiness which happens to be right for, and is the task of, their particular age. They create a new style; they prove that a certain form of life and activity is a really genuine possibility; they show experimentally that one can be a Christian even in 'this' way; they make such a type of person believable as a Christian type."

As new "styles" of saintliness unfold, the old ones retain a kind of relevance—much as the philosophers of antiquity always retain their power of provoking thought—yet in each new era the Church will have to set forth new models to show the continuing adaptability of saintliness. What the saints show are new ways of imitating Christ; together with Paul, they say in effect, "Be imitators of me as I am of Christ" (1 Cor. 11:1).[22]

Building upon Rahner's essay and on Pius XII's encyclical *Mystici corporis Christi* of 1943, Paul Molinari has developed a view of the saints as "preeminent members" of the Mystical Body of Christ. He takes issue with those "modern theologians" who see the saints as distracting from Christ, or who see the veneration of saints as a dispensable feature that Catholicism can usefully discard in the name of ecumenism. Conversely, he opposes those "maximalists" who exaggerate the saints in a way that does indeed distract from the honor due to Christ. The crucial notion in Molinari's theology is that through his Mystical Body the human Jesus attains a completion that he could not possess in his historical life. Like any other individual, Jesus had a limited individual nature that needed to be perfected through the contributions of other individuals. Unlike other persons, Christ has unbounded capacity for such perfection, as he unites himself mystically to all those who are open to his grace and become members of his Mystical Body, and thus he can live in all the specific ways that these members live. In his historical life Christ worked, prayed, and suffered on behalf of this Mystical Body; to bring Christ's work to fulfillment, his preeminent members will do the same in their individual ways. Like Paul, they "complete what is lacking in Christ's sufferings for the sake of his body, that is, the Church" (Col. 1:24). To imitate them, venerate them, and invoke them is thus not to turn away from Christocentric piety; rather, it is to maintain respect for Christ's work in this extended body of his. Christ himself, as head of the Mystical Body, takes satisfaction in being able to glorify the Father in union with all of his members. For us recognizing the efficacy of Christ in his saints is a way of affirming that the created world is not utterly vitiated by sin but is capable of aiding us in our progress toward God.

Molinari also underscores the importance of the saints' miracles. The canonized saints are not merely the Church's "most genuine and authentic children" and exemplars of the holiness the Church proposes as an ideal. Over and above this, they are individuals whose "perfect conformity with God's will" is "confirmed from on high by miracles." God himself, by manifesting his miraculous power through the saints' intercession, has singled these individuals out for special veneration. It is only the Roman Catholic church, Molinari says, that sets forth canonized saints whose worthiness is thus confirmed. The Church on earth and the saints in heaven both belong to the Mystical Body and are thus united to each other; by these miracles God points out certain saints whom he wishes to be canonized as a way of promoting consciousness of this union and fostering relationships between the Church Militant (on earth) and the Church Triumphant (in heaven). The scriptural basis for this use of miracles is Mark 16:17 f., in which Christ promises "signs" as marks of those who believe.[23]

Molinari was instrumental in framing chapter 7 of *Lumen gentium,* the dogmatic constitution on the Church issued by the Second Vatican Council. This chapter deals with "the eschatological nature of the pilgrim Church and her union with the heavenly Church." The saints are presented here, as in Molinari's own work, as preeminent members of the Church. Being "more closely united with Christ," those in heaven "establish the whole Church more firmly in holiness, lend nobility to the worship which the Church offers on earth to God, and in many ways contribute to its upbuilding." The Church has always believed that the apostles and martyrs are "quite closely joined with us in Christ," and has venerated them accordingly and asked their intercession. God manifests his presence and his face vividly in those who "shared in our humanity and yet were transformed into especially successful images of Christ." Our union with the Church in heaven is most nobly expressed in common celebration of God's majesty in the liturgy. While thus reaffirming the cult of saints, the council enjoins all members of the Church to "work hard to prevent or correct any abuses, excesses, or defects which may have crept in here and there, and to restore all things to a more ample praise of Christ and of God." Further, the council specifies, "the authentic cult of the saints consists not so much in the multiplying of external acts, but rather in the intensity of our active love." Yet this is not to relegate the saints to a purely exemplary role: the love we bear toward them leads us to seek "example in their way of life, fellowship in their communion, and aid by their intercession."[24]

The common theme running through Rahner, Molinari, and *Lumen gentium* is that the saints play an important role in the life of the Church as such; nowhere in these reflections is emphasis placed on the saints as special patrons for individuals or groups, although Molinari does recognize that specific persons will naturally cultivate relations with certain saints rather than others. Veneration of the saints does not draw the individual Christian away from the broader Church into acts of private devotion but serves as a bond uniting each individual to the total Body of Christ. By the same token, Rahner, Molinari, and *Lumen gentium* all see veneration of the saints as a means for relating to Christ and imitating Christ. Inspired in part by the Protestant challenge and by an aversion to abuses, they incorporate the cult of saints firmly within an ecclesiological and Christological setting.

These points having been established, they are more often presupposed than echoed in the theological literature written since the Second Vatican Council. René Latourelle, writing just after the council, emphasized the impact of personal holiness on the surrounding culture. In other ages prophetic witness, martyrdom, and miracles have been effective signs that have spread and strengthened the faith; in the twentieth century holiness of life holds greater cogency. Contemporary man seeks to dominate the material world but even in doing so recognizes his own weakness and instability. He thus turns to the saints, whose consecration of their life to others brings a personal fulfillment not available from the material world. Repeatedly Christian conversions in our age seem to be provoked or accelerated by some eye-opening shock, often the living Christianity of a saint or a holy community. Charles de Foucauld, Gabriel Marcel, Jacques and Raïssa Maritain, and Karl Stern were all touched by such encounters. Another convert found Christ animating a Christian community as it recited the Lord's Prayer. In short:

> In an encounter with the person sinewed in Christ, salvation becomes transparent. Holiness becomes a value which one aspires to participate in. Positively it attracts because it attests to a superior presence working in man, capable of transforming him into a new creature dominated by love.

The bearer of holiness may be an individual rather than a community, but the impact is greater when the individual belongs to a holy community: "Heroic sanctity cannot be fully efficacious unless it appears at the top of a pyramid whose base is established in collective holiness."[25]

In various ways Latourelle's article typifies the theology of sainthood produced in post-Conciliar Catholicism. For him the saint is an extraordinary person who exerts extraordinary attraction and impact on others, but it is not necessary that this bearer of holiness be a canonized saint or an obvious candidate for canonization. The force of example is central to Latourelle's argument, not the power of intercession. He sees sanctity as a "sign of revelation," a manifestation of divine presence, but it is virtuous conduct rather than miracles that show this presence. If the saint differs from other Christians, it is evidently a difference of degree rather than of kind. The holiness of the saint can be shared, and ideally *must* be shared, by broader communities. The otherness of the saint may persist *de facto* but not *de jure*.

These trends in Roman Catholic theology are very much in keeping with the interest Catholics have shown in ecumenical relations with Protestantism. On the other side there are some Protestant writers who have shown an interest in rethinking the notion of sainthood. James William McClendon, Jr., has suggested that many Protestants would like to see themselves as sharing in a wider communion of saints; while the traditional saints of Catholicism form part of this broad collectivity, inspiring Protestant figures (Dag Hammarskjöld, Martin Luther King, Jr., etc.) must also be included. The central point for McClendon is that the saints must be seen as a collectivity. Scripture commonly speaks of "the saints" (*hagioi*) in the plural, seldom in the singular, and it would be wise to follow that model rather than to single out individuals for special honor or veneration. The saints are "*all* of God's children," and worship of God must reflect this fact by celebrating the saintly community. If the life stories of individuals are told, for example in biographical sermons, these individuals are nonetheless to be seen as representatives of the entire collectivity to which the worshiping church belongs, "flesh of our flesh." They should not be subjects for public invocation; private devotion to individuals should be neither encouraged nor disdained but left to each person's conscience.[26]

If McClendon's suggestions are more radical than what most Catholic theologians have proposed, they come close to what many practicing Catholics have already come to take for granted. In the West, at least, many Roman Catholics find the veneration and legends of saints to be vestiges of a tradition in which they no longer share. If saints are important at all, it is as exemplary members of the broader Christian community. Doubtless many Catholics would be happy to recognize Martin Luther King, Jr., and perhaps even Martin Luther, as partners with Francis of Assisi and other canonized saints. Without passing judgment on this development, one must at least note that it represents more than a minor revision of the traditional concept of sainthood. As miracle workers (or means by which God works miracles) during their lives and after their deaths, and as individuals called by God to extraordinary forms of life, the saints have traditionally stood apart from the ordinary run of Christians. Their virtues might be imitable, but their special charismatic powers have been seen as marks of a special numinous presence upon the earth. The legends telling of their deeds, whatever their historical value, have served as powerful testimony to this presence. Saints perceived as essentially imitable and stripped of their "otherness" may represent a kind of democratic ideal; they also represent what one might call a "disenchantment of the Church," *Entzauberung der Kirche*. But if this has been possible, it is not because Protestantization has deprived the Catholic church of what it previously had cherished, but because Catholics living within a culture of disenchantment had already lost any vital sense of the saints as numinous beings worthy of veneration.[27]

NOTES

1. Michael Novak, "Seven Theological Facets," in *Capitalism and Socialism: A Theological Inquiry*, ed. Michael Novak (Washington, D.C: American Enterprise Institute for Public Policy Research, 1979), p. 114.

2. For general information on Christian saints and sainthood, see the excellent bibliography in Steven Wilson, ed., *Saints and Their Cults: Studies in Religious Sociology, Folklore and History* (Cambridge: Cambridge University Press, 1983). Information on specific saints, with reference to the sources for

their lives, can usually be found in Alban Butler, *The Lives of the Saints,* rev. Herbert Thurston and Donald Attwater (London: Burns, Oates & Washbourne, 1926–1938). Of the numerous studies on this topic, three may suffice to suggest the range of possibilities: René Aigrain, *L'hagiographie: Ses sources, ses méthodes, son histoire* (Paris: Bloud & Gay, 1953), a scholarly synthesis; Hippolyte Delehaye, *The Legends of the Saints,* trans. V. M. Crawford (London: Longmans, 1907), a popular classic by one of the great scholars in the field; and Phyllis McGinley, *Saint-Watching* (New York: Viking, 1969), a popularization.

3. On canonization and the role of canonized saints, see E. W. Kemp, *Canonization and Authority in the Western Church* (London: Oxford University Press, 1948); André Vauchez, *La Sainteté en occident aux dernières siècles du Moyen Âge, d'après les procès de canonisation et les documents hagiographiques* (Rome: Ecole Française de Rome, 1981); Donald Weinstein and Rudolph H. Bell, *Saints and Society: The Two Worlds of Western Christendom, 1000–1700* (Chicago: University of Chicago Press, 1982).

4. "The Martyrdom of Polycarp," in Maxwell Staniforth, trans. *Early Christian Writings: The Apostolic Fathers* (Harmondsworth: Penguin, 1968), p. 162.

5. Ronald C. Finucane, *Miracles and Pilgrims: Popular Beliefs in Medieval England* (Totowa, N.J.: Rowman and Littlefield, 1977).

6. Ewald M. Plass, ed., *What Luther Says* (St. Louis: Concordia, 1959) 3: 1251.

7. Léon-E. Halkin, "Hagiographie protestante," *Analecta Bollandiana* 68(1950): 453–463.

8. There is a good survey of methods in František Graus, *Volk, Herrscher und Heiliger im Reich der Merowinger: Studien zur Hagiographie der Merowingerzeit* (Prague: Nakladatelství Československé Akademie Věd, 1965), itself a monumental study. The best way to keep abreast of ongoing work is through reviews and notices in the *Analecta Bollandiana,* the standard journal on hagiography. See also Baudouin de Gaiffier, *Recueil d'hagiographie* (Brussels: Société des Bollandistes, 1977).

9. Sergei Hackel, ed., *The Byzantine Saint* (London: Fellowship of St. Alban and St. Sergius, 1981); Constantin de Grunwald, *Saints of Russia,* trans. Roger Capel (London: Hutchinson, 1960).

10. On the central notion of heroic virtue, see Rudolf Hofmann, *Die heroische Tugend: Geschichte und Inhalt eines theologischen Begriffes* (Munich: Kösel & Pustet, 1933). The ascetic and mystical ideals both emerged from the monastic tradition; for works on this see Giles Constable, *Medieval Monasticism: A Select Bibliography* (Toronto: University of Toronto Press, 1976). There is no single work on the ideal of active service, but many of the relevant issues are discussed in Mary Elizabeth Walsh, *The Saints and Social Work: A Study of the Treatment of Poverty as Illustrated by the Lives of the Saints and Beati of the Last One Hundred Years* (Washington, D.C.: Catholic University of America, 1936).

11. *The Complete Works of Saint Teresa of Jesus,* trans. and ed. E. Allison Peers (London: Sheed & Ward, 1957), vol. 1, p. 65.

12. Ibid., vol. 2.

13. Edward Cuthbert Butler, *Western Mysticism: The Teaching of Augustine, Gregory and Bernard on Contemplation and the Contemplative Life,* 3d ed. (London: Constable, 1967).

14. C. Grant Loomis, *White Magic: An Introduction to the Folklore of Christian Legend* (Cambridge, Mass.: Mediaeval Academy of America, 1948); Benedicta Ward, *Miracles and the Medieval Mind: Theory, Record and Event, 1000–1215* (London: Scolar, 1982).

15. Lynn White, jr., "The Historical Roots of Our Ecological Crisis," in *Brother Francis: An Anthology of Writings by and about St. Francis of Assisi,* ed. Lawrence Cunningham (New York: Harper & Row, 1972), p. 90.

16. Elizabeth Dawes and Norman H. Baynes, trans., *Three Byzantine Saints: Contemporary Biographies Translated from the Greek* (Oxford: Blackwell, 1948); Marvin Kantor, *Medieval Slavic Lives of Saints and Princes* (Ann Arbor: University of Michigan, Dept. of Slavic Languages and Literatures, 1983).

17. Charles Plummer, ed., *Vitae sanctorum Hiberniae* (Oxford: Clarendon, 1910), especially the introduction in 1:ix–clxxxviii; Charles Plummer, ed. and trans., *Lives of Irish Saints* (Oxford: Clarendon, 1922); John Morris, "Celtic Saints," *Past and Present* 11 (1957): 2–16.

18. Hans Bekker-Nielsen et al., eds., *Hagiography and Medieval Literature: A Symposium* (Odense: Odense University Press, 1981); Clare Sutcliffe, *St. Martin and His Hagiographer: History and Miracle in Sulpicius Severus* (Oxford: Clarendon, 1983).

19. Gerhard Strunk, *Kunst und Glaube in der lateinischen Heiligenlegende* (Munich: Fink, 1970), esp. pp. 138 ff.

20. Régis Boyer, "An Attempt to Define the Typology of Medieval Hagiography," in Bekker-Nielsen et al., *Hagiography and Medieval Literature,* pp. 27–36.

21. Lawrence S. Cunningham, *Saint Francis of Assisi* (Boston: Twayne, 1976), pp. 117–120, discusses Kazantzakis and Hesse's Franciscan fiction.

22. Karl Rahner, "The Church of the Saints," in Rahner's *Theological Investigations,* vol. 3, trans. Karl-H. and Boniface Kruger (Baltimore and London: Helicon, 1967), pp. 91–104.

23. Paul Molinari, *Saints: Their Place in the Church,* trans. Dominic Maruca (New York: Sheed & Ward, 1965).

24. Walter M. Abbott, ed., *The Documents of Vatican II* (Chicago: Regnery, 1966).

25. René Latourelle, "Sanctity, A Sign of Revelation," *Theology Digest* 15 (1967): 41–46; see also Lawrence S. Cunningham, *The Meaning of Saints* (San Francisco: Harper, 1980).

26. James Wm. McClendon, Jr., *Biography as Theology: How Life Stories Can Remake Today's Theology* (Nashville and New York: Abingdon, 1974), pp. 204–215; see also Max Thurian, "Le mémorial des saints: Essai de compréhension évangélique d'un aspect de la piété catholique," *Verbum Caro* 13 (1959): 7–28.

27. Richard Kieckhefer, "The Cult of Saints as Popular Religion," *Explor* 7 (1984): 41–47. It would seem fitting to close with a reference to recent Ortho-

dox work, perhaps Elie Melia, "Réflexion orthodoxe sur la sainteté," in *Saints d'hier et sainteté d'aujourd'hui* (Paris: Desclée de Brouwer, 1966), pp. 121–130. But Orthodox studies are not comparable to those of Roman Catholics and Protestants, as the Orthodox world has not felt such a need to rethink this topic radically—has not, in fact, conceived it essentially as a problem. Orthodox devotion to saints can make some claim to being *numquam reformata quia numquam deformata*.

2

Sainthood on the Periphery: The Case of Judaism

Robert L. Cohn

Ask an American Jew to identify the saints of Judaism and you will most likely be met with bewilderment. The term "saint" conjures up images of halos, shrines, and relics quite foreign to modern Jewish sensibilities. For modern Western Jews sainthood is a category irredeemably Christian. Despite this popular view, however, modern Jewish scholars have occasionally used the term "saint" to refer to various rabbis. Thus Louis Finkelstein entitled his biography of the famous second-century sage *Akiba: Scholar, Saint, and Martyr,* while Louis Ginzberg, in his book *Students, Scholars, and Saints,* treated sages from ancient to modern times without clearly distinguishing among the three rubrics.[1] More recently Jacob Neusner has identified the Babylonian rabbis as saints, using the term in the general sense of "holy man."[2] But it is not clear just what the term "saint" adds to our understanding of these figures or how they relate to saints in other religions.

If we want to employ sainthood as a category in the comparative study of religion and to investigate its application to Judaism, we must begin with a good sense of what we are looking for. "Saint" must mean more than "holy person" in general but must also be liberated from its specifically Christian definition.[3] As the term is used in this study, a saint is a type of religious authority who is both a model for imitation and an object of veneration. A saint so perfectly enfleshes the ideals and values of a religion that he or she becomes holy in a distinctive way. The life of the saint acts as a parable for others, a beacon leading to fullness of life. The sanctity of the saints inspires other people to follow them, usually by dwelling piously on their stories (hagiography) and cultically revering their memory (hagiolatry).[4]

This description characterizes entire classes of holy persons in Christianity, Islam, Hinduism, and Buddhism. In classical forms of these traditions individuals function as paradigms for piety and their holiness inspires cultic veneration. Saints are vital to Roman Catholicism and Eastern Orthodoxy, as are the *walī* to Sufism, the *ṛṣi* and *guru* to Hinduism, and the *arahant* to Theravāda and the *bodhisattva* to Mahāyāna Buddhism. These figures stand at the center of the piety of these traditions. But classical rabbinic Judaism, by contrast, never officially designated a set of human beings as worthy of special reverence or models of pious behavior. The literary genre of hagiography is nearly absent from biblical and classical Jewish literature and appears only sporadically among later mystical groups.[5] Most telling, the Jewish calendar lacks any celebration or memorial devoted to a holy person; there are no saints' days or seasons celebrated throughout the Jewish world. With rare exceptions Jewish graves did not become shrines, and relics are unheard of. Those saintlike figures that Judaism has produced have emerged not from its classical rabbinic center but from its periphery, from forms of Judaism localized in time or place. Thus North African Jewry, heavily influenced by Muslim practice, and Eastern European Hasidism, repelled by rabbinic formalism, both developed traditions of saints.

To investigate the category of sainthood with respect to Judaism, then, is first and foremost to explain why no institution of sainthood formed within rabbinic Judaism. Only then can we explore those manifestations of sainthood that do exist and see them in their proper perspective. Accordingly, we shall first examine the ways in which the shape of Judaism militates against a tradition of saints. In so doing we shall see how this comparative category aids in highlighting the distinctiveness of Jewish piety. Next, guided by Jewish specimens of hagiography and hagiolatry, we survey those figures who may be construed as saintlike. Finally, we describe the ideal human types that Judaism commends for emulation, for it is these ideals, rather than flesh-and-blood human beings, on which most Jewish aspirations have focused.

The minor role that sainthood plays in Judaism can be explained by analyzing several features inherent in the structure of Jewish religion and society. First, of major relevance is the Jewish faith's subordination of the individual to the community. The central Jewish myth sees God bound in covenant to the people of Israel as a whole; one's individual identity is discovered through membership in that people. By following God's Torah, his commandments, the Jew works toward the redemption of the whole people, toward the creation of a just society. Salvation is not primarily an individual but a group achievement. The idea of the saint as paradigm, conversely, presupposes an individualistic form of piety. The saint is a spiritual elder who has cultivated a unique path and can help followers cultivate theirs. Moreover the saints' journey to holiness endows them with the ability to aid or intercede for followers as they pursue life in this world. But Jews lack the need for individual intercession because redemption is understood to come only when society as a whole is ripe for it. One rabbinic dictum insists that the Messiah would come if all Israel would only keep a single Sabbath. No amount of saintly intercession can produce that result; it is a matter of human will and energy properly directed toward obeying the injunctions of Torah. The way of Torah is not too difficult, says Deuteronomy (30:11); the law is public and even the humblest Jew can follow it. Rabbinic Judaism has no barriers that need to be crossed with supernatural helpmates and no *gnosis* that must be supernaturally revealed. The very goal of regnant Jewish faith renders the saint superfluous.

The centrality of Torah leaves no room either for the paradigm of sainthood in many traditions: the unique founder. An impersonal law, not a personal life, molds Jewish piety. Unlike Christianity, Islam, Buddhism, and others, Judaism recognizes no superlative person whose experience and insight map the spiritual journey for everyone else. Saints often reenact the founder's life in their own by seeking to follow his path. They act as symbols who translate the founder's experience into terms that are understandable in their own time and place. Lacking such a central person, Judaism offered no master paradigm to spiritual seekers. Although Moses ("our rabbi") was seen to be the recipient of a unique mission, his life was the object of no special attention. God had assigned him a distinct role, but even Moses remained subject to the Torah, which he mediated. It, not he, focused religious devotion.

Because Jewish religion is inextricably linked to Jewish nationhood, conversion, which is a hallmark of many religious biographies, tends to be exceptional rather than standard. Most Jews become Jews by birth, not transformation, so the experience of conversion is not central to the faith of Jews as it is, for instance, for many Christians. In other religions saints provide models for potential converts by dwelling on their own experiences of conversion or transformation. Often these come as profound visions, auditions, or awakenings that suddenly or gradually change their lives.[6] Such transformation experiences are important to hagiographers for they demonstrate how the most worldly person can become the most spiritual. But in Judaism such tales of transformation generally failed to exercise the religious imagination. In fact, Jewish custom forbids the recall of the prior life of a convert; what counts is the life shared with fellow Jews. Thus the spiritual transformation, the stock in trade of hagiography, has had little appeal in Judaism.

The correlation between the Jewish emphasis on nationhood and the dearth of saint veneration emerges most clearly in the two matchless indices to Jewish piety, the calendar and the prayerbook (*Siddur*).[7] The main festivals of Judaism commemorate national events: the exodus, the giving of Torah, the wilderness wandering. Even minor holidays such as Purim and Hanukkah, though they involve the praise of individuals, celebrate national salvation.[8] In fact, the Passover *Haggadah,* which retells the liberation from Egypt, mentions Moses, the great liberator, only once—and that in a proof-text from Scripture. Similarly, the *Siddur* devotes no petitions to individuals and recalls no individual lives. Even in remembering the martyrs of Judaism, the liturgies for the Day of Atonement and the Ninth of Av view them as a group rather than as individual saints. In the *Mahzor,* the High Holiday prayerbook, individual supplications to God for forgiveness of sin are found in the first-person plural: "we have sinned." Even on these days of awe when the individual Jew seeks atonement he or she does so as part of a group—and directly, without saintly mediation.

The absence of any veneration of humans from the religious calendar and liturgy derives from a second distinctive feature of Jewish piety: its unrelenting aniconism. The second commandment's prohibitions on image making and serving other gods were interpreted to preclude also the veneration of any human being or earthly object. The abyss between God and human beings is absolute in Judaism; neither divine incarnation nor human apotheosis can occur. Thus a class of perfectly sanctified human beings rubs against the grain of Jewish faith. Like mosques, synagogues lack icons and employ few symbols in decoration. To be sure, the ban on images has been relaxed in various eras: Hellenistic synagogues, for instance, displayed zodiacs and their symbols and even had drawings of biblical figures. Nonetheless neither humans nor representations of them formed any part of Jewish worship.

Related to the prohibition of molded images and their use in worship is the biblical ban on necromancy—contact with the dead, the veneration of whom would compromise the exclusive worship of God. So the biblical tradition insists that the dead are gone for good. Deuteronomy 34:6 emphasizes that even the grave of Moses is unknown, thus precluding any cult dedicated to the dead liberator. And the shade of the prophet Samuel, the only dead man contacted by the living in the Hebrew Bible, is outraged that Saul disturbs him. But sainthood, especially in the Christian tradition, often relies on the power of the dead. The posthumous miracles of Christian saints are an important criterion for their canonization: wonders frequently occur in the vicinity of their graves or their relics. The only good saint, it has been suggested, is a dead saint.[9] But the Jewish refusal to countenance contact with the dead or to recognize their powers nearly eliminates this entire dimension of sainthood. Although from at least Second Temple times Jews commonly visited the alleged tombs of biblical and rabbinic worthies, these revered dead were not the objects of official cults.[10]

The distance that Jews kept from the dead proceeds also from a deep-seated sense of the impurity of corpses. In biblical law a dead body represents the highest degree of impurity and conveys uncleanness to everything that touches it or is in the same tent with it (Lev. 11:24–25; Num. 19:14–16). Those who have come in contact with corpses, like those who have touched lepers or had an issue from their sexual organs, must undergo purification rituals. Talmudic law extends the category "father of impurity" beyond corpses to entire burial areas.[11] These purity rules made nearly impossible any cultic contact with the dead or their relics. Jewish practice thus stands in marked contrast to the Christian fascination with corpses, their dismembered pieces, and their blood, as well as with objects that had come in contact with the dead. Indeed the rise of the Christian cult of saints took place in the cemeteries, where the faithful gathered to pay homage to and solicit the merit of the martyrs.[12] Gradually the tomb became a shrine, and the power of the dead became the foundation of the piety of the living. Eventually relics brought the power of saints to distant places. Because these developments could not occur in Judaism, there existed no real cultic basis for sainthood.

A final barrier to the development of sainthood in Judaism is sociological. Jewish piety tended to be egalitarian: all were bound by the same law and worshiped in the same synagogues. Separate and supererogatory piety, such as is represented in other religions by monasticism, played no role in rabbinic Judaism. Jews could not escape from the world to find God; they met him in their daily lives. They saw their task to be sanctifying the world as given, not leaving it to find a higher way. The rabbis' goal was to "rabbinize" Israel, not to cultivate a separate path. So by refusing to recognize a higher terrain of piety, Judaism eliminated the main breeding ground for saints. In part this position was an expression of the conviction that Jewish society as a whole was already separate from the "world"—that is, from the dominant Christian or Muslim society in which it lived. As a "nation within the nations" distinguished from them by its Torah, Judaism treasured its separateness, its higher calling. Because Israel saw itself as a "kingdom of priests and a holy nation" (Exod. 19:6) with respect to Christendom and Islam, it did not typically nurture a pious elite class within itself.

Furthermore without an official hierarchy, Judaism lacked an authoritative means to canonize saints, to declare that certain holy persons were deemed fit as exemplars. Without an institution to sponsor them local holy persons' reputations could easily wither. Indeed in Christianity it was the bishops' willingness to patronize the tombs of the martyrs and to exploit them for their own needs that created the cult of the saints out of what might have been private shrines.[13] Moreover unlike many holy persons in other religions who lived and functioned at a distance from society, rabbis lived under the constant gaze of their disciples and colleagues.[14] Thus claims to special holiness were likely to have as many detractors as defenders.

The absence of a vigorous tradition of sainthood in Judaism in no way reflects despair about the human potential for holiness. Rather the very structure of Jewish religion and society discouraged the recognition of holy persons as models and icons. The primacy of the community over the individual in covenant and cult, the abhorrence of icons and the uncleanness of corpses, and the egalitarian nature of Jewish society all worked against the production of saints. Nevertheless despite these limiting factors, certain individuals and groups of individuals in the history of Judaism may be construed as saintlike, given the impression they made on popular Jewish piety. Holy men (but not women!) have occasionally achieved a status analogous to that of saints in other religions.[15] Having explained why sainthood is rather peripheral in Jewish piety, I next look historically at the manifestations of sainthood on that periphery.

SAINTLIKE MANIFESTATIONS IN JEWISH HISTORY

Biblical personalities have always occupied a special place in the Jewish imagination. Although no single one of them could properly be regarded as a saint for ancient Israel, together they display a range of imitable and inimitable qualities typical of saints. Many project values that biblical authors considered exemplary. Thus Abraham is a model of faith, Jacob of cunning, Joseph of wisdom, Moses of humility, David of repentance, and Jeremiah of compassion. And among females the narratives praise Sarah the patient, Rebekkah the determined, Ruth the loyal, and Esther the wise. Others display supernatural powers associated with saints: Elijah and Elisha multiply food, heal lepers, and raise the dead. Even the bones of the dead Elisha have the power to raise a corpse (2 Kings 13:21). At the same time, none of these figures is idealized, much less seen as a perfected being. Indeed biblical authors go to great lengths to depict the weaknesses of their heroes: Abraham lies, Jacob cheats, Joseph boasts, Moses refuses, Jeremiah complains, David murders, Sarah laughs at God, and Elisha misuses his powers to slay some children who have offended him.

The biblical tales, moreover, cannot be regarded as hagiographical in any meaningful sense. Although biblical historiography is structured around the deeds of individual characters, the narratives focus not on praising the hero but on illustrating his or her role in the history of Israel. Biblical historiography presents a succession of characters whose lives become windows to the ramifications of biblical faith. Episodes depict the virtues and vices of the biblical worthies but never comprise a devotional vita.

Although on one level the biblical characters seem to be too much like us to be considered saints, on another level they are too different from us to warrant that title. Nearly all of them are "called," divinely designated for a certain vocation. Abraham must forsake his past, Moses must lead his people, David must reign as king, and Amos can but prophesy. Their experiences are not repeatable, as no discipline of prayer, meditation, or asceticism has made them what they are. One cannot train for their vocations. Rather, they have been struck dumb by a God who gives them power to act or speak on his behalf. The prophet is in no sense a model to imitate; one should do what he says but cannot do what he does. Biblical sources retroactively apply the title "prophet," in the sense of a unique spokesperson for and intercessor with God, to Abraham, Moses, and others, while rabbinic literature terms all of the biblical heroes prophets.[16] One rabbinic tradition counts forty-eight prophets and seven prophetesses (Babylonian Talmud [hereafter *b.*] *Megillah* 14a). Because the rabbis believed that prophecy ceased at the end of the biblical era, the designation "prophet" marks for them a unique set of inimitable individuals confined to ancient times.

In Hellenistic Jewish literature various genres elaborate hagiographically on the laconic tales given in the Bible.[17] Testament literature, for instance, attributes lengthy deathbed testaments to biblical personalities, such as the sons of Jacob, who commend particular virtues and condemn certain vices. In the many apocalyptic writings ancient worthies such as Enoch, Moses, and Ezra are credited with incredible visions that map events in the time of the Hellenistic authors. Philo's *Life of Moses* represents a third genre: sacred biography. Here Moses is represented as the ideal king, the true priest and prophet, and the perfect lawgiver. Significantly all of these hagiographical types were preserved not by Jews but by Christians.

Another Hellenistic genre, more significant for ongoing Judaism than these, is the martyr story. During the Antiochan persecution, the first time that individual Jews were persecuted and killed for adhering to Torah's laws, the martyr who died rather than violate Torah became a new kind of Jewish hero. In 2 Maccabees, for instance, the tortures and deaths of the aged Eleazar and of a woman and her seven sons at the hands of Antiochus Epiphanes are related with a Greek rhetorical flourish that celebrates their courage and exemplary behavior (6:18–7:42). Writers soon read qualities of the martyr back into the lives of prophets whose biblical stories, except in the case of Jeremiah, gave only scant attention to the matter of suffering for one's beliefs.[18] Thus the Ascension of Isaiah memorializes the martyrdom of the prophet at the hands of the evil king Manasseh. Later the *midrashim* of the *tannaim* and later rabbinic sources count nearly all biblical heroes as martyrs—from Abel and Abraham to Zechariah and Daniel. Although as prophets these figures are inimitable, as martyrs they are exemplary. In this way they reflect the basic tension found among saints in other world religions.

Within the history of Israel and biblical literature itself there is little indication that holy men formed the subjects of special devotion or cultic worship. True, miracle tales such as those that surface about Elijah and Elisha may indicate a circle of disciples who revered the master's powers, and the tomb of the patriarchs and matriarchs at Machpelah seems to have been a holy place. Yet the strong biblical animus against any cult of personality or homage to the dead meant that any real veneration would have had to operate underground, beneath the official level of biblical writers. But by the Hellenistic period sources reveal a lively cultic interest in the graves of biblical figures. Matthew 23:29 accuses the scribes and Pharisees of building and adorning the tombs of the prophets, a charge borne out by recent investigations into the role of biblical tombs in popular piety. Joachim Jeremias documents traditions about the graves of Joseph, Hulda, Isaiah, Zechariah, Rachel, David, Jeremiah, the patriarchs, and others; they were the object of pilgrimages from near and far.[19] References in Hellenistic Jewish literature and rabbinic *midrashim* indicate that on the popular level, the holy person was believed to be still present in his grave and capable of hearing the prayers of the faithful and answering them. This popular piety, however, was soon repudiated by the rabbis, and veneration of graves became an exclusively Christian practice. One source declares, "One erects no grave monuments to the dead; their lives perpetuate their memory" (Palestinian Talmud [hereafter *j*] *Shekalim* 47a). Despite this official rejection, however, pilgrimages to tombs of biblical prophets are widely attested throughout the Middle Ages and have continued among eastern Jews until the present.[20]

Classical rabbinic literature—Talmud and *midrash*—does not focus on personalities, as does biblical narrative. In fact the structure of these texts, which map debates about interpretation of law and Scripture, leaves no room for biography.[21] Not a single hagiographic sketch can be found in all of rabbinic writing. To be sure, sayings of and anecdotes about rabbinic sages appear everywhere, but nowhere is there an interest in an individual personality for its own sake. The rabbis did not see one another or their rabbinic forbears as possessors of a unique holiness worthy of devotion on the part of others. Yet rabbinic tales do attribute special qualities and merit to certain sages. The gentle Hillel is contrasted with the harsh Shammai, for instance, and Rabbi Simeon bar Yohai is known for his mystical predilections; many others are praised for their great learning and wisdom. The five disciples of Rabbi Yohanan ben Zakkai each have their characteristic virtues. The greatest of them, Eliezer ben Hyrcanus, is said to be "a plastered cistern which loses not a drop" (Mishnah *Abot* 2:8), and others are credited with far-reaching wonder-working powers. Several Palestinian rabbis, such as Rabbi Hanina ben Dosa, are given the title *ḥasid* (enthusiast) and somewhat ambivalently celebrated for their cures and rain-making powers.[22] Many tales, similarly, relate the ability of a number of Babylonian rabbis to bring fertility, exorcise demons, and heal the sick.[23] One text even claims that people used soil from the grave of Rav to bring down a fever (*b. Sanhedrin* 47b). But such powers were the stock in trade of magicians throughout the world of Late Antiquity; the influence of such Jewish magicians was primarily local and short-lived, not analogous to the lasting charisma of Christian saints.

More important for the subject of sainthood is the continued attention given to martyrs. The rabbis embraced the stories of the Maccabean martyrs and retold their stories in Talmudic literature.[24] In addition the deaths of rabbinic sages were interpreted in such a way that would swell the ranks of those who preferred death to violating the dictates of Torah. Under the persecution of Hadrian many, such as Rabbi Akiba, met their deaths, and their last moments were memorialized in tales that boast of their great courage. Rabbi Akiba, for example, is pictured reciting the *Shema* as the Roman executioner flays his flesh (*j. Berakhot* 14b). During the geonic period (seventh to eleventh century), martyr stories of ten teachers who were slain by Hadrian on a single day, according to legend, became the subjects of a special *midrash* ("The Ten Martyrs") also adapted for liturgical use.[25]

Tradition maintained that the selfless actions of these rabbinic martyrs and their biblical forebears earned merit for the community as a whole. Their deaths atoned not only for the sins of their own generation but also for the sins of their ancestors and descendants. Thus the deaths of the "ten martyrs" eventually were understood to atone for the ancient sin of the sale of Joseph, which had gone unexpiated. This idea of martyrs' merit forms part of the more general rabbinic tenet of the "merit of the fathers," the righteous biblical patriarchs.[26] As early as the Pentateuch Moses invokes the names of Abraham, Isaac, and Jacob when he seeks to avert God's destruction of Israel (Exod. 32:13). For the rabbis this merit continues to sustain Israel just as the merit of Noah sustains the Gentiles. Although there was opposition to the belief that the merit of the righteous in general and the martyr in particular might be called upon by later generations, it became anchored, nonetheless, in the prayers of fast days and the New Year. On the Day of Atonement, for instance, God is asked to remember the binding of Isaac, a near martyr, when he judges Israel. But this doctrine of merit, reminiscent as it is of the intercession of saints, focused not so much on individual persons as on the collectivity of the righteous and the martyrs. Together their merit could elicit God's mercy toward his sinful people.

Martyrs continued to be thought of as possessing saintlike virtue among the Ashkenazic Jews of medieval Europe as the Crusades led to an immense new wave of slaughtering of Jews. Outnumbered and nearly defenseless Jewish communities in the Rhineland attacked by fringe groups of Crusaders (first in 1096) resorted to mass suicide rather than die at the hands of the uncircumcised.[27] Jewish chronicles and poets present these frenzied acts of desperation as the victims' saintly self-sacrifice for the sake of the sanctification of the divine name (*qiddush ha-shem*).[28] Following the rabbinic dictum that one must choose martyrdom over the commission of an act of idolatry, sexual crime, or murder, the victims willingly chose death over baptism. Chroniclers term these martyrs "holy ones" (*qedoshim*), for their righteous deaths not only earn them a place in the world to come but also atone for the sins of later generations. In fact, the chronicler Solomon bar Simson envies that generation chosen for its merit to be a sacrifice and witness to God's great name.[29] Although these martyrs were regarded as saintly and their memories were preserved not only in chronicles but also in *piyyutim* (poems) and *Memorbuchen* (memorial books) read in Ashkenazic synagogues, their individual vitae, like those of the "ten martyrs," were not emphasized. The chroniclers' stories of their martyrdoms are so highly stylized, in fact, that their individuality tends to disappear.[30] The Spanish Jewish poet and theologian Judah Halevi, who lived during the Crusades in the north, argued that since Christians and Muslims extol their martyrs, the Jews, an entire people of martyrs, should glory in them all the more.[31] But the martyrs' *individual* identity and potential sainthood pale before their function as representatives of Israel as a whole.

In addition to revering the martyrs, the Ashkenazim admired the leaders of the Ḥasidei Ashkenaz ("pious ones of Germany"), a mystical pietistic movement that developed in the wake of the violence of the Crusades.[32] Samuel of the Kalonymus family of Speyer, his more famous son Judah (1140–1217), and Judah's disciple, Eleazar of Worms, led an ascetic and penitential group of men who sought to live a continual martyrdom by dying daily to the pleasures of this world. Although they cultivated powerlessness, the Ḥasidim, especially their leader, Judah, were credited with magical powers. Because he denied himself everything, the *ḥasid,* in the popular mind, commanded the elements. Legends about the powers of Judah the *ḥasid* form the richest hagiographical cycle in medieval Jewish literature. Judah was transformed from a model of piety for the few into a magician venerated by the many.[33] He thus functioned as a popular saintlike figure despite his esoteric mystical orientation.

The propensity to revere mystical leaders as saints is even more evident among the Sephardic Jews, both in Spain and in the lands into which they were dispersed after their expulsion in 1492. Among these Jews, who were less fundamentalist than their Ashkenazic coreligionists, *kabbalah* (mystical tradition) developed in many directions. The classical document of *kabbalah,* the Zohar, written in late thirteenth-century Spain by the mystic Moses de Leon, featured the ancient rabbinic mystic, Rabbi Simeon bar Yohai, as the expounder of esoteric doctrine.[34] His role as the fountainhead of mysticism indicates his unique position in the imaginations of Spanish mystics as a kind of patron saint. Until 1492 the *Zohar* and other mystical works belonged to a small elite, but after the expulsion from Spain they moved more into the public domain. To the new exiles mysticism offered an explanation for their fate and a discipline for bringing exile to an end. Especially in sixteenth-century Safed in northern Israel, pietists gathered under the tutelage of charismatic mystics to repent for the sins of Israel and prepare for the coming of the redeemer.

Foremost among these mystics was Isaac Luria, called Ha-Ari ("the divine Rabbi Isaac"), who interpreted the historical exile of the Jews as but a symptom of God's exile from himself and imprisonment in the material world.[35] Through prayer and fulfillment of the commandments, he thought, the Jew aids in the process of *tikkun* (restoration), whereby God is "restored" to himself, and thereby hastens the messianic age. By attributing cosmic significance to the experience of exile and the discipline he fostered to overcome it, Luria attracted a serious following who regarded him as a *tsaddiq* (saintly man). For his part he encouraged this reverence by demonstrating clairvoyant powers. He "discovered" the graves of ancient worthies and, with his disciples, communed with these honored dead. Like all *kabbalists* Luria believed in metempsychosis, the transmigration of souls, and like many, he claimed to be able to read in people's foreheads the identities of the ancient souls within them. In fact, he declared that he and his disciples reincarnated Rabbi Simeon bar Yohai and his disciples, the heroes of the *Zohar.* His lasting influence was ensured by the writing of *Toledot ha-Ari,* a collection of his sayings and habits; one of the disciples who wrote it, Hayyim Vital, also composed an autohagiography as his own claim to be Luria's successor.

Mystical enthusiasm and the tradition of open messianic speculation among Sephardic Jews gave rise to a large number of messianic claimants and movements.[36] These false messiahs illustrate the fate likely to befall a would-be Jewish saint. In the heat of apocalyptic predictions any Jewish leader recognized as especially holy may well assume the unique position of messiah in his own mind or that of his followers. But the public acclamation of a saint necessarily became the public condemnation of a sinner when the messiahship proved false. Such was the fate of all Jewish messianic pretenders: for them sainthood was an all-or-nothing proposition. Among the many figures who shared this fate, one might mention Solomon Molcho (1500–1532), a Portuguese Marrano who reverted to Judaism, preached in Salonika about the coming redemption, gathered many followers, and became convinced that he was the messiah. He even attempted to fulfill a Talmudic messianic legend by sitting in Rome as a beggar for thirty days (*b. Sanhedrin* 98a). His movement spread to Poland, and "relics" such as his banner are still on display in a Prague museum.[37] When the messianic age failed to dawn, however, his "sainthood" was discredited. As might be expected, Isaac Luria too saw himself in a messianic light, but because he was more circumspect in his claims, his messianic failure did not tarnish his kabbalistic influence. He only alluded to his belief that he was "the messiah, son of Joseph" and that he would die in fulfillment of his mission.

The most famous of these messianic personalities, Shabbatai Zevi, illustrates most dramatically how precipitously saint can become sinner in Judaism.[38] At the urging of his disciple and prophet, Nathan of Gaza, Shabbatai proclaimed himself messiah on 31 May 1665 and soon declared 18 June 1666 to be the date of redemption. His prophecies, combined with his forceful personality and bizarre antinomian behavior, won him a huge following in Palestine and Turkey, and his fame spread rapidly through the Middle East and Europe. Everywhere the glad tidings of redemption evoked mass enthusiasm. His apostasy to Islam after he was arrested by Turkish authorities, however, brought an abrupt end to the messianic hopes of the vast Jewish society that supported him. Some groups continued to believe, seeing his apostasy as another manifestation of the "holiness of sin" that he earlier espoused, and they also converted to Islam along with him. For the great majority, however, apostasy was anathema, and the sudden collapse of the Shabbatean movement greatly diminished the respectability of messianism among rabbinic authorities and the credibility of this perilous mode of Jewish sainthood from the seventeenth century onward.

The expulsion of the Jews from Spain brought the Sephardim to the lands of the third major grouping of Jews to be considered here, those who made their home in the Orient, North Africa, and the Middle East. In these Muslim lands Jewish attitudes toward sainthood were heavily influenced by Muslim practice. The ancient graves of biblical and rabbinic holy men were located there: in Palestine, Egypt, Syria, and Babylonia. The common Muslim practice of making pilgrimages to the tombs of the saints undoubtedly encouraged Jewish pilgrims to honor their dead in a similar way. Throughout the Middle Ages the itineraries of famous pilgrims from Europe were determined by these sacred tombs. The settlement of Jews in Turkey after 1492 greatly increased the number of pilgrims to the holy land. At the tomb of Samuel the prophet at Ramah, for instance, a spot also venerated by Muslims, Jewish pilgrims held annual communions and celebrations.[39] In North Africa Muslim worship at the tombs of marabouts prompted similar veneration among Jews at famous rabbis' tombs. In fact several such sites were shared by Jews and Muslims who revered the same or a different saint there.[40] Approaching such a tomb on the occasion of some important event, devotees would undergo purification, remove their shoes, light candles, kiss the tomb, eat a meal, and petition the rabbi for some favor.[41] The most famous of Moroccan rabbis so honored, Rabbi Amran ben Divan, offered God his life if his ill son would recover. After his death in 1782 his tomb became an object of veneration, and his intercession was requested especially by barren women. Similar practices can still be observed among Oriental Jews at sites such as Rachel's tomb near Bethlehem, where women pray to "Rachel our mother" for fertility.

Annual collective pilgrimages to tombs occurred on the anniversary of the saint's death. Sometimes these were festive celebrations called *hilula* (wedding). The grandest of these was the *hilula* for Rabbi Simeon bar Yohai, hero of the *Zohar,* at his grave in Meiron in Galilee.[42] This festival is still celebrated by Sephardic and Oriental Jews on Lag be 'Omer, the thirty-third day after Passover. While other Jews mark this day by lifting the restrictions in force between Passover and Shavuot, *hilula* celebrants conduct a joyful vigil at the grave of Rabbi Simeon, lighting torches and bonfires, dancing and singing, and performing special rites such as cutting children's hair.

The most recent and vigorous examples of sainthood in Judaism emerge from the Hasidic movement that took shape in late eighteenth-century Poland and the Ukraine. Led by the charismatic preacher and amulet writer Israel ben Eleazar (1700–1760), called the Baal Shem Tov, the movement appealed to simple Jews repelled by the elitism of rabbinic learning, disheartened by the failure of Shabbatai Zevi, and devastated by the harsh conditions of Poland after the Chmielnicki massacres (1666).[43] To them the Baal Shem Tov offered a warm and fervent piety rich in song and dance. In Hasidism many of the arcane notions of *kabbalah* reappear but are transformed for popular consumption to produce a practical mysticism appealing to the most unlettered soul. In the Baal Shem Tov his followers found more than a magician, a master of the divine name (*baal shem*); in him they found a living Torah, a personality that embodied the spirit of Torah and made it accessible to them directly. He showed the way to a personal redemption toward which individuals could strive by sanctifying the world around them and thus lifting their own souls to God.

After the death of the Baal Shem Tov his disciples gathered his sayings and stories but did not worship him as a dead saint. Rather, the living disciples themselves became the leaders of groups of Hasidim. In place of the one leader, then, multiple centers of authority developed, each focused on the *tsaddiq* or *rebbe*. With one important exception, Nahman of Bratslav, these *tsaddiqim* did not claim exclusive authority but were content to lead their own disciples in the tradition of the Baal Shem Tov as they understood it. Each *tsaddiq* had a distinctive personality and orientation and attracted a following only partially determined by geographical proximity. Disciples would travel great distances to "their *rebbe*," often bypassing other Hasidic communities on the way. There they would find the *tsaddiq* who reached their soul, prayed for them and with them, answered their questions, and cured their ills. The *tsaddiq*'s very life served as a model for his disciples. Said one disciple of his master: "I did not go to the Maggid of Meseritz to learn Torah from him but to watch him tie his boot laces." The *tsaddiq* characteristically taught Torah not by giving learned commentaries on it but by telling evocative tales that appealed to the emotions.

But if the *tsaddiq* was an exemplar, a living Torah, he was also inimitable, a saint whose powers transcended those of normal men. Then and now—for Hasidic communities still flourish—the *tsaddiq* functions as an *axis mundi,* a channel through which divine grace flows to the community and the agent through which the community approaches God.[44] A disciple of the Maggid of Meseritz reported that whenever he and his companions reached the town limits of Meseritz all their desires were fulfilled. Because the *tsaddiq* practices *devekut* (clinging to God), he can raise his disciples' prayers with dispatch. One influential Hasidic doctrine asserts that to be truly effective the *tsaddiq* must descend from the realm of purity in which he dwells and encounter the evil world of the masses in order to lift up his followers with him. Although he remains inwardly bound to God, he goes out to the people to feel their sorrow, needs, doubts, and hopes and then to lead them from their current rung on the spiritual ladder to the realization of their highest potential.[45]

The inimitability of the *tsaddiq* reached its most extreme form in the Hasidic sect centered on Nahman of Bratslav.[46] Nahman considered himself an absolutely unique *tsaddiq* who rendered his contemporaries obsolete. He claimed to be the *tsaddiq ha-dor,* the sole *tsaddiq* of his time, and the last in a series that included Moses, Rabbi Simeon bar Yohai, Isaac Luria, and Baal Shem Tov. He held, moreover, that as the final link in the chain he heralded the messiah. Whereas the writings of other Hasidic sects portray their *tsaddiqim* as guides, teachers, healers, protectors, and intercessors, only the writings about Nahman depict the *tsaddiq* as a redeemer who battles sin for his disciples' sake.[47] One even finds among the Bratslavers the hope that he will return from death as the Messiah ben David. This Hasidic sect honored Nahman's claim to uniqueness by never recognizing a successor. Whereas in all of the other Hasidic sects a descendant of the *tsaddiq* became the link between God and community, in Bratslav Nahman reigned even after his death.

In the contemporary world the *tsaddiqim* continue to function as living saints. To witness the *rebbe* addressing his followers or casting scraps of food to them from his plate is to be shocked into the recognition that some Jews in the contemporary world venerate saints. To observe the *hilula* for Rabbi Simeon bar Yohai at Meiron similarly convinces one that despite modernity and Judaism's characteristic antipathy toward sainthood, ancient holy men continue to exercise influence over Jews today.

We have seen that although traces of sainthood in Judaism are meager, it is undeniable that saints have been popularly acclaimed, especially by mystical groups. Here the stress on personality over law and on emotion over rationality has produced figures both imitated and venerated. And despite Judaism's abhorrence of veneration of the dead, the graves of the ancient heroes and their later descendants have proved to be powerful magnets drawing the faithful to commune with their holy past. Yet the saints that we have identified do not constitute the main focus of piety even for those who revere them. Even the Lurianic *kabbalists* followed the standard Jewish calendar; even the Hasidim read the Torah and soon studied Talmud as well; even North African Jews prayed out of a *Siddur*. To understand the human ideals that shape Jewish piety we must look beyond the disconnected instances of Jewish sainthood. We must realize that although the sources of Judaism have much to say about the ideal Jew, they rarely dwell on specific human beings as models of perfection. Instead they talk about the ideal man in the abstract, using episodes from the lives of particular individuals to illustrate this or that quality. In the Hebrew Scriptures humans are directed to be holy, not perfect (Lev. 19:2; cf. Matt. 5:48). Thus the tradition stresses paths by which everyone can attain sanctity, rather than the special attainments of individuals who live a life apart.

THREE SPIRITUAL IDEALS

Plato understood the human soul to consist of three faculties: the spirited, rational, and appetitive, or, in other words, the will, mind, and heart. Recently Robert Neville has used these Platonic categories as the basis for three models of spiritual perfection: the soldier, exemplar of psychic integrity; the sage, paragon of enlightenment; and the saint, embodiment of perfect love.[48] He analyzes the stages on the way to the development of their three perfections—a good will, a profound understanding, and a pure heart. Interestingly Judaism offers three human ideals that correspond closely to Neville's categories: the *tsaddiq,* or just man, the *talmid ḥakham,* or scholar, and the *ḥasid,* or enthusiast.[49] Although these types are not always clearly distinguished from one another in Jewish sources, they may usefully be separated here for purposes of discussion.

Without doubt the premier ideal of Jewish piety is the *talmid ḥakham,* literally, the pupil of a sage. This ancient rabbinic term for "scholar" emphasizes the continued studentship of even the greatest sage, for he always remains subordinate to the Torah he studies. Because Torah and its ongoing explication, interpretation, and application disclose the will of God, the ability to learn and teach it is Judaism's most prized skill. In the *talmid ḥakham* the mind traverses the most direct road to God, a road that beckons all to follow. Because Torah proceeds from God, to study it is to think God's thoughts after him. And Torah is never complete: each generation must appropriate, refine, and extend it as the flux of history demands. Talmudic reasoning seeks the principles behind every ruling, thus aiming to understand the basic structure of the universe. This process, as Jacob Neusner has said, represents the "perfect intellectualization of life."[50] God too studies Torah, rabbinic legend asserts; thus by applying his mind to Torah, the *talmid ḥakham* imitates God.

Rabbinic sages often viewed the study of Torah as an end in itself: *talmud torah lishmah.*[51] It should be studied for its own sake, not for the earthly or heavenly awards attendant thereupon. Rabbi Simeon bar Yohai went so far as to condemn farmers who did not study but worked in the field: "They forsake eternal life and busy themselves with temporal life." Interestingly the same comment is ascribed to another sage, Rava, on the occasion of his observing Rabbi Hamnuna at prayer (*b. Shabbat* 10a). By saying what he is supposed to have said, he accounted prayer less significant than study. Indeed study becomes in Judaism a ritual act, a formalized mode of behavior through which the participant contacts God through his written word. The centrality of the rabbinic intellectual ideal is highlighted also by the abuse the rabbis heap upon the uneducated man, the *ʿam ha-ʾarets*.[52] Not to avail oneself of the chance to study Torah and thereby to merit eternal life makes one a stupid boor, and to study Torah in the presence of such an uncouth person, one source avers, "is as though he raped his betrothed before him" (*b. Pesahim* 49b). Although other spokesmen for the rabbinic tradition are more charitable, such calumny reveals the importance of the ideal of the *talmid ḥakham*.

The rabbinic sage, as his image was recorded in the Talmuds of Palestine (400 C.E.) and Babylonia (500 C.E.), became the dominant model of religiosity for all Judaism in the centuries that followed. No Jew could hope to attain a position of authority without thorough training in the classics of Torah literature. Whether he was a physician like Maimonides or a statesman like Don Isaac Abravanel, every ambitious Jew had the model of the *talmid ḥakham* before him. Even radical mystics like Isaac Luria began their careers studying Torah and continued to do so. The ancient biblical heroes too were transformed through legend into rabbinic sages: Abraham studied the whole Torah before it was given to Moses, and David donned phylacteries and prayed like a rabbi. Moses the greatest prophet became *Moshe rabbenu,* "Moses our rabbi," the spiritual forebear of all later sages. For most Jews through history the great names—the "saints"—have been the names of great scholars such as Hillel, Rashi, Rambam, and the Vilna Gaon. Often their biographies were nearly unknown. Instead they were remembered and revered because of their contributions to Torah, the repository of Jewish wisdom. In fact, even the names of many rabbinic authorities were displaced by the titles of their commentaries.

Judaism's moral ideal crystallized in the figure of the *tsaddiq,* the righteous person. In Talmudic literature the term carries a variety of meanings: a man free from sin, a man who obeys Torah, a man declared not guilty at a trial, a man who gives charity (*tsedaqah*).[53] Some traditions hold that any person who does his best to obey the law is to be accounted a *tsaddiq*. He may fail time and time again, but if he keeps his duty always before him and does not give up, he is righteous. Even a wicked person who repents of his sins may become a *tsaddiq*. In Talmudic literature there are tales of individuals deemed *tsaddiqim* because of a single righteous act. For example, a certain Pentakaka (whose name means literally "five sins"), though the resident manager of a brothel, is called a *tsaddiq* for selling his own bed to ransom from prison the husband of a penniless woman who would otherwise have been forced into a life of prostitution in order to ransom him (*j. Ta'anit* 1,4,64b).

The righteous benefit not only themselves but the world at large. Their deeds bring blessings to the world, and they intercede with God on behalf of humans. Through the notion of merit the effect of righteous beings on others is held to persist even beyond their deaths.[54] As we have seen, the merit of the patriarchs was in some quarters believed to sustain Israel. The martyrs form a special class of *tsaddiqim*: spiritual soldiers *par excellence*. Their moral courage stands in the tradition as an example of what every Jew ought to do in similar circumstances.

The ethical ideal of the righteous person is highly elaborated in medieval and modern philosophical and ethical literature. Just as the preeminence of a written revelation fostered the ideal of the scholar, so too the focus on the prophetic and social dimension of the commandments encouraged the development of the exemplary *tsaddiq*. Maimonides (1135–1204), for instance, sees the righteous man as the one who chooses the middle way. Everyone, he says, is free to become as great a *tsaddiq* as Moses or as infamous a *rasha'* (wicked man) as Jeroboam, the apostate king of Israel (*Mishneh Torah Teshuvah* 5:2). Medieval moralists wrote ethical tracts that were meant to instill righteousness through rabbinic examples. For instance, the *Mesillat Yesharim* (*The Path of the Upright*) of Moses Hayyim Luzzatto (1707–1746), written on the eve of the modern period, declares itself a guide to *ḥasidut* (piousness) but understands that condition largely in terms of moral training.[55] Luzzatto laments pietistic practices such as reciting psalms, fasting, and soaking in ice and snow, which had given *ḥasidut* a bad name. Instead he offers a step-by-step program through which the learned person can cultivate proper traits of character and achieve true piety and, finally, holiness. Sanctity, for Luzzatto, results from the proper motivation in observing Torah's dictates.

In the nineteenth century an educational movement called Musar (moral) aimed at inculcating ethical ideals in Eastern European Jewish society,[56] but its influence was felt primarily in the Lithuanian *yeshivot* (academies). Founded by Israel Lipkin Salanter, the Musar movement sought to resist the disintegrating trends of Haskalah (enlightenment), Hasidism, and Reform by infusing the study of Talmud and the practice of a traditional Jewish life with a high and dignified moral tone. Using Luzzatto's works and other ethical writings, Musar teachers had their pupils chant passages with plaintive melodies in semidarkness to create the proper emotional atmosphere for the internalization of their ethical teachings. In addition, sermons and other group activities encouraged the achievement of ethical goals. These practices created solidarity among the pupils and between each pupil and Torah, and these *yeshivot* successfully produced rabbinic leaders of high character and scholarship.

Although, as Gershom Scholem argues, the *tsaddiq* is by and large an ideal to which all can aspire, a fullness of moral virtue that all can attain with effort, nonetheless a different and richly developed strain in Jewish mysticism sees the *tsaddiq* as a supernormal person.[57] According to this tradition the *tsaddiq* is an individual whose existence sustains the world (*b. Berakhot* 17b). Rabbi Yohanan said, "The world exists for the sake of a single *tsaddiq,* as it is written: 'The *tsaddiq* is the foundation of the world' (Prov. 10:25)" (*b. Yoma* 38b). The Talmudic rabbis speculate about the number of *tsaddiqim* necessary in any generation to outweigh the world's sin; their estimates vary from forty-five to thirty. Rabbi Simeon bar Yohai, with characteristic audacity, includes himself in their number and claims that even if there is only one *tsaddiq,* that one is he (*Genesis Rabbah* 35:2). This notion evolves, as we saw earlier, into the mystical idea of the *tsaddiq ha-dor,* the unique sustainer of the world in his own and even in many generations. A final twist on this theme is the Yiddish legend of the *lamed-vovniks,* the thirty-six "just men" who covertly sustain the world though they themselves may not be aware of their true identity.

This tradition of the exceptional, inimitable *tsaddiq* brings us close to the third ideal of Jewish piety, the *ḥasid,* a figure usually also regarded as a unique individual. The *ḥasid* is a devotee who seeks an individualistic path to God, one that goes beyond knowing God's Torah (like the *talmid ḥakham*) and doing his will (like the *tsaddiq*). Whereas the *tsaddiq* is restrained, doing only what is right, the *ḥasid* is radical, going beyond the call of duty. The *ḥasid* displays the extremes of *ḥesed*: love, mercy, unbounded generosity. He follows the way of fervent prayer, ascetic discipline, or mystic rapture. Until the eighteenth-century Hasidic movement, the title *ḥasid* was given only to lone individuals, not to a social group.[58] In lists of Ashkenazic martyrs, for instance, some names are followed by the designation *ḥasid* or *ḥasidah* (fem.) to convey the highest honor. But even as extremists, *ḥasidim* were understood as part of their communities and were not organized into exclusive pietistic conventicles. Not everyone was encouraged to be a *ḥasid*; emotional enthusiasm was an ideal for the few.

In Mishnah and Talmud the name *ḥasidim rishonim* (*ḥasidim* of old) denotes men distinguished by the austerity of their halakhic rulings and their lengthy prayers.[59] "The *ḥasidim rishonim* used to tarry an hour before they prayed, that they might direct their hearts toward God" (Mishnah *Berakhot* 5:1). These men were also known for their wonder working. Honi the Circle Drawer, for instance, is credited with controlling rainfall. One can understand why miracles would be attributed to such pietists; spiritual intensity in religion often overflows into salvific acts.

More clearly illustrating the extremist's vocation are the medieval German pietists (Ḥasidei Ashkenaz). Out of the *Sefer Ḥasidim,* a book of popular teachings and examples, comes a radical ideal.[60] Although preserving his family life, the *ḥasid* was to renounce ordinary pleasures and aim toward such emotional equilibrium that would permit him to bear shame and insult without flinching. It is said, in fact, that the more he is abused, the greater will be his reward in the world to come. The *ḥasid* revered Torah yet marched to a different drummer, the "heavenly law" (*din shamayim*). His altruism forced him beyond the law, to a stricter interpretation: he might concentrate on the performance of a single commandment or undertake a radical act of penance such as sitting in an icy pond for an hour daily. By erasing all trace of ego the *ḥasid* thus sought to do God's will out of pure love, and when his heart burned with this love, he was deemed worthier than a scholar.

If the medieval *ḥasidic* ideal stressed emotional control, the modern *ḥasidim,* the followers of the Baal Shem Tov, applauded emotional extravagance as the way to love God. In place of ascetic deprivations, joyful singing and dancing and fervent prayer became central. In this case, as Scholem notes, the term *ḥasid* referred no longer to the single religious enthusiast but to the mass following of a "super-*Ḥasid,*" the *tsaddiq*.[61] Yet, as Arthur Green argues, although *ḥasid* and *tsaddiq* might seem to have been transposed in meaning in modern Hasidism, in fact the figure of the supernormal and exceptional *tsaddiq* has clear precedents in Talmudic and mystical tradition. Moreover, the new application of the title *ḥasid* to the many still carries with it the connotations of emotionalism and individualism of the old *ḥasidic* ideal. These new *ḥasidim* too looked beyond Torah, or rather found Torah in the person of the *tsaddiq,* with whom they felt a deep emotional attachment. Each *ḥasid* needed to find his own master, his own link to God. As a group the modern *ḥasidim,* like the earlier individuals given this title, sought a piety more intense than that available to them through the normal rabbinic channels. They took refuge in the fervor of a popular mysticism. In this movement, then, the narrow ideal of the *ḥasid* is opened and becomes a life-style for the many.

The three ideals that I have sketched as distinct entities are not separated so neatly in Jewish sources. The *tsaddiq* and the *ḥasid* overlap, and the scholar should be a righteous and generous man. The Jew is encouraged to work toward all of the ideals at once: to study, observe, and pray. Indeed the *Shema,* the pivotal demand of Jewish faith, enjoins these ideals upon every person: "You shall love the Lord your God with all your heart, with all your soul, and with all your might" (Deut. 6:5). If we interpret this verse in a midrashic fashion, we may identify "heart" (the biblical seat of intelligence) with mind, "soul" (life) with will, and "might" (strength, energy) with enthusiasm. Thus the Jew is to love God with the mind, like a *talmid ḥakham*; with volition, like a *tsaddiq*; and with the emotions, like a *ḥasid.*

The study of the category of sainthood as applied to Judaism has yielded, in one sense, rather meager results. Saints—holy persons understood as models for imitation and subjects for veneration—have been an exceptional rather than a normal feature of Jewish religion. Characteristically, Jewish piety has not focused on the lives of paradigmatic and perfected human beings. Jewish tradition reveres many sages for their learning and wisdom but knows little about their spiritual lives. And tradition credits numerous holy men with gnostic, wonder-working, and even salvific powers but rarely enshrines them in any cultic devotion. If it recognizes extraordinary figures such as Rabbi Simeon bar Yohai, it almost never holds them up as models for the pious. There is little intersection between the paradigmatic and the perfected in Judaism. Only biblical personalities are universally recognized as simultaneously inimitable because they are chosen, and yet exemplary, though in no way perfect, in the virtues they display. On the other end of Jewish history, the *tsaddiqim* of modern Hasidism represent the best examples of a tradition of personalities whose spiritual power rests in the tension between inimitability and otherness.

But if the yield of Jewish saints has been small, the light that the category sheds on Jewish piety has been substantial. For in trying to account for the dearth of Jewish saints, we were forced to examine some basic features of Jewish religion and society that inhibit the development of sainthood. Moreover, we saw that Judaism does not revere exceptional human beings but rather sets forth ideals of learning, righteousness, and enthusiasm for which all—not merely the few—can aim. On the whole it is these holy ideals, rather than holy persons, that have guided Jewish society on its road to redemption.

NOTES

*I am grateful to Professors Manfred Vogel and Jon Levenson for their helpful suggestions on earlier drafts of this essay.

1. Louis Finkelstein, *Akiba: Scholar, Saint, and Martyr* (Philadelphia: Jewish Publication Society, 1962); Louis Ginzberg, *Students, Scholars, and Saints* (Philadelphia: Jewish Publication Society, 1928).

2. Jacob Neusner, *There We Sat Down* (Nashville and New York: Abingdon, 1972), pp. 79–86.

3. For a contemporary treatment of the idea of saints in Christianity with implications for cross-traditional studies, see Lawrence Cunningham, *The Meaning of Saints* (San Francisco: Harper & Row, 1980), esp. pp. 65–85.

4. Joachim Wach stresses the impress of the saint on society by the force of his personal example and his posthumous effect in forging a new social entity. *Sociology of Religion* (Chicago: University of Chicago Press, 1944), pp. 357–360.

5. See Haim Zafrani, "Hagiography," in *Encyclopedia Judaica* [hereafter *EJ*] (Jerusalem: Keter, 1972), vol. 7, cols. 1116–1121.

6. Cunningham writes about Christian saints: "A saint is a person so grasped by a religious vision that it becomes central to his or her life *in a way that radically changes the person* and leads others to glimpse the value of that vision" (emphasis added). *Meaning of Saints,* p. 65. See also Jonathan Sumption, *Pilgrimage: An Image of Medieval Religion* (London: Faber and Faber, 1975), p. 18.

7. See Joseph H. Hertz, trans., *The Authorized Daily Prayer Book,* rev. ed. (New York: Bloch, 1959).

8. In the realm of popular custom, however, the deaths of certain "martyrs" such as Rabbi Meir and Jeremiah the prophet were commemorated in past eras. Also the death of Moses on 7 Adar was marked by reading the story of his death in Deuteronomy 34:5 once every three years, when that passage fell on that date in the ancient triennial cycle of Torah readings. Certain Jewish groups also commemorated the deaths of other figures such as Rabbi Simeon bar Yohai (on this see later text). Eric Werner, "Traces of Jewish Hagiolatry," *Hebrew Union College Annual* 51 (1980): 51, 55–58.

9. This is the thrust of G. van der Leeuw's discussion of the posthumous powers of saints. See *Religion in Essence and Manifestation: A Study in Phe-*

nomenology (New York and Evanston, Ill.: Harper & Row, 1963), pp. 236–239.

10. For a general discussion of Jewish holy graves, see James W. Parkes, Raphael Posner, and Saul Paul Colbi, "Holy Places," in *EJ*, vol. 8, cols. 921–922.

11. See "Purity and Impurity, Ritual," in *EJ*, vol. 13, cols. 1405–1414; Johs. Pedersen, *Israel: Its Life and Culture I–II* (London: Oxford University Press; and Copenhagen: Branner Og Korch, 1926), pp. 481–484.

12. See Peter Brown, *The Cult of the Saints* (Chicago: University of Chicago Press, 1981), pp. 1–12; and Michael Perham, *The Communion of Saints* (London: Society for the Propagation of Christian Knowledge, 1980), pp. 15–21.

13. Brown, *Cult of the Saints,* pp. 23–49.

14. For a discussion of the organization of rabbinic disciple circles and assemblies in Babylonia, see David M. Goodblatt, *Rabbinic Instruction in Sasanian Babylonia* (Leidon: E. J. Brill, 1975), pp. 267–285.

15. Aside from the biblical heroines and Beruriah, the pious wife of Rabbi Meir, very few Jewish women attained positions of influence in society or were celebrated in Jewish literature. This fact is simply part and parcel of the masculine-centered focus of *halakha* and Jewish piety. See Paula E. Hyman, "The Other Half: Women in the Jewish Tradition," *Conservative Judaism* 26, no. 4 (1972): 14–21.

16. See Louis I. Rabinowitz, "Prophets and Prophecy," in *EJ*, vol. 13, cols. 1175–1176.

17. For a brief introduction to these writings, see Leonhard Rost, *Judaism outside the Hebrew Canon: An Introduction to the Documents* (Nashville and New York: Abingdon, 1976).

18. See H. A. Fischel, "Martyr and Prophet (A Study in Jewish Literature)," *Jewish Quarterly Review* 37, no. 3 (1947): 265–280.

19. Joachim Jeremias, *Heiligengräber im Jesu Umwelt* (Göttingen: Vandenhoeck and Ruprecht, 1958), esp. pp. 118–143.

20. See E. N. Adler, *Jewish Travelers* (London: G. Routledge and Sons, 1930), for example, pp. 64–99.

21. See William Scott Green, "What's in a Name?—The Problematic of Rabbinic Biography," in *Approaches to Ancient Judaism: Theory and Practice,* ed. William Scott Green, vol. 1 (Missoula, Mont.: Scholars Press, 1978), pp. 77–96.

22. See Geza Vermes, *Jesus the Jew* (New York: Macmillan, 1973), pp. 58–78; William Scott Green, "Palestinian Holy Men: Charismatic Leadership and Rabbinic Tradition," in *Aufstieg und Niedergang der Römischen Welt,* ed. H. Temporini and W. Hasse, vol. 19: 2, pp. 619–647.

23. See Neusner, *There We Sat Down,* pp. 79–86.

24. Gerson D. Cohen, "The Story of Hannah and Her Seven Sons in Hebrew Literature," in *Mordecai M. Kaplan Jubilee Volume,* ed. Moshe Davis, vol. 2 (New York: Jewish Theological Seminary of America, 1953), pp. 109–122 (Hebrew).

25. Haim H. Ben-Sasson, "Kiddush Ha-shem," in *EJ*, vol. 10, cols. 981–982;

"The Ten Martyrs," in *Jewish Encyclopedia* (New York and London: Funk and Wagnalls, 1916), 8: 355.

26. See the discussion of Ephraim E. Urbach, *The Sages: Their Concepts and Beliefs* (Jerusalem: Magnes, 1975), pp. 496–511.

27. Salo W. Baron, *A Social and Religious History of the Jews,* vol. 4 (New York: Columbia University Press; and Philadelphia: Jewish Publication Society, 1957), 89–106.

28. Baron, *History,* 4: 139–147. See the chronicles now translated in Shlomo Eidelberg, *The Jews and the Crusaders* (Madison: University of Wisconsin Press, 1977).

29. Baron, *History,* 4: 144.

30. See, for instance, the Chronicle of Solomon bar Simson in Eidelberg, *The Jews,* pp. 34, 43–44, 55–58.

31. See Hartwig Hirschfeld, trans., *Judah Hallevi's Kitab al Khazari* (London: George Routledge and Sons; and New York: E. P. Dutton, 1905), p. 78.

32. For background, see Gershom Scholem, *Major Trends in Jewish Mysticism* (New York: Schocken, 1954), pp. 80–87.

33. Scholem, *Major Trends,* pp. 98–99.

34. Again, for background, see Scholem, *Major Trends,* pp. 156–159.

35. Scholem, *Major Trends,* pp. 273–275, 284–286.

36. Gerson D. Cohen, "Messianic Postures of Ashkenazim and Sephardim," in *Studies of the Leo Baeck Institute,* ed. Max Kreutzberger, (New York: Ungar, 1967), pp. 121–125, 133–142.

37. Joseph Schochetman, "Molcho, Solomon," in *EJ,* vol. 12, cols. 225–227.

38. The career of Shabbatai Zevi is dealt with broadly in Scholem, *Major Trends,* pp. 289–299, and in great detail in his *Sabbatai Sevi: The Mystical Messiah,* Bollingen Series 93 (Princeton, N.J.: Princeton University Press, 1973).

39. "Pilgrimage," in *Jewish Encyclopedia,* vol. 10, cols. 35–38.

40. For a detailed list and description of these tombs, see L. Voinot, *Pèlerinages judeo-musulman au Maroc* (Paris: Larose, 1948).

41. See A. Chouraqui, *Between East and West: A History of the Jews of North Africa* (New York: Atheneum, 1973), pp. 71–79.

42. See Eric Werner, "Traces of Jewish Hagiolatry," pp. 56–57; "'Omer Lag be-," in *Jewish Encyclopedia,* 9: 399–400.

43. Scholem, *Major Trends,* pp. 34–50.

44. See Arthur Green, "The *Ẓaddiq* as *Axis Mundi* in Later Judaism," *Journal of the American Academy of Religion* 45 (1977): 327–347. Green shows that *axis mundi* symbolism is richest in the case of the *tsaddiq* Nahman of Bratslav.

45. This is the doctrine of Yaakov Yosef of Polnoy, the earliest Hasidic writer and the main source for the teachings of the Baal Shem Tov. His idea of the "descent of the *tsaddiq*" is explained in Samuel R. Dresner, *The Zaddik* (New York: Schocken, 1960), pp. 148–190.

46. Arthur Green, *Tormented Master: A Life of Rabbi Nahman of Bratslav* (University, Ala.: University of Alabama Press, 1979), esp. pp. 135–220.

47. Green, *Tormented Master,* p. 183.

48. Robert C. Neville, *Soldier, Sage, Saint* (New York: Fordham University Press, 1978).
49. My analysis largely follows that of Gershom Scholem, "Three Types of Jewish Piety," *Eranos-Jahrbuch* 38 (1969): 331–348.
50. See Neusner's suggestive analysis in *Invitation to the Talmud: A Teaching Book* (New York: Harper & Row, 1973), pp. 223–246.
51. On the importance of study, see Urbach, *Sages*, pp. 603–620.
52. On the *ʾam ha-ʿarets*, see Urbach, *Sages*, pp. 632–639.
53. On the righteous man, see Urbach, *Sages*, pp. 483–495.
54. See Urbach, *Sages*, pp. 496–511.
55. Moses Hayyim Luzzatto, *The Path of the Upright*, trans. and ed. Mordecai M. Kaplan (Philadelphia: Jewish Publication Society, 1966).
56. Haim H. Ben-Sasson, "Musar Movement," in *EJ*, vol. 12, cols. 534–537.
57. See Green, *Tormented Master*, pp. 117–119; 132, n. 71.
58. This point is stressed by Scholem, "Three Types of Jewish Piety," p. 343.
59. See S. Safrai, "Teaching of Pietists in Mishnaic Literature," *Journal of Jewish Studies* 16, nos. 1–2 (1965): 15–33.
60. See Scholem, *Major Trends*, pp. 91–99.
61. Scholem, "Three Types of Jewish Piety," p. 346.

Professor Cohn participated in the original seminar on sainthood that initiated this volume, and a version of his chapter appeared also in *Saints and Virtues* (Berkeley, Los Angeles, London: University of California Press, 1987). The editors wish to thank John S. Hawley, who edited that work, for his assistance in making Professor Cohn's scholarship more widely available.

3

"God's Friends:" The Sanctity of Persons in Islam

Frederick M. Denny

To talk about sainthood in English is to talk about the holiness, sanctity, and sacrality of persons. In Islamic-Arabic terminology the words that could be translated "holy" or "sacred" rarely occur in explicit references to persons. Perhaps this is partly because they are not frequently used when speaking of God either. The Arabic root for holy, *q-d-s,* is rare in the Qur'an and applies to God in only three of ten occurrences, as in 59:23, "He is God; there is no god but He. He is the King, the All-holy (*al-quddūs*), the All-peaceable, the All-faithful, and All-preserver, the All-mighty, the All-compeller, the All-sublime."[1] In this passage holiness is but one of a number of attributes. The Qur'an never speaks of the holiness of persons, be they human, *jinnī,* or angelic. Another root that can mean "sacred" or "holy" is *ḥ-r-m,* from which we get *ḥarām,* "prohibited, unlawful"; also "sacred," as in *al-masjid al-ḥarām,* "the sacred mosque." Note the ambivalence of the term. A *muḥrim* is one who is in a state of ritual purity and consecration, as on the Pilgrimage. *Ḥaram* is a "holy place" or "sanctuary" and preeminently refers to Mecca and Medina, the "Two Sanctuaries" (*al-Ḥaramayn*). *Ḥarīm* also means "sanctuary," but it extends to include the secure quarters of a home where the female members are and, indeed, refers to those people themselves as an inviolable group. The root *ḥ-r-m,* then, can apply to humans, although it does so rarely in the Qur'an except in the sense of being forbidden something (e.g., 6:146 concerning dietary regulations and prohibitions), or in senses that do not mean sacrality. In pre-Islamic Arabia a *ḥaram* was a sacred enclave where holy people were buried or a special family heritage was memorialized.[2]

When we use the term "saint" to apply to Islamic cases of the holiness of persons, we must do so with the understanding that we are importing a foreign notion that only partially fits the data. The conventional Islamic-Arabic word that is most often translated as "saint" is *walī,* which literally means, particularly in its Qur'anic occurrences, "friend," "patron," "benefactor," "protector," "helper," "one who is near." It can also mean "relative." It is really only by extrapolation that we can translate *walī* as "saint."[3] And there is extremely little support within the Qur'an itself for this, the *locus classicus* for those who would discern a scriptural foundation for Islamic sainthood being 10:63: "Surely God's friends (*awliyā'*)—no fear shall be on them, neither shall they sorrow." This passage refers to pious persons who, because of their devotion, do not need to fear final judgment or punishment. The Jews and Christians are castigated by the Qur'an (62:6, 5:56) for asserting that they are the special friends of God in an exclusive sense. All who obey God and hope for the hereafter are *walīs* (pl.: *awliyā'*), friends of God, who in turn is *walī* to them (as in 4:45, where God is *walī* in the sense of protector). *Walī* in the Qur'an, then, can apply both to God and to humans. It expresses more a living relationship than a quality or virtue and is thus typical of the dynamic character of Qur'anic religion. If any other than God is taken as *walī,* those who do so will be regarded as deniers of God and be consigned to hell (18:102). Of especial loathing to God in the Qur'an is the practice of seeking intercession (*shafāʿa*) of others than God (10:19, 13:17, 39:44), who are called *shurakā'*, "associates" (sc. idols). The one unforgivable sin in Islam is *shirk,* "association" of anything with God. This was the basis of the draconian reforms of the Wahhābīs in eighteenth-century Arabia, when they pulled down mosque-tombs and desecrated the graves of "saints" in the name of a stern unitarianism. *Awliyā'*, "saints," then, can be regarded in an idolatrous manner, for God is the only *walī* for the believers according to a strict construction of the Qur'anic text.

According to the Qur'an, no creature can intercede with God on behalf of humans, except for Muhammad, depending on how certain verses are interpreted (e.g., 2:256, 19:90, 20:108, 34:22; compare 39:45—"Intercession is wholly with God"). The Hadith[4] contain explicit statements of Muhammad's intercession, which the strict Wahhābīs insisted would be available only with God's permission, and on the Last Day, not before. We shall see that the cult of saints in Islam features intercession on a grand scale.

Before taking up specific examples of Muslim saints and their varieties, it will be useful to examine the issue that was raised at the outset, namely the holiness of persons within the Islamic worldview. Granting that the terms "holy" and "sacred" are rarely employed, there is nevertheless a vocabulary of high religious value that is available and active. Knowledge of this vocabulary will enable one to discern something of the peculiar character of Islamic piety, in that it renders the believer worthy to traffic in sacred things and speak to his Lord. There are titles, terms, and concepts by which we can set out to describe the holiness of persons in Islam. These can be conveniently divided into two major categories. The first consists of roles, qualities, and states that can be earned by the believer to a large extent, granted that the very conditions of human existence—especially that *fiṭra,* the God-given, innate, sound human constitution (30:30)—come from God in the first place. The second category consists of virtues and statuses that are bestowed upon or attributed to selected individuals. There can be overlap between the two categories, especially in the sense that the second tends to embrace the first, as will become clear. For convenience the two categories are presented in parallel columns. No attempt has been made to include all possible examples, but a representative sampling has been attempted.

Earned	*Bestowed or Attributed*
roles/titles	roles/titles
shaikh (various meanings, e.g., old man, religious scholar)	*shaikh* (especially in Sufism)
walī (in the Qurʾanic sense)	*sayyid* (descendant of Muhammad, therefore inherited; compare *sharīf*—noble, and *ahl al-bayt*—people of the house)
ḥājjī (one who has made the Pilgrimage)	*walī* (in the elaborated sense of "saint": compare *mawlā,* master from the same root)
imām (of Ṣalāt or of a mosque)	*ḥujja* and *burhān* in the sense of proof
ghāzī (warrior)	Imām, as in Shiʾism
shahīd (martyr)	*quṭb* (pole in sense of *axis mundi* and head of the hierarchy of saints)
ʿālim (Islamic legal expert)	
qualities/states	
muḥrim (ritual purity as in Ṣalāt or on Ḥajj, with proper garb)	

Earned

mukhliṣ (sincere)

ṣāliḥ (pure, sound)

muṭahhar (ritually pure)

zāhid (ascetic)

sālik (wayfarer)

faqīr (poor dervish; compare *sā'iḥ*)

muslim (submitter)

mu'min (believer)

taqiyy (devout)

ʿābid (worshipper)

rāhib (fearer; monk in Christian Arabic)

Bestowed or Attributed

murshid (spiritual guide)

nabī (prophet)

rasūl (apostle)

mujaddid (renewer of religion)

qualities/states

ʿiṣma (sinlessness of the prophets and, for the Shiʿa Imams also; infants possess a sinless nature, too, as established in their *fiṭra*)

fiṭra (humankind's primordial state as sound and sinless)

majdhūb (attracted; that is, enraptured mystic, who attains all the states and stages of the *ṭarīqa* without effort, because of having been chosen by God)

This list of titles, qualities, attributes, and so forth shows how very wide a range there is in Islam for exhibiting piety, and in the left-hand column alone. If the Bible, and especially the New Testament, harps on how unholy humankind are, the Qur'an (and Islamic literature in general) hastens almost in every verse to remind humans of their marvelous possibilities as *homines religiosi*. But common run-of-the-mill piety is not the same as saintliness in the sense in which saints exude a special quality, a power, sometimes regardless of observance or nonobservance of the normal forms of piety and morality. Most, if not all, of the individuals who could be listed in the right column also would have already attained several or even most of the titles or states in the left column, but the reverse is not the case. A pious Muslim view would claim that all of the examples in the left-hand column are made possible and actual only by the will of God and that no one can truly earn them on his own. An additional example of this sort would be *tawba,* "repentance," which according to a close reading of the Qur'an can be shown to be ultimately linked to divine initiative.[5] And yet there is a sense in which human capacity is deeply involved in "turning" toward God in repentance. The "earned" column's titles and qualities are not all on the same level, for there are degrees. A *shahīd,* "martyr," is a very special kind of Muslim, who will be granted instant entry into Paradise.[6] A *mu'min,* "believer," is superior to a mere *muslim,* "submitter," as the Qur'an itself states in a frequently quoted passage: "The Bedouins say, 'We believe (*āmannā,* i.e., "we are *mu'mins*")!' Say: 'You do not believe; rather say "We surrender" (*aslamnā,* i.e., "we are *muslims*"); for belief has not yet entered your hearts'" (49:14). All *mu'mins* are *muslims,* but the reverse is not the case.

All that is necessary for succcss, in this world and the next, is available in the left-hand column. This is not to suggest that one earns salvation; rather, it is to affirm that guidance has been provided for the people as a whole and spiritual elitism lies beyond. The *walī* is a case in point. The Muʿtazilite "rationalists" of high Caliphal times affirmed "that all Moslems are friends (*awliyā'*) of God when they are obedient to Him."[7] But the Muʿtazilites did not have their way, for they tended to conceive of God and his will in rational terms.[8] In their celebrated struggle against anthropomorphism, the Muʿtazilites ironically raised their own intellects to the divine level and as a result undermined the transcendent mystery of the divine-human encounter. The majority of Muslims could not follow this trend and probably did not even know or care about it. Goldziher credited the rise of saint veneration, which is based on the existence of unusually potent individuals, to the vast abyss that separates humans from God.

> The helpless creature looks longingly to the limitless heights, to the realm of infinity and fate which is unattainable to it. No human perfection can participate in the realm of infinite perfection, no supernatural gift of a privileged individual can mediate between the two spheres, which are linked only by the relations of causality and dependence. No creature has part, even in a finite and qualified measure, in the might which pertains to God . . . etc.[9]

If Sufism (Islamic mysticism) was born from a frame of mind that wished for "a closer walk with God," then saint veneration—and, antecedently, saint production—must have been engendered in a similar context. In fact, Sufism and saintliness are closely related historically, conceptually, and temperamentally, although it would be a mistake to consider them as completely coterminous. On the folk religious level are many saint-related phenomena that are not really part of Sufism, as we shall see.

Granted that God is far above his creatures and practically unapproachable, his Prophet was very much a human being who over the course of several generations after his death became idealized, gradually, as an immaculate and exemplary model for attitudes and behavior. The evolution from the Muhammad of history to the Prophet of faith has been well documented by Tor Andrae and others.[10] Against the express instructions and warnings both of the Qur'an and the Prophet's own statements, Muslims developed their image of Muhammad into a kind of supersaint who would thenceforth be adored and emulated in all times and places through the cultivation and application of his Sunnah, or "custom." Indeed, the Muslim personality has been definitively influenced and even molded by the Prophet's Sunnah to the point at which criticisms of and attacks on the memory of Muhammad are felt as assaults on Muslims themselves. This is because of the penetration of Muhammad's approved pattern of behavior into even the homely, intimate details of individual life, such as family relations, toilet, and conversation. The followers of the Sunnah experience a kind of spiritual grafting through which Muhammad's essence is nurtured and celebrated in ongoing communal life. This extends to the naming of children. While the Prophet is reported to have said that God most approved such names as ʿAbd Allāh (Servant of God) and ʿAbd al-Raḥmān (Servant of the Compassionate),[11] he also is reported to have said: "There is no people holding a consultation at which there is present one whose name is Moḥammad or Aḥmad (a variant), but God blesseth all that assembly."[12] He also is reported to have said: "Whoever nameth his child by my name, or by that of any of my children or my companions, from affection to me or to them, God (whose name be exalted) will give him in Paradise what eye hath not seen nor ear heard."[13]

To a very marked degree, the cohesiveness of the Islamic Ummah worldwide, which has been sustained without benefit of clergy or institutional hierarchy, is attributed to the conformation of Muslims to their hero's Sunnah. This was achieved through that enormously powerful source of Islamic ideas of correctness known as *ijmāʿ*, "consensus." "Indeed," Muhammad is reported to have said, "my Community shall never agree together upon an error." This sort of *vox populi vox dei* conviction itself led to the triumph of the Prophet's example in the hearts and habits of his community to the present. And the law schools and theologians came to defend the development of Muhammadan supremacy in the face of the sheer force of enthusiasm for it on the mass level. As Goldziher summarized the situation when writing about Muhammad as a miracle-worker,

> It is one of the most curious phenomena in the development of Islam to observe the ease with which orthodox theology also adapts itself to the needs of popular belief, though this entails open contradiction to the unambiguous teaching of the Koran. The power of *ijmāᶜ* here scored one of its biggest triumphs in the whole system of Islam, insofar as the belief of the people succeeded in penetrating into the canonical conception of the Prophet and, so to speak, forcing it to make him into a fortune-teller, worker of miracles, and magician.[14]

Was that not enough for the Muslims? Why was it felt desirable and permissible to acknowledge additional supermundane individuals across the Islamic world when Muhammad himself seemed to be so omnicompetent? With the considerable range of pious qualities and states and roles that were accessible to ordinary Muslims (listed earlier), and with the added perfection of the Prophet's Sunnah as guide, as well as the promise of his intercession at the Last Judgment, one would perhaps think that additional holy persons would be strictly supernumerary at best and *shirk* at worst. (Indeed, the Wahhābīs considered veneration of the Prophet to be idolatry.) Probably the main reason the Muslims embraced so many additional persons beyond their beloved Muhammad as sources of power and sacrality is that widespread religious communities need more than official, transcendentally oriented doctrines and generalized, ubiquitous models, as Muhammad came to be. As great as the celebration of the Prophet's birthday (*mawlid al-nabī*) can be for gaiety and colorfulness, it is nevertheless a pan-Islamic observance and not intimately connected with any specific localities, with the ironic exception of Mecca and Medina, where it has not been celebrated since the coming to power of the fanatically antisaint veneration Wahhābīs some two centuries ago.

There is much more to saint production and veneration than mere locality, but this dimension is of fundamental importance for it provides a means of close identification of persons with special places where ancestors, neighbors, leaders, teachers, spiritual advisers, friends, and even enemies have lived and been active and, more important, have died. Traveling through the Egyptian countryside, for example, one is struck by the proliferation of saints' tombs, ranging from humble little mud-brick affairs with their squat, knobby domes to grand stone and masonry edifices with extensive grounds and sometimes attached mosques. Any hamlet without a saint's tomb, or *qubba,* is a place without a center or a soul. It is not the place that gives sanctity to the tomb, but the saint whose remains sacralize the place, endowing it with power and prestige, which are then available to the people round about who come for blessing and comfort. The complex of saintly remains, adoring people, and place reinforces the efficacy of Qur'anic piety and following the prophetic Sunnah while going beyond them in certain respects. Following the American anthropologist, Robert Redfield's useful distinction between "great" and "little" traditions, canonical Islam finds a foothold in local situations by means of an identification with them in a blend of classical doctrine and regional folklore. The great tradition of world Islam stoops to conquer in Egypt by allowing and even embracing otherwise deviant or at least idiosyncratic local saint cults, which in turn have their analogues throughout much of the rest of the Islamic world. The little tradition is, in its own way, a great tradition in its very ubiquity, although any official recognition and rationalization of its myriad varieties of expression—from Morocco to Indonesia—comes from a scripturalist and transcending authority structure.

The following is a true story with the force of parable. The most outspoken opponent in the struggle against saint veneration in Islamic history was Ibn Taimīya, the Hanbalite jurist who lived in the thirteenth and fourteenth Christian centuries.[15] So vitriolic were his attacks on the cult of saints, centering on the visits to their tombs in search of blessings and intercession, and so independent was he as a jurisconsult and reformer that he was frequently imprisoned by indignant authorities both in Cairo and in his native Damascus. Although most of his incarcerations are not attributable to his attacks on the cult of saints, everything he did bore the stamp of zealous guarding of what he considered to be the pure Islam of the Qur'an, the Prophet's Sunnah, and the early generations of jurists, before Sufism, saint veneration, and elaborated styles of rationalist theology had established secure, institutionalized roots in the soil of Muslim attitudes and behavioral patterns. Ibn Taimīya championed the forms of piety that were listed in the "earned" column earlier in this chapter. All may draw nigh unto their Lord through the channels that have been revealed in holy writ and prophetic example. There is no need, in the first place, and no warrant, more particularly, for saints. All Muslims are already sufficiently well equipped, both through their ontological constitution (*fiṭra*) and a clearly marked path—the Shariᶜa—to enjoy the blessings of the true religion to the utmost in what for lack of a better phrase could be called the "ecstasy of obedience" to God's commands. Ibn Taimīya was highly regarded in his own day, however controversial his views were, but he had little success in his crusade against the cult of saints. Yet his influence was fundamental in the Wahhābi reforms four centuries later in Arabia: his writings were like a time bomb planted in the fourteenth and detonated in the eighteenth century whose shocks are still reverberating across the Islamic world.

The supreme irony of Ibn Taimīya's life was what happened after his death. His funeral was attended by an estimated two hundred thousand men and fifteen thousand women at the Sufi cemetery in Damascus, and admirers adopted the custom of visiting his tomb in ever increasing numbers to venerate his memory, seek his intercession, and share in the *baraka* (spiritual power) of his now holy remains. The reluctant saint was a victim of his own virtues. Perhaps Ibn Taimīya's reckless audacity in the face of worldly authority imbued him with that antinomian quality that is so frequently a mark of Islamic holy personages. It can be seen as a sign of God's working in the world. But one must hesitate to consign Ibn Taimīya to that special class of "saintly fools" (*bahālil*), whose numbers contain a wide range of deviant types.[16]

Several centuries before Ibn Taimīya a similarly austere and correct student of the Qur'an and Sunnah developed the intricate and ingenious methodology for the use of prophetic traditions (*ḥadīth*) which was to dominate Islamic jurisprudence to the present. His name was Muḥammad Ibn Idrīs al-Shāfiᶜī, and he was born in 768 C.E. in Gaza and died in 820 in Cairo. He was a master of the entire Qur'an by heart at age seven, qualified to render legal opinions at fifteen, and a celebrated jurist and teacher over a long and productive professional life with nothing in the least unorthodox in his record; nevertheless his remains have been venerated in a manner unusual even in saint-intoxicated Egypt. From his life story one can focus on a few incidents that contributed to his enduring renown.[17] Once, when he was on the verge of being executed for pro-Shiᶜite sympathies in Baghdad, al-Shāfiᶜī spoke up to the attending caliph and for his boldness was freed while his companions were beheaded. Another time, when visiting Mecca from his post as court jurisconsult in Yemen, he dispensed ten thousand dirhams because his mother had once told him always to empty his pockets in that holy city (he was often observed to give away his last coin during his Cairo years). Al-Shāfiᶜī lived a rather ascetic life and freed his slave upon his death. He enjoys membership in the very front rank of Arabic stylists (he had spent ten years as a youth with a Bedouin tribe learning poetry and the manly arts). He left Baghdad, the capital of the Caliphate, for Egypt when he was at the height of his fame as a jurist because, as he told people, "of my fondness for sugar cane." He wanted to be buried in Old Cairo, and when an attempt was made to move his remains back to Baghdad, a strong odor was said to have emanated from them, causing the enterprise to be abandoned.

The Imām al-Shāfiʿī reposes in a majestic domed chamber in the southern cemetery of Cairo, which pilgrims visit from all over the world. There is a curious dichotomy in the manner in which his burial place is approached and regarded by those who visit it. From personal observation, when learned scholars and shaykhs are around—as they are each Friday afternoon, for example, attending a Qur'an recitation session—there is little overt veneration of the more exuberant peasant variety and what there is tends to be low key and modest, marked by dignified comportment and the attending to meditation and prayer in a manner found in all mosques. The actual tomb chamber—a mosque with the saint's tomb enclosure at the center—adjoins an even larger public mosque, which is usually occupied, often to capacity, during the canonical prayers. The tomb chamber is emptied of the types of people—women especially from the surrounding streets and neighborhoods—who rub the beautiful wooden screen enclosure, soaking up *baraka* and spreading it to others with gestures and embraces, or who drop into the space surrounding the displayed coffin letters beseeching the saint's intercession. But when the orthodox religious and their followers are absent, the setting becomes indistinguishable from other famous centers of spiritual power and folk practices. There is a colorful birthday celebration (*mawlid*) each year, when the streets nearby are bedecked with lights and banners and special foods and diversions are available.

One of the most interesting things about the cult of al-Shāfiʿī is that for centuries people have been addressing letters to him. Most of the letters are concerned with questions of injustice that the senders have experienced. It seems that the great man's fame as a thoroughly orthodox Sunnī law expert is somewhat appreciated even by the unlearned. And his name, which means, quite coincidentally, "intercessor," clearly carries in the minds of his supplicants great weight, for they address the dead but living saint: "Yā Shāfiʿī" ("O, my intercessor!"). A fascinating study of a large number of letters was done by an Egyptian sociologist and published (in Arabic) in 1965.[18] Most of the requests were for vengeance, but many are for cure of diseases, especially blindness.

My impression, after discussing the Shāfiʿī phenomenon with Egyptian friends and colleagues, especially those of a more orthodox turn of mind, is that the cult of the saint does no harm and, because of the saint's own indisputably orthodox Sunnī pedigree, actually serves to keep people on a straight course. A father who was in the habit of taking his five-year-old son to the Qur'an recitation sessions every Friday afternoon said that he did so because of the inspiration of al-Shāfiʿī's own example, who memorized the text by age seven. I asked if going to the tomb would bring about a similar result in his boy, and he said that it certainly would not by itself because mastering the Qur'an is largely a matter of hard work. The Imām al-Shāfiʿī is indeed an intercessor and more, perhaps, a bridge to the worship of God. His cult is very close to normative Islam and in fact tends to reinforce it, if anything.

A quite different saint complex is that of Sayyid Aḥmad al-Badawī in the large Egyptian delta city of Ṭanṭa. "Sīdī Aḥmad," as the saint is called, was born in Fez, Morocco about the year 1200 C.E. to parents said to be descended from ʿAlī, the Prophet's son-in-law (thus his right to bear the title Sayyid). He traveled with his family to Mecca when still a boy. There he was educated and grew into young manhood, excelling at horsemanship and the martial arts, which earned him nicknames such as "the Intrepid Horseman" (*al-ʿAṭṭāb*) and "Champion Bruiser" (*Abū 'l-Fityān*).[19] At about age thirty al-Badawī experienced an inner transformation and became a mystic, withdrawing himself from society and cultivating spiritual states, including trance. He and his devoted older brother began a series of pilgrimages to the tombs of great saints, such as those of Aḥmad al-Rifāʿī and ʿAbd al-Qādir al-Jilānī in Baghdad, two "poles" (*quṭb*) whose spiritual lineages to this day remain intact and widely cultivated in the Islamic world.

Refusing a proud woman's offer of marriage, Aḥmad at length received a vision to travel to Ṭanṭa in Egypt, where he migrated about 1237 and remained for the rest of his life, dying there in 1276. The Egyptian period was the most significant. A standard description of his life there tells of his standing on the roof of a house, motionless, staring at the sun until his eyes became like "fiery coals," and going without food or drink for forty days. At times he would be silent and at others would scream continuously. Although he had rivals and enemies in Ṭanṭa, he managed to attract able disciples, who for the first twelve years lived with him on a roof. His miracles and signs outdistanced those of his contemporary fellow masters in Ṭanṭa, so that gradually his fame spread across the Islamic world. The mother of one of his disciples (ʿAbd al-ʿĀl), who was strongly opposed to her son's involvement with Aḥmad, repented after the saint saved the boy from a charging bull by rushing in and wrestling it to the ground using brute strength. (A variant source has him receiving the nickname "Champion Bruiser" when, upon arriving at the outskirts of Ṭanṭa for the first time, he and his brother were confronted by a gang of toughs, whom Sīdī Aḥmad proceeded to beat up one by one, thus establishing himself as a force to be reckoned with.)[20] After forty-one years of leadership and yogi-like meditation and experiences in Ṭanṭa, Sīdī Aḥmad died, having either driven away or won over his adversaries. His chief disciple, ʿAbd al-ʿĀl, who had served his master in domestic as well as administrative matters for many years, together with others managed to establish Sīdī Aḥmad's cult as an enduring feature of Egyptian popular Islam, to the point that Sīdī Aḥmad is in some ways the most powerful spiritual force in Egypt to this day, especially on the peasant level.

Each autumn the greatest of Sīdī Aḥmad's three *moolids* (colloquial Egyptian for *mawlid*, birthday festival) is held in Ṭanṭa. Hordes of people, mostly rough country folk from all over Egypt, converge on the city, where day and night they occupy nearly every square foot of the central quarter near the great mosque-tomb complex that houses al-Badawī's and other saints' remains. Significantly, this *moolid* is scheduled according to the non-Muslim solar calendar, at harvest time, thus suggesting a very old tradition extending back well before the coming of Islam to Egypt in the seventh century C.E. The agricultural and fertility symbolism is varied and emphatic, including visits of barren women seeking to be made pregnant through the intercession and plain vigor of Sīdī Aḥmad.

The *moolid*, which lasts a week, is in fact a large agricultural fair, whose economic dimensions are only beginning to be studied by specialists. The economic and spiritual aspects of the autumn *moolid* reinforce each other in a way that has been part of Egyptian life since the time of the pharaohs. The number of pilgrims runs well over one million each year, thus rivaling the turnout for the annual Mecca Pilgrimage. When I was in attendance in October 1976, the official estimate was that one and a half million were present on the final day, which climaxes the whole *moolid* with a colorful procession (*zeffa*) of Sufi brotherhoods, soldiers, military bands, and tradespeople through the streets of the city. Sīdī Aḥmad bestows his blessing on the whole event in the person of his *khalīfa,* or "deputy," who is the present head of the Badawiyya order. This important person rides at the end of the long parade on a fine caparisoned horse. He wears a flowing scarlet robe and a large round white headgear. He is accompanied by two bedouins on gorgeously bedecked and blanketed camels who beat on great copper tympani. Around the *khalīfa* is a sort of bodyguard that helps keep him on his horse and interposes between him and the pressing crowds along the way. The parade ends with the *khalīfa* entering the great mosque for special prayers, *dhikrs,* sermons, and offerings.

Significantly, at the autumn *moolid* the government is very much in evidence in the form of military units in the parade, posters, allowing meat to be sold even on meatless days (because of rationing), and great fireworks displays. The final day is always a Friday, the day on which Muslims congregate for prayer and sermons. The night before is called "the Great Night" (*al-layla al-kabīra*), when the festive and commercial as well as religious activities reach their climax in the stalls and streets of central Ṭanṭa. Among the last are Sufi *dhikrs,* spiritual concerts centering in the ecstatic recitations and songs of the representatives of Egypt's various Dervish orders, which set up tents and hold open house, so to speak, throughout the *moolid.* This is the only time when outsiders have a chance to see the colorful banners and flags of the orders displayed publicly. Positioned right against the ancient walls of the mosque are a number of circumcision booths, with their owners calling to parents in the crowds to bring their boys forward to be "purified," as the practice is interpreted (*ṭahāra*). Parents often wait until the Badawī *moolid* to have their children circumcised because of the additional blessing it brings in that context.

It needs to be said that Ṭanṭa, far from being merely the site of a stupendous religioagricultural fair, is the second most prestigious center of orthodox Islamic learning in Egypt and one of the foremost in the world. No less a figure than the modernist Shaykh Muḥammad ʿAbduh (d. 1905) was trained there. While the remains of Sīdī Aḥmad repose in Ṭanṭa, his name is invoked all over Egypt by such phrases as "*Yā Shaykh al-ʿArab! Yā Sayyid*!" ("O, Shaykh of the Arabs! O Sayyid!") and "Yā Abū Farāg!" ("O Deliverer!"). One day when I was in the reception room of an important religious education official in Cairo enjoying tea, cigarettes, and conversation with a number of other supplicants, most of whom were of the more humble classes, I was questioned about why I, a foreigner and obviously a professional person, was waiting for an audience with the big shaykh. It was late September and I was eager to obtain information on the time of the Ṭanṭa *moolid,* so I inquired whether any of the group knew anything about Sīdī Aḥmad. There was an astonished silence, followed by friendly questions about how I came to hear of him, why I wanted to know about him, and so forth. I had the strong impression that the group members regarded the shaykh of the Arabs as being present in the room and that one must be very discreet in mentioning his name, at least in the presence of an outsider, lest the saint's power be unleashed in an unpredictable and possibly hazardous fashion. Yet during my stay in Ṭanṭa the following month, when some companions and I were being entertained by educated upper-class citizens, there was barely concealed amusement that we were interested in mingling with superstitious peasants at an old-fashioned *moolid.* On the day of the parade such sophisticated Ṭanṭawis may at most take their young relatives by the hand and watch the procession go by while buying them colorful paper *moolid* hats and sweets. The truth is, the Badawī cult is a complex, multilayered phenomenon embracing religious, social, economic, cultural, political, and personal elements in an intricate interrelationship. The site of Ṭanṭa seems to have been especially potent before the arrival of Sīdī Aḥmad, but his long residence and ultimate interment there provided a unique focus that intensified and sustained the traditional as well as the new dimensions of that power center in a nation that for three thousand and more years had lavished its praises while it pinned its hopes on Osiris and Isis.

It is significant that in a country that is at once warmly hospitable to outsiders and fiercely devoted to its own kind two of its greatest saints should have come from outside: Imām al-Shāfiʿī and Sīdī Aḥmad al-Badawī. Saint cults will arise anyway and in any place, but it is perhaps because of the universalizing brotherhood of Islam that a Palestinian jurist and a Moroccan pugilist could become integral and potent parts of the Egyptian religious matrix. In terms of Egyptian importance purely, Sīdī Aḥmad outranks al-Shāfiʿī, even to the point of being numbered among the four "poles"[21] (*axes mundi*) recognized in Egypt, the others numbering two foreigners—ʿAbd al-Qādir al-Jilānī and Aḥmad al-Rifāʿī—and one native—Ibrāhīm al-Dasūqī—all founders of the most prominent international Sufi brotherhoods followed in Egypt. But with respect to the past, present, and most likely future fortunes of orthodox Islam, the Imām al-Shāfiʿī is without doubt far weightier than any of the Sufi-designated poles. Although such comparisons are problematic, it would not be far from the truth to parallel al-Shāfiʿī's role in the development of Islamic legal theory (*fiqh*) with the combined contributions of the church fathers Irenaeus, Athanasius, and Augustine in theology; not, to be sure, with regard to content but with respect to their determinative influences in the realms of sources, the identification of central issues, and methodologies. This comparison is at most heuristically useful, but it suggests to the reader who is not familiar with the development of Islamic thought and institutions a rough idea of how very significant al-Shāfiʿī is as a figure of world, not merely Islamic, religious history.

As an afterthought and before moving beyond Egyptian cases, Coptic Christian saints are also energetically venerated by means of pilgrimage and *moolid* in all parts of Egypt, and Muslim and Christian alike frequently share in the festivities and *baraka.* Coptic saints are buried within the grounds of a monastery or in a church, and additional monasteries and churches may be dedicated to their memory and in their names. When a particular saint is equally venerated by both Muslims and Christians, the burial is set off by itself in a separate building or area. Even if the adherents of the two religions do not visit or venerate each others' saints, there is a strong sense that the saints nevertheless can exercise power over anyone. Winnifred Blackman writes that when either a Muslim or Christian wrongs a saint of either tradition in Egypt, he or she must borrow a pair of shoes of the kind worn by the poorest peasant (*fellāḥ*), suspend them around his or her neck, and do penance before the altar or the prayer niche (*qibla*) of the church or mosque, as the case may be, by asking for pardon. The shoes represent abasement.[22]

At this point it is well to consider two issues: How may we compare the saint with the prophet? How is a saint known as such? On the first there is uniformity of opinion. The prophet is superior to the saint because he is the bearer of a special message from God to humankind, at least in the case of the apostles among the prophets (those who were entrusted with a message). While both the prophet and saint perform miracles, they are understood to be different kinds and are called by different names. The miracles of the prophet are known as *muʿjizāt.* They are few in number and considered evidentiary in nature, in that they are public confirmations of the prophet's mission. They can be performed only by the prophet, the word *muʿjiza* meaning, literally, "rendering impotent"—namely the adversary of the prophet. It carries the sense of inimitability as well. The Qur'an itself does not contain this term but uses *āyāt,* "signs," to express what might be called "miracle," at least in some passages. The Qur'an does not appear to claim miracles for Muhammad. As we read in Sura 29:50:

> They say, "Why have signs (*āyāt*) not been sent down upon him from his Lord?" Say: "The signs are only with God, and I am only a plain warner." What is it not sufficient for them that We have sent down upon thee the Book that is recited to them? Surely in that is a mercy, and a reminder to a people who believe.

But the prophetic *ḥadīth* and biography (*sīra*) attribute wondrous deeds to Muhammad, although the word *muᶜjiza* does not appear in either, being a later technical term. The *muᶜjizāt* (miracles) of the prophet confirm the mission, whereas the *karāmāt* (gifts of grace) of the saint "establish both the prophecy of the apostle and his own saintship," as al-Hujwīrī expressed it. Miracles are discussed at great lengths in the works on theology and mysticism, but al-Hujwīrī, reflecting the general view, asserts categorically that "the pre-eminence of the prophets depends on their exalted rank and on their being preserved from the defilement of sin, not on miracles or on evidentiary miracles or acts which violate custom."[23]

The Muslims regard the Qur'an as the central, if not the sole, miracle of their Prophet. But later sources attribute to Muhammad also such miracles as causing an enemy's horse to sink into hard ground, providing water at al-Hudaibiya, feeding three hundred men from a single cake, causing a wooden pillar to weep and almost split in half because the Prophet did not lean against it, curing a broken leg by a touch, and others.[24] Many other miracles of those who came before the Prophet Muhammad are contained in the various works that make up the "Tales of the Prophets" (*qiṣāṣ al-anbiyā'*).

Ibn Battuta tells of a Syrian saint who lived the life of a recluse in the mountains and to whom pilgrimages were made for blessings. This "shaykh of shaykhs," as he was known, once claimed to be superior to Muhammad in that he could live without women, while the Prophet's proclivities in that respect were well known. The shaykh's injudicious expression of this opinion brought down upon himself the death sentence.[25] Long before, al-Hujwīrī had spelled out the relative positions of the two types of holy personages:

> You must know that, by universal consent of the Ṣūfī Shaykhs, the saints are at all times and in all circumstances subordinate to the prophets, whose mission they confirm. The prophets are

> superior to the saints, because the end of saintship is only the beginning of prophecy. Every prophet is a saint, but some saints are not prophets. The prophets are constantly exempt from the attributes of humanity, while the saints are so only temporarily; the fleeting state (*ḥāl*) of the saint is the permanent station (*maqām*) of the prophet; and that which to the saints is a *maqām* is to the prophets a veil (*ḥijāb*).[26]

The prophets are generally regarded as free from sin, a state known as *ʿiṣma* (impeccability), which they share with infant children. Saints are not sinless as a class, although on the whole the *walī* is regarded as one who is exemplary in his devotion and selflessness. According to Sufi doctrine, some saints are "protected" (*maḥfūẓ*) and "preserved" (*maʿṣūm*) from sin, and these, along with the prophets, are superior to the angels.

> A Gabriel, who worships God so many thousands of years in the hope of gaining a robe of honour, and the honour bestowed on him was that of acting as Muḥammad's groom on the night of the Ascension—how should he be superior to one who disciplines and mortifies his lower soul by day and night in this world, until God looks on him with favour and grants to him the grace of seeing Himself and delivers him from all distracting thoughts?[27]

Of course the comparison in that passage is with Muhammad, the greatest of saints and prophets. But the same source also says that "the elect among the true believers are superior to the elect among the angels, and the ordinary believers are superior to the ordinary angels."[28]

How does one know who is a saint and who is not? Al-Hujwīrī declares that "a saint is known only to a saint," arguing that if one wishes to know the depth of this mystery he must be willing to sacrifice all in the quest. But al-Hujwīrī represents an elite and refined stratum of Sufism and seeks always to represent such subjects as sainthood in terms acceptable to orthodox Muslim opinion. On the popular level there is no hesitation to acknowledge people as saints, whether in this life or after they have died. And frequently the saints themselves have boldly proclaimed their status to their contemporaries, as in the words of the prominent Egyptian saint, Ibrāhīm al-Dasūqī:

> God showed me what is in the heights when I was seven; at eight I read the well-guarded tablet; at nine I solved the talisman of heaven and discovered in the first sūra of the Koran the letter

> which dismays men and demons; at fourteen I was able to move what rests and to make rest what moves, with the aid of God.[29]

Even such a sober Sufi master as al-Junayd could say of himself, "God has given no knowledge to man and allowed them no entry to it without letting me participate in it."[30]

The making of a *walī* is considered to be wholly God's doing, and no amount of pious observance, study, and reflection will bring it about without God's will. Most commonly *walīs* are discovered to be persons who have been spontaneously enraptured by God. These are *majdhūb,* "charmed" or "captivated" individuals whom God has selected for the ranks of saintliness without their having had to exert the usual forms of effort by means of a spiritual discipline. This phenomenon of being enraptured is sometimes associated with a certain kind of madness, which comes and goes. Lawrence Durrell has described such a saint.

> Even Narouz shuddered as he gazed upon that ravaged face, the eyes of which had been painted with crayon so that they looked glaring, inhuman, like the eyes of a monster in a cartoon. The holy man hurled oaths and imprecations at the circle of listeners, his fingers curling and uncurling into claws as he worked upon them, dancing this way and that like a bear at bay, turning and twirling, advancing and retreating upon the crowd with grunts and roars and screams until it trembled before him, fascinated by his powers. He had "come already into his hour," as the Arabs say, and the power of the spirit had filled him.[31]

The *majdhūb* in this story had no regard for the rank or status of those against whom he lashed out. He even attacked a venerable shaikh with a green turban, indicating descent from the Prophet's family. The "Magzub" shouted at the old man, who was walking on the outskirts of the crowd:

> "He is impure." The old sheik turned upon his accuser with angry eyes and started to expostulate, but the fanatic thrust his face close to him and sank those terrible eyes into him. The old sheik suddenly went dull, his head wobbled on his neck and with a shout the Magzub had him down on all fours, grunting like a boar, and dragged him by the turban to hurl him among the others.[32]

The crowd was outraged at the treatment of the old man, but the old shaikh did not complain. To be sure, this is a fictional story. But Durrell, who lived in Egypt a long time, has an unusually sharp eye for significant detail, and the episode is true to life.

Lane complained over a century ago that many imposters claimed the rank of sainthood by means of feigned insanity.

> For, a reputation for sanctity being so easily obtained and supported, there are numbers of persons who lay claim to it from motives of indolence and licentiousness, eager to receive alms merely for performing the tricks of madmen, and greedy of indulging in pleasures forbidden by the law; such indulgences not being considered in their case as transgressions by the common people, but rather as indications of holy frenzy.[33]

Lane was pestered by many people from the streets of Cairo, it seems, and he had a somewhat severe outlook on the religious and moral life anyway. Another strict observer who did not suffer fools gladly nevertheless was capable of making certain judgments that were beyond Lane. This was Ibn Khaldūn, the great historian of culture and civilization (d. 1406), who wrote:

> Among the adepts of mysticism are fools and imbeciles who are more like insane persons than like rational beings. Nonetheless, they deservedly attain stations of sainthood and the mystic states of the righteous. The persons with mystical experience who learn about them know that such is their condition, although they are not legally responsible. The information they give about the supernatural is remarkable. They are not bound by anything. They speak absolutely freely about it and tell remarkable things. When jurists see they are not legally responsible, they frequently deny that they have attained any mystical station, since sainthood can be obtained only through divine worship. This is an error. "God bestows His grace upon whomever He wants to."[34]

Ibn Khaldūn distinguishes such persons from the insane in that they have rational souls that are intact, whereas those of the insane are corrupt. The saintly fool lacks intellect (*ʿaql*), but the possession of a healthy rational soul is his grasp on reality. One of the ways to distinguish between saintly fools and plain lunatics is

> that fools are found devoting themselves constantly to certain *dhikr* exercises and divine worship, though not in the way the religious law requires, since, as we have stated, they are not legally responsible. The insane, on the other hand, have no (particular) devotion whatever.[35]

There is some disagreement among scholars as to whether a saint's power is greater during life or after death. Goldziher insisted that the living *walī* was generally more potent than a dead one, citing the opinion of Shams al-Dīn al-Ḥanafī (d. 847).

> When a *walī* dies, his power over nature with which he was able to lend help ceases. If however pilgrims to his grave nevertheless obtain help or achieve the fulfillment of their desires, this is Allāh's deed wrought through the mediation of the respective *quṭb* who sends help to the pilgrim according to the degree of the saint's grave that was visited.[36]

Blackman, who based her generalization on anthropological fieldwork rather than on medieval texts, asserted that "however great may be the veneration paid to a saint in his lifetime, the honour he receives after his death is far greater."[37] The degree of veneration is proportionate to the amount of power a saint is regarded to possess, and this power is believed to continue expressing itself down through the ages. Usually a saint's tomb enclosure is erected only after his death and after some sort of dream or visionary experience is had by a living person to the effect that the deceased saint demands the honor of a proper tomb.

> A dead sheikh may appear to some man in a dream, or even when he is awake, and tell him to build a tomb on such and such a spot, and may even personally conduct him thither. It may happen that the inhabitants of a village possessing a venerated sheikh have been guilty of misconduct, or have offended the holy man by neglecting to pay him the respect which he considers his due. In such a case, it is believed, the sheikh will appear to a man in a distant village and instruct him to build another tomb.[38]

There are many stories of dead shaikhs visiting unsuspecting individuals by night and demanding a proper burial place or threatening some dire consequences if the people do not improve the quality of their veneration of him.

In the 1920s in Algeria, a living saint exercised enormous influence on his fellow Muslims, who often came from great distances to be of service and to be near their master. Dr. Marcel Carret, who became the Shaykh Aḥmad al-ʿAlawī's personal physician, describes the building of the *zāwiyah,* or Sufi compound, that facilitated the work of the order the shaykh headed in Mostaganem.

> There was neither architect—at least, not in the ordinary sense—nor master-builder, and all the workmen were volunteers. The architect was the Shaikh himself—not that he ever drew up a plan

> or manipulated a set-square. He simply said what he wanted, and his conception was understood by the builders. They were by no means all from that part of the country. Many had come from Morocco, especially from the Riff, and some from Tunis, all without any kind of enlistment. The news had gone round that work on the zāwiyah could be started once more, and that was all that was needed. Among the Shaikh's North African disciples there began an exodus in relays: masons some, carpenters others, stonecutters, workers on the roads, or even ordinary manual labourers, they knotted a few meagre provisions in a handkerchief and set out for the far-off town where the Master lived to put at his disposal the work of their hands. They received no wages. They were fed, that was all; and they camped out in tents. But every evening, an hour before the prayer, the Shaikh brought them together and gave them spiritual instruction. That was their reward.[39]

This remarkable project continued for two years, until the *zāwiyah* was built. Workers came and left in shifts without any specific planning or administration of the process. The whole affair is an example of what anthropologist Victor Turner has called "communitas," that open, spontaneous, egalitarian type of human collectivity that is the opposite of hierarchy and structure. Of course the shaykh is an overarching authority figure, but he led without leading and designed without designing. That is, his *baraka* seemed to inhabit the whole proceeding, including especially the workers, thus drawing all together in a powerful spiritual and communal bond.

The visiting of the graves of persons can be traced back long before Islam in North Africa and, indeed, before Christianity.[40] Early in this century Edward A. Westermarck conducted extensive (one is almost tempted to say exhaustive) fieldwork on popular religion in Morocco. His massive and monumental *Ritual and Belief in Morocco* contains a great deal of information on the cult of saints. More recent scholarship on the region has sought to show the interrelationships of the symbols, roles, and relics of sainthood within the culture as a whole.[41]

In traditional Morocco the most prevalent form of sainthood has centered in the "marabout," a French rendering of the Arabic *murābiṭ*, whose root means "to tie, bind, moor, fasten, attach, hitch, connect," and so forth. A *murābiṭ* is thus bound in some way to something, in the case of maraboutism, to God. In military terms the *murabīṭ* is one who is garrisoned in a particular place, such as a frontier fortress. The marabout possesses *baraka,* and his close shackling[42] to God makes people in turn seek a close tie with the saint. Social and political legitimacy are intimately woven into the complex interrelations of marabouts and maraboutic shrines and the peoples of Morocco. The marabout has been made and/or discovered in two main ways: through wonder-working and through descent from the Prophet as a *sharīf,* or both. The marabouts of Morocco have had a close association with holy warfare and indeed gave their name to one of the most brilliant medieval dynasties: the Almoravids or, more correctly, the *murābiṭūn* (marabouts). When a marabout dies, his *baraka* continues to be active at his tomb and especially in his living descendants, some of whom will in their turn be regarded as saints. These individuals engage in a wide range of cult activities, such as animal sacrifice, intercessory prayer, healing, and divination. There are reports of saints being able to fly, changing shapes, becoming invisible, bringing rain, and many other things.[43] Marabouts can be dangerous as well as beneficial, and it is necessary therefore to propitiate them. Geertz recounts the story of the saint Lyusi's fateful collision with the Sultan Mulay Ismail, who had ordered the saint from his city because of some disturbing acts, including a mortal insult to the sultan. Upon hearing that Lyusi had not left Meknes, he sent a messenger to inquire the reason.

> "Tell him," Lyusi said, "I have left your city and I have entered God's." Hearing this, the Sultan was enraged and came riding out himself on his horse to the graveyard, where he found the saint praying. Interrupting him, a sacrilege in itself, he called out to him, "Why have you not left my city as I ordered?" And Lyusi replied, "I went out of your city and am in the city of God, the Great and the Holy." Now wild with fury, the Sultan advanced to attack the saint and kill him. But Lyusi took his lance and drew a line on the ground, and when the Sultan rode across it the legs of his horse began to sink slowly into the earth. Frightened, Mulay Ismail began to plead to God, and he said to Lyusi, "God has reformed me! God has reformed me! I am sorry! Give me pardon!" The saint then said, "I don't ask for wealth or office, I only ask that you give me a royal decree acknowledging the fact that I am a sherif, and that I am a descendant of the Prophet and entitled to the appropriate honors, privileges, and respect."[44]

Lyusi then left and preached to the Berbers in the Middle Atlas, where he died and, after burial, was transformed into a *siyyid,* a term that refers both to the dead saint and to the burial place, together with the cultic complex attached to it.

The close association between the saint and the Prophet Muhammad is the main way in which Moroccan maraboutism is linked to global Islam of the great tradition. As Ernest Gellner has forcefully expressed it, the saints of Morocco are "the Prophet's flesh and blood. Koranic propriety emanates from their essence, as it were. Islam *is* what they do. They *are* Islam."[45] Here we see the distinction, made earlier in this chapter, between the ubiquitous model of the Prophet and the local presence of the saint transcended in the unification of the two. This is frequently the case throughout the Muslim world, for in connection with Sufism especially and in all cases in which the saint is also a descendant of the Prophet, the *baraka* of Muhammad continues to reach down to the local level and extend itself into common life at many levels. Recall the earlier discussion of the respective miracles of prophets and saints in which the latter "establish both the prophecy of the apostle and his own saintship," as al-Hujwīrī put it. So, far from being a deviation from the central foci of Qur'an and Prophet, local sainthood activities can be observed to reinforce the authority of the Messenger and the Message, particularly among provincial Muslims such as the Berbers of the Atlas ranges in Morocco. Inevitably much else of local character and of questionable provenance gets carried along as well.

Islamic sainthood is not a vast miscellany of holy persons rising up from local contexts in a random manner across the world; or at least it is not considered to be such, for there is a general hierarchy that is acknowledged. Al-Hujwīrī writes that God has appointed saints as

> the governors of the universe; they have become entirely devoted to His business, and have ceased to follow their sensual affections. Through the blessing of their advent the rain falls from heaven, and through the purity of their lives the plants spring up from the earth, and through their spiritual influence the Moslems gain victories over the unbelievers.[46]

Four thousand of the saints are hidden from humankind and do not know either one another or their own exalted state. God uses them as he wills. Then there is a special group of 355 saints who constitute God's court. In ascending order, this hierarchy composed of three hundred *akhyār* (good), forty *abdāl* (substitutes), seven *abrār* (pious), four *awtād* (pillars), three *nuqabā'* (substitutes), and, at the apex, the *quṭb* (pole, axis), also known as *ghawth* (succor, aid). There is a tendency to regard the *quṭb* as greater than the *ghawth*. This saintly hierarchy lives in full knowledge of its members and acts only by mutual consent. The *quṭb,* or Pole, is at the center of the cosmos, around which the created order revolves and from whom it draws its energy and being.[47] It is closely linked with Muhammad, although in each successive age it takes on the clothing of a different individual. Many mystics have claimed to be the *quṭb* of their time, to the extent that the notion became somewhat weakened and diffused. The Shiʿa has claimed a close relationship between the Pole and the "hidden Imam," who will reappear at the close of history. The Sunnis have held a strong view of the Pole, too, as may be seen in the words of Rūmī: "He who does not know the true sheikh—i.e., the Perfect Man and *quṭb* of his time—is a *kāfir,* an infidel."[48] At this level of theory the saint becomes the highest form of being apart from God. This has raised interesting questions of the relative value of prophethood (*nubūwa*) and sainthood (*wilāya*). Sufis and Shiʿas have tended to consider *nubūwa* as being finally caught up in *wilāya* functionally. The former is passive, receiving revelation without active participation, whereas the latter is dynamically creative and timeless.[49] The timelessness of the saint has been expressed in provocative fashion by al-Junayd:

> The saint hath no fear, because fear is the expectation either of some future calamity or of the eventual loss of some object of desire, whereas the saint is the son of his time (*ibn waqtihi*); he has no future that he should fear anything; and as he hath no fear so he hath no hope, since hope is the expectation either of gaining an object of desire or of being relieved from a misfortune, and this belongs to the future; nor does he grieve, because grief arises from the rigour of time, and how should he feel grief who is in the radiance of satisfaction (*riḍā*) and the garden of concord (*muwāfaqat*)?[50]

The Poles are real persons who engage in normal human activities and interrelationships; however, their identity is not usually known except by the spiritually aware and advanced. Ibn al-ʿArabī tells of his strange encounter with such a figure:

> In the year 593 I met the Pole of the time in the garden of Ibn Ḥayyūn in Fez. God had given me an inspiration concerning him and told me who he was. He was with a group of people none of whom took any notice of him, he being a stranger to them from Bugia, a man with a withered hand. . . . The company were discussing the Poles, so I said, "My brothers!, I will tell you something amazing about the Pole of your own time." As I said this I

> turned to look at the man whom God had revealed to me as being the Pole. . . . He said to me, "Tell what God has shown to you, but do not reveal his identity"; then he smiled.[51]

At various points in this essay miracles have been named and discussed. Much more could be added on the descriptive level, for example, of how certain miracles are specialties of specific saints. The performance of miracles is not always considered to be of importance, as, for example, in the hard-nosed view of the Sufi master Abū Saʿīd ibn Abī 'l-Khayr (d. 1049 C.E.). He wrote, concerning true sainthood,

> When God makes a man pure and separates him from his selfhood, all that he does or abstains from doing, all that he says and all that he feels becomes a wondrous gift (*karāmāt*).[52]

In another passage he gave his opinion of the value of miracles:

> They said to him, "So-and-so walks on the water." He replied, "It is easy enough: frogs and waterfowl do it." They said, "So-and-so flies in the air." "So do birds and insects," he replied. They said, "So-and-so goes from one town to another in a moment of time." "Satan," he rejoined, "goes in one moment from the East to the West. Things like this have no great value"; and he proceeded to give the definition of the true saint . . .—a man who lives in friendly intercourse with his fellow-creatures, yet is never forgetful of God.[53]

This essay has ranged over a wide variety of saintly types in Islam. The chief examples have been drawn from the Arab and Berber regions, but similar cases could be cited from Iran and Central, South, and Southeast Asia. In each region of the Muslim world can be seen certain local patterns and emphases native to their contexts. In East Java, for example, one saint's tomb complex is guarded by *nāgas,* carved representations of Hindu serpent divinities that have protected sacred compounds—Hindu, Buddhist, and Muslim—since time immemorial in Indonesia. Instead of calligraphic or geometric decorative design on the tomb enclosure itself, there is a carved lotus motif. Indonesian sainthood carries forth a considerable amount of the older Hindu-Buddhist symbolism, but there is no doubt in the people's minds that any saint in question is a true Muslim, even if such be actually regarded simultaneously as an authentic embodiment of the region's ancient traditions and values as well.[54]

Finally, it should be pointed out that female saints have also been known since the earliest periods of Islamic history to the present.[55] They are not as numerous as male saints, but their existence and activities have always been considered as important. They are often connected with institutional Sufism and convent life, for example, in Egypt and North Africa. A hallmark of female saintliness has often been religious scholarship of a high order, which distinguishes them from male saints, who are not normally admired for scholarly pursuits. The miracles and after-death honors paid to female saints are the same as for males. One great *shaykha,* Sayyida Nafīsa, who was the great-granddaughter of Hasan, son of Ali and Fatima, was renowned for her spiritual energy and devotion. She made the Pilgrimage to Mecca thirty times, fasted frequently, observed night prayer vigils regularly, and was so thoroughly versed in the Qur'an and its exegesis that no less a personage than the Imām al-Shāfiʿī is said to have greatly admired her. She dug her own grave and, before expiring, recited the Qur'an 190 times, finally committing her soul to God on the word *raḥma,* "mercy."[56]

NOTES

1. In addition to 59:23, *q-d-s* refers to God also in 2:30 and 62:1. In 2:87, 253; 5:110; and 16:102 it refers to the Holy Spirit (*al-rūḥ al-qudus*), while 20:12, 79:16, and 5:21 refer to holy territory (e.g., *al-wād al-muqqadas,* the holy valley).

2. See R. B. Serjeant, "Haram and Hawtah, the Sacred Enclave in Arabia," in *Mélanges Taha Hussein,* ed. Abdurrahman Badawi (Cairo: Dar al-Maaref, 1962), pp. 41–48.

3. Arab Christians use the term *qaddīs* for "saint," and *al-Kitāb al-Muqaddas* for the Holy Bible. (It is only relatively recently that translations of the Qur'an have begun to appear under the title "The Holy Qur'an." The scripture of Islam is never called that within its own text or in traditional sources. Rather, it is usually called "The Noble Qur'an" [*al-qur'ān al-karīm*].)

4. Reports of the Prophet Muhammad's sayings and actions, ranking second only to the Qur'an in authority for Muslims.

5. See Frederick M. Denny, "The Qur'anic Vocabulary of Repentance: Orientations and Attitudes," in "Studies in Qur'an and Tafsir," *Journal of the American Academy of Religion* thematic issue, ed. Alford T. Welch, Vol. XLVII, no. 4S (December 1979): 649–664.

6. E.g., 2: 154 and 3: 170–171.

7. ʿAlī b. ʿUthmān al-Jullābī al-Hujwīrī, *The Kashf al-Maḥjūb: The Oldest Persian Treatise on Sufism,* trans. Reynold A. Nicholson, new edition (London: Luzac, 1936), p. 215.

8. A reliable introduction to the subject is the article "Muʿtazila," in the *Shorter Encyclopedia of Islam,* ed. H. A. R. Gibb and J. H. Kramers (Leiden: E. J. Brill, 1953), pp. 421–427.

9. Ignaz Goldziher, "The Veneration of Saints in Islam," in the author's *Muslim Studies,* vol. 2, trans. and ed. S. M. Stern (London: Allen & Unwin, 1971; first published in German in 1890), pp. 256–257. This classic study contains references to a great range of original sources and secondary literature.

10. Tor Andrae, *Die Person Muhammeds in Lehre und Glauben seiner Gemeinde* (Stockholm: P. A. Norstedt, 1918). See also Annemarie Schimmel, *And Muhammed is His Messenger: The Veneration of the Prophet in Islamic Piety.* (Chapel Hill and London: University of North Carolina Press, 1985).

11. See *Mishkat al-Masabih,* ed. and trans. James Robson (Lahore: Sh. Muhammad Ashraf, 1966), III:994–999.

12. Edward William Lane, "Studies from the Thousand and One Nights," in *Arabian Society in the Middle Ages,* ed. Stanley Lane-Poole (London, 1883; reprint New York: Barnes and Noble, 1971), p. 190. See also Lane's *An Account of the Manners and Customs of the Modern Egyptians,* (1836; New York: Dover Publications, 1973), *pp. 53–54.*

13. Lane, *Arabian Society,* p. 190.

14. Goldhizer, "Veneration of Saints," p. 262.

15. For a sketch of his life and work, see the article "Ibn Taimīya" in the *Encyclopedia of Islam,* (Leiden: F. J. Brill, 1960), III: 951–955. Ibn Taimiyya's views on saint veneration have been fully aired in Muhammad Umar Memon, *Ibn Taimiyya's Struggle against Popular Religion, with an Annotated Translation of His Kitāb Iqtidā' al-Ṣirāṭ al-Mustaqīm Mukhalafat Aṣḥāb al-Jahīm* (The Hague and Paris: Mouton, 1976).

16. On this see later in the chapter.

17. On the life of al-Shāfiʿī, see *Ibn Khallikan's Biographical Dictionary,* trans. M. de Slane (London: 1843), II: 569–574; and Philip K. Hitti, *Makers of Arab History* (New York: Harper Torchbooks, 1971), pp. 167–183. The biographical details in this paragraph are drawn from both.

18. Sayyid ʿUweis, *Min malāmiḥ al-mujtamaʿ al-Miṣrī al-Muʿāṣir. Ẓāhira irsāl ilā ḍarīḥ al-Imām al-Shāfiʿī* (Some characteristics of contemporary Egyptian society. The phenomenon of sending letters to the tomb of the Imām al-Shāfiʿī) (Cairo: National Center of Social and Criminological Research, 1965).

19. Joseph Williams McPherson, *The Moulids of Egypt* (Cairo, 1941), p. 288. See also "Aḥmad al-Badawī," *Shorter Encyclopedia of Islam,* pp. 22–24; ʿAbd al-Ḥalīm Maḥmūd, *Al-Sayyid Aḥmad al-Badawī* (in Arabic) (Cairo: Dār al-Shaʿb, n.d.). On the mosque-school complex of al-Badawī in Ṭanṭa, see Muhammad ʿAbd al-Jawād, *Ḥayāt mujāwir fī al-jāmiʿ al-Aḥmadī* (Life in the vicinity of the Aḥmadī Mosque) (Cairo: Maṭbaʿa al-Iʿtimād, 1366/1947). For a description of the *moolid* of al-Badawī, see the primly disapproving article of George Swan, "The Tanta Mulid," *The Moslem World* IV (1914): 45–51.

20. McPherson, *Moulids of Egypt,* p. 288.

21. The notion of "pole" (*quṭb*) is treated later in this chapter.

22. This paragraph is based largely on Winnifred Blackman, *The Fellāhīn of Upper Egypt* (London: Frank Cass, 1968; first published 1927), pp. 248–251. See also Michael Gilsenan, *Saint and Sufi in Modern Egypt* (Oxford: Clarendon Press, 1973), for a recent anthropological study that treats sainthood in relation to Sufi organization and practice.

23. Al-Hujwīrī, *Kashf al-Maḥjūb,* p. 219.

24. Thomas Patrick Hughes, *A Dictionary of Islam* (London, 1885; reprint 1935), p. 351.

25. Goldziher, "Veneration of Saints," p. 267.

26. Al-Hujwīrī, *Kashf al-Maḥjūb,* pp. 235–236.

27. Ibid., p. 240.

28. Ibid., p. 241.

29. Goldziher, "Veneration of Saints," p. 265.

30. Ibid.

31. Lawrence Durrell, *Balthazar* (New York: Pocket Books, 1961), pp. 150–151.

32. Ibid., pp. 151–152.

33. Lane, *Arabian Society in the Middle Ages,* p. 60.

34. Ibn Khaldūn, *The Muqaddimah: An Introduction to History,* 3 vols., trans. Franz Rosenthal (London: Routledge & Kegan Paul, 1958), I: 224–225.

35. Ibid.

36. Goldzhizer, "Veneration of Saints," pp. 264–265.

37. Blackman, *The Fellāhīn of Upper Egypt,* p. 240. Compare Edward Alexander Westermarck, *Ritual and Belief in Morocco,* 2 vols. (London: Macmillan, 1926; reprint 1968), I: 159.

38. Blackman, *The Fellāhīn of Upper Egypt,* p. 240.

39. Martin Lings, *A Sufi Saint of the Twentieth Century,* 2d ed. (Berkeley and Los Angeles: University of California Press, 1973), pp. 18–19.

40. See Peter Brown, *The Cult of the Saints: Its Rise and Function in Latin Christianity* (Chicago: University of Chicago Press, 1981).

41. See the standard work by Émile Dermenghem, *Le culte des saints dans l'Islam maghrébin* (Paris: Gallimard, 1954), which has details of ritual activities. See also Ernest Gellner, *Saints of the Atlas* (Chicago: University of Chicago Press, 1969); Dale F. Eickelman, *Moroccan Islam: Tradition and Society in a Pilgrimage Center* (Austin and London: University of Texas Press, 1976); Clifford Geertz, *Islam Observed: Religious Development in Morocco and Indonesia* (New Haven: Yale University Press, 1968); and Fredrik De Jong, "Les confréries mystiques musulmanes au Machreq arabe: centres de gravité, signes de déclin et de renaissance," in *Les ordres mystiques dans l'Islam: Cheminements et situation actuelle,* ed. A Popovic and G. Veinstein (Paris: Editions de l'École des Hautes Études en Sciences Sociales, 1986), pp. 205–244.

42. Geertz's translation in *Islam Observed,* p. 43.

43. Westermarck, *Ritual and Belief,* I: 153 ff.

44. Geertz's *Islam Observed,* pp. 34–35.

45. Ernest Gellner, "Sanctity, Puritanism, Secularisation and Nationalism in North Africa. A Study," *Archives de Sociologie des Religions* 15 (1963): 71–87. As quoted in Geertz, *Islam Observed,* p. 51.

46. Al Hujwīrī, *Kashf al-Maḥjūb,* p. 46.

47. For a detailed discussion, see Reynold A. Nicholson, *Studies in Islamic Mysticism* (Cambridge: Cambridge University Press, 1978; first published 1921), chap. 2, "The Perfect Man."

48. Annemarie Schimmel, *Mystical Dimensions of Islam* (Chapel Hill: University of North Carolina Press, 1975), p. 200.

49. J. Spencer Trimingham, *The Sufi Orders in Islam* (London: Oxford University Press, 1971), p. 163.

50. Quoted in al-Hujwīrī, *Kashf al-Maḥjūb,* p. 216.

51. *Sufis of Andalusia: The Rūḥ al-quds and al-Durrat al-fākhira of Ibn ʿArabī,* trans. R. W. J. Austin (Berkeley, Los Angeles, London: University of California Press, 1977), p. 31.

52. Nicholson, *Studies,* p. 67.

53. Ibid.

54. For a brief overview of Sufism, and saint-related matters in Indonesia, see Denys Lombard, "Les *tarékat* en Insulinde," in Popovic and Veinstein, *Les ordres mystiques dans l'Islam,* pp. 139–163. A perceptive analysis of how spiritual power is mediated among the Muslim Gayo people of Aceh is John R. Bowen's "Graves, Shrines, and Power in a Highland Sumatran Society," a paper delivered at the conference on "Saints and Sainthood in Islam," University of California, Berkeley, April 3–5, 1987. The papers presented at this conference, when published, will make a significant contribution to our knowledge of sainthood in Islam.

55. See Goldziher, "Veneration of Saints," pp. 270–279. Still useful, also, is Margaret Smith's *Rābiʿa The Mystic and Her Fellow Saints in Islam* (Cambridge: Cambridge University Press, 1928; reprint San Francisco: Rainbow Bridge, 1977). An interesting recent popular survey is Charis Waddy, *Women in Muslim History* (London and New York: Longman, 1980).

56. Ibid., p. 102.

4
Indian Developments: Sainthood in Hinduism

Charles S. J. White

INTRODUCTION

The Hindu religion is often characterized as polytheistic, by which it is meant that the Hindu worshiper seems to have a wide range of distinct deities from which to choose for worship. In point of fact the deities (or deity) of the locality are most often the faith objects of the local people, with individual preferences and propensities given some latitude. For the deities, known throughout India, there are ample resources of literary myth that give pertinent information concerning appearance, actions, relationships, residence, and the like. Exclusively local deities or some new cults may require special investigation using informants to come to an adequate understanding.

The main deities of the pantheon are anthropomorphic fully or in part, and all can be related to as though they were capable of experiencing the human situation, though from a very high level. The history of the growth of the polytheistic form of Hinduism is beyond the present study, but it is important to have in mind the Hindu expectation that deity will exhibit anthropomorphic characteristics, for it is a general phenomenon in the history of Indian religions that when the deity appears most desirably human, and there is justification for it in the myth, "highly evolved" human beings come to be regarded as manifesting the divine nature in a particularly vivid way.

This is the underlying factor in the broad picture of the Indian "saint" from the earliest period of which we have record. Yet in the age-long history of the development of the Indian holy man or woman the specific roles, geographic dominance, and the like have changed considerably. A note of caution is in order here because the ancient history of Indian religion is susceptible of very uncertain delineation. Indians themselves have believed in an antiquity for their civilization which greatly outdistances what could be accepted by modern scholarly authority. Another problem that we shall have to face is the fact that Hinduism has developed the role of the holy man or woman in a wide variety of forms; it is inevitable that as we leave the most ancient historical period behind, we shall find a number of these complementary or contrasting structural elements come within view, as it were, simultaneously. Here one should exercise selectivity in facing the challenge of meaningfulness and intelligibility, although in this chapter I certainly want to try to cover as many examples as possible. I shall try to find common links to join the reconstruction.

Whenever one discusses the religious outlook of India, it is necessary to make some reference to the caste system. I do so here only to call attention to the fact that a well-known mythic justification for the caste system defines each person's social role as the product of the division of an ancient divine being who sacrificed himself in order to create the cosmos.[1] Such a theory suggests that all human beings participate in the divine nature. Of course such an idea is profoundly associated with the Indian spiritual outlook in all directions and gives strong theoretical support to the specifically Indian idea of the saint. Nevertheless the myth and the real caste system itself also inculcate a hierarchical view of human relationships in which the Brāhmaṇas, or priest caste, come out on the top of the social ladder. In this position the Brāhmaṇas are also presented in a way that suggests that they embody divinity in a unique manner. The theory behind the Brāhmaṇical dominance has influenced other attitudes in Indian society and religion. Although this essay will not further elaborate upon caste, it is useful to keep in mind that a particular social class had already in ancient times institutionalized the idea that the divine could inhabit the very leadership of the social hierarchy.[2]

Another point that we shall find in common from one age to the next in the evolution of Hinduism is the manner in which the religion has proved resilient in the face of internal tension and a threat posed from outside. In one direction this propensity includes the capacity to extrude religious movements that cannot comfortably be contained even within the very tolerant confines of Hinduism itself. For example, although they influenced the course of Hindu religious history, the Buddhist, Jaina, and Sikh religions ultimately had to acquire a separate identity. As we go forward in time within Hinduism, individual men and women, the saints of the Hindus in a wide variety of emphases, seem more and more to serve the function of giving leadership and providing new expressions in periods of crisis. This reactive mode, so typical of the Hindu, is characteristically the vehicle for the achievements of the spiritual, literary, and social leadership roles of Hindu saints.

THE PROTOHISTORICAL PERIOD

The literature about early Indian religion almost invariably begins with some discussion of the mysterious artifacts that remain from the period prior to the advent of the so-called Aryans or Indo-Europeans in India. The first excavations of these ancient remains at Mohenjo-Daro and Harappa began only in the twentieth century.[3] Prior to that time this widespread, culturally unified protocivilization had been lost to the memory of the Indian peoples themselves, who recorded in their earliest literature references to so-called Dāsyus, or "slaves," with whom the Aryan kings fought and who are now sometimes thought to have been the people of the Indus Valley civilization.[4] In any case the Indus Valley civilization, the largest in extent of the protocivilizations known from the ancient past, left scanty written records, and thus far these have not been translated. The arrangement of the cities of the time suggests a hierarchy of classes, and this has led some to suggest a so-called theocratic government. Oddly enough, as compared with ancient Egypt and Mesopotamia, no buildings are recognizable as set apart for religious use—aside from the great bath of Mohenjo-Daro, whose putative religious function is unknown. Similarly images and other cult objects are remarkably minimal. The most fascinating materials overall for religious thought are certain stamp seals that portray animals and possibly anthropomorphic divine beings. Many suggest symbols of fertility in other ancient cultures, and these are thought to be prominent in the religious outlook of the Indus Valley. Relevant to the theme of our chapter, however, is the group of seals that seems to portray a human (or divine human) dressed in an animal getup and squatting on its haunches. Whether male or female (most likely the former), the body's posture and possibly ithyphallic, if male, display correlate with elements in the post-Vedic concept of the deity called Śiva as well as with the Indian ascetic tradition of the yogis.[5]

THE VEDIC PERIOD

Most of the important elements in Indian religious history developed from material already present in the earliest historical period of Indian religious history or suggested therein. The function and ideas surrounding the Indian holy man or woman are no exception. It is perhaps possible to divide the material to be examined into two different categories. The first has to do with the priestly leadership of the society and its relationship to the so-called Ṛṣis and Munis, from whom the divine revelation in the Vedic scripture depends and who are looked up to as semidivine human beings. The second has to do with the first recorded presence of uniquely gifted individuals whose powers are acquired from ascetic practices or from magical or initiatory training or experience with the suggestion of fraternal organization.

Ṛṣis

The source to which we look for information about the Vedic period is the literature that has given the period its name.[6] The Vedas, presently written down, in ancient times were the exclusive possession of the Brāhmaṇa priestly fraternities that passed prescribed sections of the literature orally from one generation to another. The oral transmission goes on today. In turn the clans of Brāhmaṇas regard the source of the literary expression to have been a particular Ṛṣi who was, so to speak, the eponymous ancestor of the clan from whom the revelation was originally transmitted.

Not all of the Ṛṣis (sages or seers) were thought to have a direct relation to the Vedic hymns. The term *Ṛṣi* is a very broad one and the line between divinities and "men" exceedingly fine in the elaboration of the myth. To mention examples of the literarily prominent Ṛṣis, one would have to include Atri, held to have been the author of Vedic hymns in honor of Agnī, Indra, the Aṣvins, and the Viśvadevas. His son was the famous sage, Durvāsas. Complementing Atri as founders of the orthodox Brāhmaṇa *gotras* and other castes and tribes are Agastya, Aṅgira, Bharadvāja, Bhṛigu, Jamadagni, Kaṇva, Kaśyapa, Vasiṣṭha, Mārichi, Pulastya, Pulaha, Kratu, and Gautama. Gālava, Gritsamada, Kuśika, Mahīdāsa, Parāśara, Uddālaka, Vāmadeva, Viśvāmitra, Yājñavalkya, Bharata, Satyakāma, Sunaḥśephas, and others were all mentioned as among those who composed Vedic hymns. Some of the Ṛṣis are identified with the stars; perhaps most famous, the seven who make up the constellation of Ursa Major. All of the Ṛṣis are renowned for their wonder-working powers. In many cases, through austerities lasting for centuries they have been able to accumulate such powers that the gods themselves are bound by their demands and can suffer the consequences of their anger under a curse. "The fierce black-visaged rishi named Bhuti . . . had so violent a temper that all nature trembled in his presence. In his hermitage the wind did not dare to blow hard, the sun to shine too strong, the wind to raise any dust. Even the river trembled when he approached to bathe."[7]

On the whole the Ṛṣis are thought to occupy a lower place in the spiritual hierarchy than the gods themselves, although they might on occasion have intimate relations with the gods or even acquire power over them. The Hindus down through the ages have looked to the Ṛṣis as the first and greatest of the human spiritual heritage—especially as the authority for the sacred scriptures, beginning with the Veda itself through the major works of the classical period, the epics, and the Purāṇas. Many of the ideas that we associate with the saintly vocation in India, such as austerity, wonder-working, the ability to curse and bless, are prominent in the stories that are told about the lives of the Ṛṣis in ancient times. In a special sense he was supremely wise, a *maharṣi,* a title of respect that continues in use to the present day and which is bestowed on a rare few among the saints of contemporary India.

Śrāmanas and Munis

One cannot separate the tradition of the ascetic monk completely from that of the Ṛṣi, for obviously an underlying motive remains the same—that of attaining dominance over the physical body so that a degree of special power can be attained. A practical difference lies in the fact that the Ṛṣi tended to represent the dominant culture, that of the Aryan, no doubt with some additions by historical times from the suppressed so-called indigenous religious stratum, whereas the lineages of ascetics, celibate śrāmanas (as they are called by an early title), seem at least initially to represent an independent line of development.

Having already outlined aspects of this configuration elsewhere,[8] here

I emphasize the general characteristics of asceticism that have deeply influenced the Hindu outlook and have created the expectations of perfection that are realized in the lives of the holy men and women of the land. Renunciation as an aspect of asceticism is a theme that is widespread in Indian myth, religious practice, and everyday life. Some authors have referred to renunciation as a kind of passive asceticism. At its most obvious it has been incorporated into the manners of upper-caste and middle-class Indian behavior. It influences the training of children, child-parent relationships, adolescent relationships, husband-and-wife relationships, and many other areas of behavior. Essentially it requires restraint in the display of emotion. Smiles are hoarded. Vigorous physical movement, as in walking or dancing, is shunned. At least in public, gesture and other accoutrements of animated conversation, together with varied facial expressions, are rather rare. Human relationships tend to put others at a distance. There seems to be an excessive concern for what in the West could be called propriety.

In reality the motives are of a deeper nature. For through all such accidental disciplines the inner life of the individual may also be brought under restraint, such that he or she will experience greater inward calm and thus be prepared for meditation and the harder task of controlling the activities of the mind. Of course the training of whole segments of society to be calm has both a positive and a negative aspect. Speaking of contemporary life, one suspects that individuals involved, greatly varied in natural temperament as they must be, suffer considerable frustration under the tutoring of the ideal of renunciation.

But the ideal itself is of ancient origin and is regarded as essential in the ascetic disciplines that are held to lead eventually to the experience of transcendent states of consciousness, the acquisition of unusual psychomental powers, and the like. The positive side of renunciation or its corollary, rather, is the active engagement in extraordinary measures to bring the body out of one stage or mode of existence to another. Here the restraints imposed upon the body enter quite a new dimension altogether. Various positive disciplines are accepted, often accompanied by vows. In the religious or mendicant life this mainly has to do with abandoning a settled family life and the traditional work of one's class or caste in favor of a homeless, wandering existence. Outward symbols of distinctive clothing, or lack thereof, together with daubing the body with ashes, dressing the hair with cow urine and dung, and having the bare minimum of personal possessions (perhaps a water pot and a staff) complete a first level of commitment. Beyond that the disciplines of loneliness, abstaining from speech, fasting, limiting sleep, and the like take one a certain distance in the positive direction. Specialization may follow thereafter and the varied techniques of always standing, holding the arm in an upright position until atrophied, hanging suspended upside down from the branches of a tree for long periods, piercing the body with sharp instruments, consuming repulsive material, and other such attempts at overcoming natural human inclinations may be employed.[9] Extremists in ascetic practice seem to have had their place throughout Indian religious history, just as they have had in the ascetical disciplines of Christianity; nevertheless the theory stoutly insists that all such behaviors are but means to an end.

Jainism and Buddhism

The divergence between the two great orders of ascetics, the Jaina and the Buddhist, create certain models, which, together with their theoretical elaboration, affect India's subsequent experience of religious value. It is also important to note that both founders of these Indian religious movements lay much clearer claim to real historicity than the Ṛṣis and other similar figures from Indian legend and myth both before and after their times.[10]

No doubt the stories of Mahāvīra, founder of the Jaina faith, and of Gautama, founder of the Buddhist faith, contain a good deal of legendary material that cannot be directly evaluated historically. Nevertheless no serious question has ever been raised as to the underlying historical existence of these men. It is important to mention this for reasons other than the obvious one raised by historicity. It is simply that Mahāvīra and the Buddha are, among Indian prototypes, unimpeachable examples of the human person himself becoming the supreme focus of religious value. Thus the trend toward anthropomorphization that we saw as a dominating aspect of Hindu polytheism reaches downward from the realm of theology, myth, and legend and, after their time, fully embraces certain actual historical persons; therefore Hinduism finds it difficult to dismiss the claimant to divine or saintly status. Nevertheless, the Buddha and Mahāvīra, the Tīrthāṅkara, because of the attitude that they took toward the formal religious practices of the Brāhmaṇical caste, and because Buddhism allowed for the conversion and easy assimilation of the numerous foreign invaders who entered India for a period of nearly nine hundred years from toward the end of the pre-Christian millennium onward, were rejected by so-called orthodox Hinduism. The Hindus therefore sought in their own manner to determine the precise way that a human being would be elevated to the level of sainthood or divinity.

We can look at the outline of the type given to us by the Buddha and the Tīrthāṅkara for elements that are presented later in the concept of the Hindu saint, even if in a negative manner. By the latter I mean that both Buddha and the Tīrthāṅkara were of princely background, thus representing an assertion by the Kṣatriya caste of the right to lead in the spiritual as well as the military realm. Although Brāhmaṇas did enter the orders of these men, there is a certain anti-Brāhmaṇical tendency in the development of such movements which came to be regarded by the orthodox as heretical religions because they worked against both the established values of religious observance among upper-caste Hindus and allowed the mixing of castes within the religious order.

In later Hindu expressions of the saintly vocation, the disregarding of caste and orthodox religious observances is often countenanced while at the same time there may be an attempt to legitimate the low-caste status of a saintly individual, or some other apparently aberrant behavior or symbolism, by introducing a disguised Brāhmaṇical element—for example, ascribing natural parenthood of the saint to Brāhmaṇas but adoption by the individual in infancy by persons of lower caste.[11] On the contrary, in the theory, for example, of Jaina Tīrthāṅkaras it is asserted that only those conceived in Kṣatriyan wombs may be Tīrthāṅkaras even though birth may occur by miraculous means from the wombs of non-Kṣatriyas.[12]

Because I have discussed the life structure of the Indian saint elsewhere, I need only allude to the fact here that biography is important in the realization of the saintly function for the religious community.[13] So in the case of the Buddha and the Tīrthāṅkara, close attention is paid to the details of conception, birth, childhood, early youth-adolescence, possibly marriage, children, other family members (including parents, wife, friends), the immediate circumstances of the quest for spiritual emancipation, and the subsequent life histories of the individuals up to and including death.[14] If it is important and appropriate to do so, discussion of the close disciples of the saintly figure and the effect that he had on the persons attracted to him for one reason or another will also be emphasized.

In the case of both the Buddha and the Tīrthāṅkara, extraordinary philosophies, including highly suggestive cosmologies, are attributed to them together with a vast amount of other kinds of scriptural material that tell their life stories and interpret them from more than one point of view.[15] Thus in the theological sequel to the lives of the Buddha and the Jina an amazing sectarianism arose, particularly in the case of the former; and this, too, becomes a possibility in the later history of the Indian saint, though never to the same degree as in the case of Buddhism, which became a worldwide religion.[16]

We can say, then, that the Buddha and Mahāvīra continue the tradition of the "realized" saintly teacher, analogous to the Ṛṣis and Munis mentioned in the different strata of the Vedic text, including the Upaniṣads, the most important of which appear to many scholars to reflect the religious life of the Hindu community about the time that the Jaina and Buddhist heresies arose. What put the Jainas and Buddhists beyond the pale of orthodoxy, in addition to what we have mentioned previously, was insistence upon the role of the mendicant as the central focus of religious life and of a crucial experience of enlightenment as usurping all religious value, previously considered the final domain of the Brāhmaṇa priest's dominance and direction. The Order of Jaina monks and nuns—the Order of Buddhist monks and nuns: these became the focus of religious life. The universe was completely reinterpreted to accommodate the archetypal religious experience and claims of the founders and chief models of the new religious movements. Although there were other, competing heretical movements contemporaneous with the Buddha and Mahāvīra,[17] none was similarly capable of attaining the universal acceptance or providing a satisfying way of life for a broad spectrum of humanity—together with hope in a profound spiritual reality and experience beyond the realm of the merely mundane.

Women's Contribution

It is common in the handbook literature about Hinduism to point out that the role of women in social and religious terms was much higher in the Vedic and early classical period than it was in the interval prior to modern times. The evidence is more or less clear in the scriptures themselves that some women had achieved the highest levels of learning and sanctity. Indeed, the theological perspective of the Hindus from very ancient times gave due weight to both feminine and masculine modes in deity, the most illustrative perhaps being the classical icon of Śiva, Ardhanārī, showing the god as half male and half female. A modern writer on the role of religious women in ancient India writes as follows:

> In the *Ṛig-Veda* we find names of so many women who realized the highest spiritual truths. They are recognized as seers of Truth, as spiritual teachers, divine speakers and revealers. In the *Ṛig-Veda* alone there are a large number of inspiring hymns called *suktas* ascribed to as many as twenty-seven women seers or *ṛishis* or *brahma-vādinīs*. The one hundred and twenty-sixth hymn of the first book of the *Ṛig-Veda* was revealed by the Hindu woman, Romaśā, and the one hundred and seventy-ninth hymn of the same book by Lopāmudrā. It is remarkable that several of them rose to great heights of spiritual experience. One of the seers, called Vāch, who was the daughter of the sage Ambhrina, realized her oneness with the absolute, and cried out in spiritual joy: "I am the sovereign queen. . . . He who eats does so through me; he who sees, breathes or hears does so through me. Creating all things, I blow forth like the wind. Beyond heaven, beyond the earth am I—so vast is my greatness."[18]

It is somewhat startling to be reminded by the same author that in the classical period Śaṅkara himself added the name Bhāratī to his own in honor of the female scholar of the same name who served as judge in the debate between her own husband, the Mīmāṃsist, Maṇḍana Miśra, and Śaṅkara the Vedāntist. Bhāratī judged that Śaṅkara won in the debate![19] The Rāmayāṇa and Mahābhārata make reference to the power and wisdom of certain yoginīs that lived lives of extraordinary asceticism, but in later times it devolved more and more upon the Bhakti tradition to provide women the opportunity for ecstatic communion or union with Ultimate Reality.[20]

THE CLASSICAL PERIOD

Assuming therefore that Hinduism is to some extent "treading water" in the period of the rise and dominance of Buddhism during the four or five centuries that bracket either side of the beginning of the Christian era, we can begin to piece together a peculiarly Hindu tradition of reliance upon the leadership of humans who teach their own view of the universe, interact with the dominant religious trends of the time and place, and forge the bridges that will build into the future from the past. As the term is defined, the classical period extends from approximately the time of the Buddha and Mahāvīra to the advent of the Muslims in the twelfth Christian century. This is a very long period indeed and might well be subdivided into Buddhist and post-Buddhist periods. Although the development of which I wish to write here spans both subdivisions of the period, several elements must be examined separately before any general statement can be made about the period.

One of the difficulties in coming to a clear understanding of what the concepts of saint and sanctity might mean in India is that there are few persons of any consequence in the intellectual life of the Indian people who were connected with religion who did not also acquire some of the patina of the saintly individual. This is because the writers on philosophy, the founders of the great classical intellectual schools, modeled their views of reality on the same pattern as that put forward by the Buddha and others: namely, that the secret of the universe lies in discovering the means to overcome the bondage of human existence and thereby to escape the endless wheel of rebirth with its suggestion of repetition of unpleasant experiences and suffering. Therefore however coldly analytical their writings may appear to be, they nevertheless reflect first and foremost the experience of a mystic—or the accumulated wisdom of a school of mystics—who, like the less organized spokespersons for spiritual emancipation in the Upaniṣads, have attempted through systematic analysis of the method or technique and the resultant states in consciousness, or of the spiritual entity, the soul, to provide a generally accurate picture of reality.

The intellectual tradition forged in these centuries of competition with counterparts in the Buddhist tradition has tended to shape the whole experience and expectation of the Hindu religious tradition, such that even today we find the contemporary saints of India attempting to provide adequate metaphysics, or restatement of classical models, to explain what they have gone through.[21] To put the doctrine into so many words was in some respects the most important aspect of the saintly vocation in ancient times. This continues throughout Indian religious history to be a dominant motif, although the express form of the presentation may change and, instead of being discursively analytical, may be sung in poetry.

Philosophy and Theology

The six Darśaṇas of orthodox Hindu philosophy, as the Sanskrit word suggests, give six points of view upon the nature of ultimate reality, the structure of the cosmos, and the purpose and end of human existence under these terms. At the same time that the *Darsaṇas* were attaining some degree of clarity—being the province of Brāhmaṇa pandits who taught their doctrines often in conscious opposition to their Buddhist rivals—the great liturgical systems of classical Hinduism were coming into existence, and there was a degree of reciprocity between the worship of deity and the philosophical vision of reality. In this respect the classical period sees the rise to prominence of the two deities Viṣṇu and Śiva. The story of this development is a long and complicated one having more than one major point of emphasis. Here we might say that the growing experience of the Indian devotee led Hinduism out of the nascent anthropomorphism of the Vedic period, with respect to transcendent forms of deity, and gradually allowed the coalescence of a wide variety of story, legend, and rich symbolism around two independent and, to some extent, mutually exclusive personal manifestations of transcendent godhead, Viṣṇu and Śiva. In this process although nothing could be excluded from or be alien to either of the two great deities, emphasis could and did differ. Herein lies a crucial aspect of the way that the individual was thought to achieve his or her fullest spiritual potentiality. Viṣṇu was most often depicted in the myth as being actively concerned to prevent the destruction of the cosmos through the depredation of demons—hence his popular title of preserver. The image of Viṣṇu is of a deity of transcendentally eternal but active love, seeking by every means possible to preserve what may otherwise be destroyed. Perhaps borrowing from Mahāyāna Buddhism as well, Viṣṇu is seen to be concerned to give happiness and to accord fulfillment to the humanly natural needs and desires while employing such in the conquest of perfection and immortality.[22]

Śiva, on the contrary, who is the perennial inspiration for the Indian ascetic tradition, although he certainly has a benign aspect, is depicted with the symbols of negative power.[23] He reveals the essentially transitory nature of all human values and even of the cosmic forms themselves. In one of his most famous iconic forms he dances the dread Tāṇḍava dance, which is at the same time a dance of creation and of destruction. But although he is dynamic, Śiva is typically withdrawn, the passive, self-contemplating mystic power at the center of the universe.[24] He is but rarely disturbed from his abstracted state. As with so much else in the Indian religious setting, however, Śiva at the same time reveals the underlying sexual potency in the very nature of things. The puzzling sculptured erotics that begin to appear in the early classical period, to be developed thematically throughout the classical period of Indian cultural history, are suggestive of the world of matter and energy changing form of which eroticism is for humans the most compelling and personally meaningful manifestation. So in the case of Śiva, his benignity, his passive benevolence, is complemented by his destructive movement together with a highly controlled but potentially uncontrollable sexual dynamism.[25]

*Ś*AṄKARA

Although there are Hindu personalities in the period dating from the rise of Jainism and Buddhism, as compared with Buddha and Mahāvīra, no great religious figure is so noteworthy until the time of Śaṅkara. It may be no exaggeration to say that the history of the Hindu saint begins with him, if we are speaking in the strict sense about a person who is sufficiently well known to history to be unquestionably historical and whose work and life story constitute a development *in extenso* of the model of human behavior for the religion in which the person functions. In all these respects Śaṅkara sets the course for the historical saints of Hinduism.

His dates are usually given as 788–838, although it is widely believed in India that he lived to be only thirty-two years of age. He was born in South India in what today is called the State of Kerala on the Malabar coast. He came from a Brāhmaṇa family; yet it is important to emphasize that although his religious vocation contributed to the revitalization and the reassertion of Brāhmaṇical orthodoxy as normative for Hinduism, he accepts the vocation of mendicancy precisely when the decadence of Buddhism in India was commonly regarded to have reached an advanced stage. From childhood Śaṅkara was motivated toward the ascetic life. He barely escaped fulfilling his family obligations through marriage, but he was able to do so and received permission from his widowed mother to take the formal vows of renunciation that made him a Sannyāsī.[26] His intellectual abilities were of the very highest, and he was soon able to advance the cause of his monist, Advaita philosophy against the most brilliant minds of the age, including representatives of other, competing Hindu schools as well as certain late Buddhist philosophies—notably the Mādhyāmika. In his relation to the teaching of the latter he is sometimes referred to as a "Pracchanna-Bauddha," or "crypto-Buddhist."[27] Because of the possibility as well that Śaṅkara might have learned about the teachings of Islam, which was beginning its earliest missionary activity in India during his period, some writers have also attributed an Islamic influence to Śaṅkara's teachings.[28] It is quite a feat to be able to stimulate correspondences between two such apparently distinct religious approaches. The fact is that in the history of religions Islam and Buddhism probably come closest in structural terms, one stating its position through absolute negation, the other through absolute assertion.

If we examine the sectarian affiliation, the life story, and the consequences of Śaṅkara's life, we will be well on our way to establishing the pattern that repeats itself throughout the history of the well-known saints of Hinduism. Because much of the detail of Śaṅkara's life is conventional and available in readily accessible publications, let us concentrate here on pointing out how the elements mentioned earlier tend to take on an independent character and shape the formation of the saintly destiny from age to age. As one can see from the basic elements themselves, there is a "predestined" quality to them, in that the givenness of human life is reflected in them. They could be applied to any human being with interesting results.[29]

It is very difficult to extrapolate the motivation, the inner experience, the unifying factor in the personality that is reflected in the life story, except as these may be directly discussed by the saintly subject or commented on through inference by the contemporary reporters upon the life of the saintly subject. Moreover the conventional model itself is so powerful, with its elements of legend and myth—in the Indian case based upon models that by the eighth or ninth century A.D. were already of great antiquity—that what is of real interest may be only what is perceptibly novel yet possibly within what the interpreter might intuitively believe to be the realm of human possibility. In the matter of religious affiliation there is no reason to doubt that Śaṅkara was a Śaivite, as his name so clearly shows and his dedication to the sannyāsī vocation. Śaivite mendicancy may be the earliest form of ascetic discipline in the Indian tradition. That it already tended to excesses in the Vedic period is shown in the disdainful references to phallic worship; and the symbolism in the *lingamyoni* icon of the Śaiva sanctuary of later times carried on the tradition.[30] The split between the passive, meditative Śiva and his powerful sexual side has often elicited comment.[31] It is a statement made perhaps as much about human beings as about the god. A prevailing motive in the saintly vocation is to channel the sexual energy, to become "liberated" from its most trying consequences—living in a family and the reproduction of offspring; at the same time that sexual dynamism is sublimated in another direction and Śiva is said to operate in the world through his feminine form, the Goddess. So that devotion to the Goddess—whether Kālī, Dūrga, or one of the more benign forms—is a modality of the sanctification process, an instrumentality of the ordinary worshiper's reliance upon the Goddess to respond to the day-to-day trials of human existence.[32] Śaṅkara's devotion to the Goddess as well as his insistence that the ultimate form of the godhead is pure spirit and that such personal forms of god as the Goddess herself participate in the illusion of Māyā are very clear signs that his sectarian affiliation helped to determine the general shape of his saintly vocation.

The life story tells us that Śaṅkara was born evidently to a younger woman married to an older man—his "legal" father, a Brāhmaṇa—who had not expected to have children. Thus the taint of scandal hung about his birth, the knowledge of its unusual nature not to be hidden from the observant Indian community around, however much the mother might insist on the intervention of Śiva.[33] When his mother died, Śaṅkara, already dedicated to asceticism, was prohibited by custom from performing the funeral rites. Yet because his mother was alone in the world, he defied the rule of Sannyāsī exclusion and did perform the rite: this act of individual self-assertion was ever after remembered and commented on in the Śaṅkarite tradition. This veridical anecdote tells us something about the wider ramifications of Śaṅkara's life story, for he appears in the light of the history of Hinduism as The Reformer—the one who got Hinduism back in the mainstream after centuries of an ineffectual backwater kind of existence. In doing so he traveled around India and established regional centers of orthodoxy where his successors, the incumbents of the seats of authority, designated as the Śaṅkarācarya of Badrināth, Purī, Dvāraka, Śṛṅgeri, and possibly Kañcipūram, maintained a quasi-papal dominance over the rest of the Hindu faithful, not always acceptable as *primus inter pares*; for the founders of rival sects after Śaṅkara were sometimes bitterly opposed to the suzerainty, and particularly the teaching, of Śaṅkara and his Maths.

We can see from this that Śaṅkara's vocation had both an active side as well as an intellectual one. To know about his spirituality, and presumably the depth of his spiritual experience, we turn to his commentaries on the *Bhagavad Gītā*[34] and the *Brahma Sūtra* in which he sets forth his "uncompromising monism." To one uninitiated in the spiritual path with which Śaṅkara is identified—namely, the Jñāna Mārga—because of its very nature it appears to be difficult to express meaningfully. To become emancipated from the world of the *upādhi,* or limiting condition, involves discrimination, or *viveka.* The shorthand for this path is sometimes put as *na-iti* or *neti,* the path of the "not-this." By gradually disabusing the intellect of absorption in the interlinking phenomena of perception, it is said, one may unravel the web of Maya and, seeing beyond, know the Self or Ātman as one with the Universal Self, Brahman.[35]

Rāmana Mahārshi

It may be useful for our discussion of this type of Indian sainthood to make reference to the life of the most famous monist or Jñanī saint of recent Indian religious history, Rāmana Mahārshi. The saint of Arunachala in South India was born on 29 December 1879 and died on 14 April 1950. At the time of his death he had attained recognition both in Indian circles and abroad as one of the most compelling examples of the Hindu saint. It will be apropos to quote here from the description in Rāmana Mahārshi's own words of his experience of monistic separation or realization:

> It was about six weeks before I left Madura for good that the great change in my life took place. It was quite sudden. I was sitting alone in a room on the first floor of my uncle's house. I seldom had any sickness, and on that day there was nothing wrong with my health, but a sudden violent fear of death overtook me. There was nothing in my state of health to account for it, and I did not try to account for it or to find out whether there was any reason for the fear. I just felt "I am going to die" and began thinking what to do about it. It did not occur to me to consult a doctor or my elders or friends; I felt that I had to solve the problem myself, there and then.
>
> The shock of the fear of death drove my mind inwards and I said to myself mentally, without actually framing the words: "Now death has come; what does it mean? What is it that is dying? This body dies." And I at once dramatized the occurrence of death. I lay with my limbs stretched out stiff as though *rigor mortis* had set in and imitated a corpse so as to give greater reality to the enquiry. I held my breath and kept my lips tightly closed so that no sound could escape, so that neither the word "I" nor any other word could be uttered. "Well then," I said to myself, "this body is dead. It will be carried stiff to the burning ground and there

> burnt and reduced to ashes. But with the death of this body am I dead? Is the body I? It is silent and inert but I feel the full force of my personality and even the voice of the "I" within me, apart from it. So I am spirit transcending the body. The body dies but the Spirit that transcends it cannot be touched by death. That means I am the deathless Spirit." All this was not dull thought; it flashed through me vividly as living truth which I perceived directly, almost without thought-process. "I" was something very real, the only real thing about my present state, and all the conscious activity connected with my body was centered on that "I". From that moment onwards the "I" or Self focussed attention on itself by a powerful fascination. Fear of death had vanished once and for all. Absorption in the Self continued unbroken from that time on. Other thoughts might come and go like the various notes of music, but the "I" continued like the fundamental *sruti* note that underlies and blends with all the other notes. Whether the body was engaged in talking, reading or anything else, I was still centred on "I". Previous to that crisis I had no clear perception of my Self and was not consciously attracted to it. I felt no perceptible or direct interest in it, much less any inclination to dwell permanently in it.[36]

Śaṅkara's Effect

The effect of Saṅkara's life upon Hindu India has been incalculable, not only because of his intellectual and spiritual gifts but because in his life's consequences we see the vitalization of two dominating aspects of the Hindu modality. From Śaṅkara's time onward Hindu values are authoritatively reinterpreted by gifted individuals who, in their own right, become the models of behavior and leadership for large numbers of people in the society. This element of novelty perhaps allows for the regrouping of socially distinct entities into homogeneous units, or the easing of relationships between social groups that had been antagonistic toward one another. Even Śaṅkara, who is sometimes held up to criticism because of his tendency to adhere strictly to the rules of Brāhmaṇical behavior, is cited anecdotally for the recognition he gave to a person of the untouchable caste:

> One morning, Śaṅkara was going to the temple of Lord Visvanatha, accompanied by his disciples, after a bath in the sacred river. [Ganges at Banaras] A caṇḍāla (untouchable) followed by dogs and with a pot of liquor in his hand came near him. Śaṅkara

> asked the caṇḍāla to get out of his way. The caṇḍāla enquired as to which should go away, the body or the self. As for the body, it is the same in composition in the case of every person. As for the self, it is one and all pervading. Śaṅkara realized at once that this was no ordinary caṇḍāla. In fact, it was Lord Śiva Himself that had come in the guise of an untouchable. Śaṅkara prostrated before the Lord and sang a hymn in which he declares that the one who has realized non-duality is his master, be that one a brahmin or a caṇḍāla.[37]

The second consequence of his life was the development of a formal social organization with a strong leadership and an effective method for maintaining high standards at the leadership and community levels from one generation to another. Here Śaṅkara is mentioned as having borrowed ideas from the Buddhist monastic order. Be that as it may, the model that Śaṅkara gave to the Hindu community and the order with its numerous initiated Sannyāsīs, drawing their lineage from the Maths established by Śaṅkara, have been imitated and valued from his time onward.

Reaction to Śaṅkara

After Śaṅkara's time a strong countermovement to the monistic forms of philosophical analysis, based upon the orthodoxy created by adhering to the principle that nothing could be taught that was not inherent or explicit in the Veda (thus the Vedānta philosophy which took its course through commentaries on the Upaniṣads and other similar canonical works), arose among those who wanted to give respectability and a more extensive intellectual base to their devotional attitude toward God.

The counterattack against the monists came primarily from the ranks of those orthodox Hindus, likewise Vedāntists, who advocated some form of dualist philosophy with its ritualistic and theological consequences. If the first great crisis (an extended one, to be sure) of a Hinduism emerging from the background of Vedic religion was that posed by the sudden efflorescence of Buddhism, Jainism, and other *nāstika* or heretical sects, the second was a crisis immediately perceived in the setting and aftermath of the brilliant career of Śaṅkara. It was simply this: whereas the first crisis cut too radically at the social and theological roots of the Hindu masses, the second was of the nature of a very threatening judgment upon the whole panoply of custom, religious observance, and theology-mythology growing out of the union of temple worship, and the Āgama canonical writings, with the Purāṅic scriptures, which told the sacred stories of the lives of the gods, especially Viṣṇu and Śiva. Indeed a relevant anecdote is recorded concerning Śaṅkara's passing. "It is said that on his deathbed he craved pardon of God for three sins: for confining Him who is without form to stone and mortar; for describing Him, Who transcends all qualities; and for having frequented temples, since by so doing he had denied the omnipresence of His divinity."[38]

If Hinduism had been of the nature of those religions that accept final judgments on "mistakes" of the past, it is possible that the authority of Śaṅkara could have brought about a fundamental reform in the Hindu life of worship and theology. Instead, however, one could say that the crisis was rationalized hierarchically. Śaṅkara's position remained authoritative, but other options gained ground until, on the whole, the influence of Śaṅkara directly was relegated to an upper corner of the total edifice.

THE MEDIEVAL PERIOD

Thus the second great movement in the history of Indian saintly heroes and heroines is closely connected both with the dualist Vedānta and with the so-called devotional movement of Bhakti Hinduism. The Bhakti movement, taken as a whole, was an all-out effort to provide a great number of alternative scenarios of salvation for both Śaivas and Vaiṣṇavas, employing all the available sources of mythology and theology, and, last but not least, building centrally upon the experience of many devotees who in all ages to the present have illustrated over and over again the main themes of the Bhakti movement. Within the Bhakti movement there is a perceptible dialectic between the saints of poetry and the saints of theology. The movement achieves a certain supreme moment of clarity in the rise of the Āḻvār poets of Tamil literature and those of the Śaiva Siddhānta;[39] but especially in the case of the former they provide the basis for the *paraṁparā* of Vaiṣṇava Ācāryas and poets that reaches from roughly the time of Śaṅkara nearly until the end of the eighteenth century, or before the rise of modern Indian vernacular literatures that are partly modeled on European prototypes.

Because the interpretation of the Bhakti movement and its various representatives has already reached extensive proportions, we shall try to find a typical example that illustrates the style and contribution of this particular saintly vocation to the history of Indian spirituality. Because the Śaivite material is of a special nature and, though it does give rise to a very significant devotional form, is closely linked to the monist outlook, the contrasting example will be that of the Vaiṣṇava tradition in northern India. Perhaps the most significant breakthrough in the northern Bhakti tradition was the elevation of the householder life to equal status with that of the sannyāsī as far as the possibility of achieving the supreme state of the beatific vision, which for the Vaiṣṇavas meant to live in eternal communion with the form of Viṣṇu (usually Rāma or Kṛṣṇa) that inspired their devotion.

Rāmānujā, Madhva, and Vallabha

If Śaṅkara was the supreme model for the monist viewpoint on mystical experience and his impact of the highest magnitude, it is not an exaggeration to say that Rāmānujā is his counterpart and equal in the dualist Vaiṣṇava tradition.[40] His philosophical viewpoint, as well as his unique organization of the community of his followers with its emphasis upon a married membership, has had a profound impact on later forms of the expression of Vaiṣṇava sanctity and on the generations of Hindus who organized often competing Vaiṣṇava sects but perforce being cognizant of the forms that Rāmānujā gave to the Vaiṣṇava reaction to Śaṅkara.[41]

Perhaps next to Rāmānujā in the effect that his interpretation of Vedānta philosophy and his organization of the Vaiṣṇava community had had on the later history of Hinduism was the philosopher-saint Madhva,[42] whose militant stance vis-à-vis Buddhists, Jainas, and other Vedāntists is well known. Interestingly, though, Madhva must equally be remembered as one of the greatest liturgists of the Bhakti tradition and as one who had a genius for establishing ranks of religious hierarchy; as a result, the Madhva community is one of the most homogeneous and extensively organized of all such groups in India. The Sampradāya, or sect, of Vallabha in north India represents yet another departure and interpretation of the underlying themes of the Vaiṣṇava schools.[43] It was through Vallabha and Śrī Hitharivaṁś,[44] the poet-saint founder of the Rādhāvallabha Sampradāya, that the householder leadership of the Vaiṣṇava community became most clearly expressed.

The Nimbārka Sampradāya

For the purposes of this chapter I will make special mention of the remaining great Sampradāya of the Vaiṣṇavas—namely, the Nimbārka,[45] founded by an outstanding philosopher who influenced one of the great poets of the late medieval Hindi period, the writer Ghanānand. Nimbārka was approximately a contemporary of Rāmānujā (twelfth century) and advocated a philosophical doctrine that is sometimes called Bhedābheda Advaita, from the two Sanskrit words meaning "difference" and "nondifference." The implication is that the supreme deity, Brahman, is simultaneously the same as and different from the universe of his creation. Nimbārka, it is taught by the sect, was the incarnation of Viṣṇu's discus and thus, in a sense, an *avatāra* of the supreme Lord. He is also noteworthy as the founder of one of the orders of Vaiṣṇava ascetics, who have the generic name Bairāgis and in the Nimbārka case, the special appellation Nimāvats.[46] Theologically speaking, Nimbārka's greatest contribution was to bring forward the divine couple, Rādhā-Kṛṣṇa, as the center of Vaiṣṇava devotion, at least in the form that is most evocative and literal and for which the poem *Gīta Govinda* by the poet Jāyadeva, possibly influenced by Nimbārka, is the archetypal expression.[47] In his own right Nimbārka composed treatises in Sanskrit of which the very brief *Daśaśloki* outlines the main points.[48] Therein he makes very clear the prominent place he gives to Rādhā and Kṛṣṇa in their mature or Mādhuryabhakti forms. Nimbārka settled down in Vṛndāvana, which is the center of the north Indian Bhakti movement and the earthly place associated with the stories of Kṛṣṇa's deeds as expressed particularly in the *Bhāgavata Purāṇa*. In the long period since Nimbārka flourished, the sect that he founded has tended to divide into two divisions, one of householders and the other of ascetics or mendicants.

My own experience of the contemporary organization of the Sampradāya in Vṛndāvana in 1979 included visits to the Srījī temple, which is regarded as a principal cult center, and opportunities to witness the morning worship celebrated by the Ācārya of the Sampradāya, who was visiting Vṛndāvana at that time from his headquarters in Rajasthan.[49] Because I am trying in these pages to capture the ethos of the Indian saint, I mention in the case of the Nimbārka Sampradāya that the special mood of devotion to Rādhā and Kṛṣṇa remains at a high and joyful pitch. The cry "Radheśyam" ("O Rādhā, O Śyām [Kṛṣṇa]!"), heard in the temple, is repeated over and over again in rollicking hymns that are sung throughout the day by groups of devotees gathered in the temple. This speaks at least of the viability of the original impetus to such devotion. It also seems to bear out one of the points in the tenth *śloka* of Nimbārka's Daśaślokī that the devotee should experience, "the feeling of enjoyment consequent on Bhakti or love." The temple atmosphere was generally very open and friendly. I was given liberal permission to photograph and make tape recordings and to film most of the rituals in the inner sanctuary of the shrine—the only exception being that I was not allowed to photograph the temple's Śaligrāma stone, which is one of the most sacred objects in any Vaiṣṇava shrine because it is thought to be a "natural" incarnation of Viṣṇu himself.[50]

A group of young Bairāgīs was anxious to share with me their technical competence in the skills of Hāṭha yoga, which they demonstrated in a room set aside for such exercises at one side of the temple compound. The presence of a fairly numerous group of Vaiṣṇava ascetics with matted hair and their faces adorned with different versions of the Vaiṣṇava *tilak* in the company of a much larger group of householders and families with small children, all of whom took part in the enjoyment of the singing and the rituals, seemed to demonstrate an intermingling of the alleged divisions of the Nimbārka Sampradāyā rather than their separation, as suggested by Bhandarkar. The main images in the temple were of Rādhā and Kṛṣṇa in their Śṛṇgāra forms. As with several other Vaiṣṇava groups in Vṛndāvan, the structure of the divine-human relationship is thought to mirror on the mundane sphere the ideal situation of the transfigured earth with Rādhā and Kṛṣṇa actually present to their devotees, who identify with the Sakhīs, the female companions of Rādhā, who witness the divine dance of Rādhā and Kṛṣṇa and to some extent participate in it.[51] Some among the devotees, male and female, sitting and waiting in front of the curtained shrine for the formal ceremonies to begin, rose and danced to the accompaniment of the drums, harmonium, and the singing of the praises of Rādhā and Kṛṣṇa. Both householders and ascetics participated in that expression of devotion.

Nimbārka and Jāyadeva—the one a philosopher, the other a poet—are special sources from which the later, widespread enthusiasm for Rādhā-Kṛṣṇa devotion arose. However, as with a large number of the Bhakti cults throughout India, a wide variety of intellectual and literary talents was attracted to the life of devotion. One might compare the situation with that of Christianity in which, at least until recently, every generation of believers has had its share of great theologians, preachers, and hymn writers, sometimes one person displaying all three talents.

GHANĀNAND

The Bhakti period in literature reached a high point in the sixteenth century and then gradually gave way to movements in which form and content became more important than sincerity of feeling. This can be detected in the elaboration of technique and the emphasis upon technical competence, although great brilliance as a writer does not necessarily preclude sincerity of emotion. Thus in the period when the artificiality of expression in poetry of the Mādhurya-bhāva mode of the Rādhā-Kṛṣṇa relationship had begun to replace true devotion, a greatly competent poet whose sincerity of feeling is not questioned is thought to have arisen among the members of the Nimbārka Sampradāya, and we might close this section on Nimbārka's contribution to the function of the saintly role in Hinduism by reference to Ghanānand's special qualities. I say that he is thought to have arisen because Ghanānand is one of a group of poets whose precise sectarian affiliation is perhaps less important than the depth of his or her religious feeling. Besides Ghanānand, Mirābaī and Raskhān are other examples of the type. One might call them "independent saints." Nevertheless there is a strong tradition in the Nimbārka Sampradāyā that Ghanānand had been initiated into the sect. His poetry reflects the values of the Śṛṇgara mode of Bhakti as exemplified in the teaching of the sect.[52]

The known biography of Ghanānand is fairly limited. He is thought to have been born in A.D. 1689 and to have died about fifty years later, killed in Vṛndāvan during the invasion of Nadirshah. Prior to moving to Vṛndāvan he had worked as chief clerk in the court of the emperor of Delhi, Muhammad Shah. His position suggests his caste, that he was of the Kāyasthas, who, though Hindus, held important administrative posts in the medieval Muslim bureaucracy and who have continued to emphasize business, law, and money-lending in their caste professions in modern times. His poetic gift was already evident during his days in the royal court, and, as was usual under the circumstances, he was also a singer with a wonderfully melodic voice. The story of Ghanānand's downfall at court, though possibly true, reflects a theme that recurs in the biographies of other poets both of the medieval and modern periods. He fell in love with the leading courtesan of the royal entourage and began to compose and sing poems that reflected this passion. It came to the attention of the emperor that his chief clerk was a very gifted singer, and he requested Ghanānand to perform in the court, but the latter refused. However, at the entreaties of Sujān, the courtesan, he finally agreed to the emperor's request and sang the praises of his beloved before the highest nobles of the land. By then the emperor had grown annoyed and he ordered Ghanānand into exile. Sujān refused to accompany him, and so the poet went alone to Vṛndāvan, where he adopted the life of the Vaiṣṇava ascetic and became an initiated disciple of Śrī Vṛndāvan Devācārya of the Nimbārka sect.

Thereafter Ghanānand lived in Vṛndāvan singing the praises of Rādhā and Kṛṣṇa in superb poetry that contains an intriguing ambiguity of reference in that the poetry continues to be addressed to Sujān, the name of Ghanānand's earthly beloved but taken by all authorities in the field to refer, depending upon the context, to various aspects of the divine-human context: Lord Kṛṣṇa, Rādhā, Rādhā and Kṛṣṇa together, Dear Man, God the Lover, and others. Tradition reports that in his ecstatic fervor Ghanānand wandered the roads of Braj, immersed in the feeling of union and separation from his beloved Lord Kṛṣṇa. He laughed and wept by turns and at times seemed to lose consciousness as he contemplated the sacred waters of the Yāmuna River. Such a delirium of devotion is the extreme and at the same time the archetypal outcome of the Bhakti ideal. Those who through poetry and autobiographical record make accessible to succeeding generations of devotees the ideal of such intensity are deserving of the title of saint. But their "yoga" is repeatable in the common experience of the devotee, who, as in the case of the modern follower of the Nimbārka Sampradāya, can go to the Srījī temple in Vṛndāvan and joyfully join in singing the hymns of Rādhā and Śyām.

Women in the Bhakti Movement

Two Indian women, one from the earliest period of Bhakti in south India and the other a north Indian mystical genius of the Middle Ages, are often compared for the intensity of their devotion to Kṛṣṇa. Although it is overtly the case that the Ācāryas and the great majority of the poet saints of the various Bhakti groups are men, the supreme *bhāva* or *rasa*, the corresponding intensity of emotional state that the devotee experiences in a particular relationship to God, is in the Mādhurya or Śṛṇgāra mode. To enjoy this *rasa* the devotee of God usually adopts the stance of the feminine lover in relation to the masculine Supreme Being who loves. The existential fact of this point of view is that feminine erotic emotions are presented as the norm of the devotional experience (to be sure, in a sublimated fashion). Thus when the Śṛṇgāra rasa of devotion is exemplified in a female devotee of exceptional gifts, there is a kind of breakthrough to a greater reality of the archetype. The renowned male devotees also exhibit the fruits of the Śṛṇgāra bhāva, but it can only be perceived, as it were, indirectly—

there is a greater inwardness or hiddenness about it. In the female devotee the real and the ideal are overt to a greater degree. This provides a particular kind of exemplary model that is greatly admired among the devotees. For this reason, and the excellence of their writing, Āndāl, the south Indian Āḷvār, and the poet Mīra Bāī in the north are among the most famous saints of the Bhakti tradition.

MUSLIM INFLUENCE

In all fairness, there is another aspect of the medieval Indian situation that deserves comment before moving on. If we continue to think of the development of Hinduism as following a line provoked in part only, but yet significantly, by response to crisis and thus the rise of Śaṅkara's reform and reorganization as a response to the effects of Buddhism, and the growth of Bhakti devotion and the rise of the forms of Vaiṣṇava organization and modes of sanctity as a response to Śaṅkara's thought and possible impact on theistic forms of Hinduism, we cannot disregard the direct Muslim influence on the shaping of religious thought of the epoch in which Islam prevailed as the dominating religion of the rulers of the land. Once again, I have covered aspects of the specifically Islamic contribution through the Sūfī movement and do not wish to go over the same ground again.[53] Here I will content myself with references to examples of how the intermingling of Muslim and Hindu ideals contributed to the further development of Hindu sectarianism as well as the specific role of the saint in the Hindu tradition.

The theme I wish to emphasize concerns the way in which the monist conception of God could be seen by some important religious persons of the medieval period to break through the structure of caste and theistic sectarianism to provide a unique Hindu outlook on the spiritual quest and the possibility for human transcendence to the category of enlightenment. The first tradition to which I refer is that of the so-called Sant of whom the lineage of Vaiṣṇava saints of Maharashtra provides the typical example. These have been much favored and written about both by Indians and by foreign students of Indian religion and literature.[54] There is another group of such "saints" in north India in the Hindī- and Punjābī-speaking areas who grew out of the missionary work of a great early medieval saint, named Rāmānanda, formerly a member of the Rāmānujā sect but ostracized because he was believed to have broken the sect's quasi-caste rule against eating food in a public manner. As a consequence he set about to attract a large number of devout persons to a pure kind of Bhakti, centered upon Rāma, one of the incarnations of Viṣṇu and the hero of the Indian epic *Rāmayāna.* Among Vaiṣṇavas Rāma had gradually acquired the theological potency of the nondual God, reflected in the moral and psychological atmosphere of the later Rāmite mythology—for instance, the poetry of Tulsidās. Although God took form in Rāma, his form was only expediently relevant to his godhead, which shone through the physical, Avatāra guise with uncompromising purity.[55]

Perhaps it was inevitable that certain Rāmites should come to the view that God in purity of essence without human embodiment and hence without recourse to idol worship should be the true goal of Bhakti. That influence from the Maharashtrian Vaiṣṇavas figures in this development is patent. It is also clear that Monist Vedānta was adaptable to more than one expression in the same way that Tantrism found a logical accommodation with certain types of Bhakti that emphasized the Mādhurya-bhāva mode. Islam with its uncompromising monotheism can likewise not be denied in the total developmental process leading to the Sant (saint) form of Bhakti. Perhaps most radically Sant Bhakti denied the efficacy of icon worship altogether and relied wholly upon the devotee's personal relationship with the one God, who might be addressed under the titles of Rāma and Govinda but also Allah or the Faqīr, a name for the guru in the Sūfī tradition.[56]

Guru Nānak

Building, therefore, on this unitary vision of the Bhakti mode, one of the great revitalization movements of the medieval period takes form gradually around the teachings of Guru Nānak (fifteenth century). There can be little doubt that he was a Sūfī, of the type that flourished in India, heavily influenced by the terminology and mythology of the Hindu environment but ultimately employing the concepts of Islamic theology and mysticism in speaking to the spiritual quest of the devotee. Guru Nānak had both Hindu and Muslim devotees and self-consciously set about to bridge the sectarian differences between Hindus and Muslims. Ultimately the path he set forth grew to be an independent religious expression, today called Sikhism, embodying the teachings of Guru Nānak as well as those of the founders of the Sikh religion. The military aspect of the Sikh religion is a unique character among the major Bhakti movements of the Indian Middle Ages.[57]

Kabīr

But among all the religious figures of the Sant type in north India, Kabīr holds a place of special importance because of the singular way in which he combined the gift of great poetry with a unique ability to synthesize the values of Muslim Sūfism within a doctrinal expression that was as acceptable to Hindus as to Muslims. He also is regarded as the founder of a division of medieval Hindu groups of quasi-ascetic membership with the title of Kabīr-panthis. These groups appear to have arisen out of a combined membership of Hindus and Muslim devotees who regarded themselves as Kabīr's original followers.[58]

The main emphasis in Kabīr's religious experience is on the realization of God in the inner self. He writes, "People say that Hari lives in the East and that Allah resides in the West. / Search in your heart, search in your heart—there is his dwelling and his residence!" But this knowledge is not without paradox. He goes on to say, "I believed him to be exterior to myself—and, near, he has become distant to me!" The problem is that with the mystics of the world Kabīr affirmed the essentially incommunicable nature of his experience of the divine. In a manner highly reminiscent of the Sūfīs, Kabīr often speaks of the brightness of the mystical illumination: "All darkness was dissipated when the lamp shown in the depths of the soul." Sometimes the imagery of light is joined with some other motif as in the lines, "Kabīr says, the striking of the Eternal is like the rising of a whole succession of suns. / Near the bridegroom the bride has arisen, and a marvelous spectacle has appeared to her."[59]

Kabīr often refers to the absorption of the self in God, and he has been considered to be a *nirgūnī* monist, an adherent of the nonqualified Absolute in contrast with the majority of Vaiṣṇavite bhaktas who adore a personal, qualified *saguṇa* God. Kabīr was poised in the paradox familiar to the religions of the world. His devotion to God was the experience of the personal, breaking through the forms of the impersonal world and into the consciousness of the yogi, who would have liked to find all aspects of the personal dimension of God superfluous for his salvation but in the end has had to admit the copresence of a divine person in the experience of union. Kabīr, more than other Indian mystics, was able to hold the two elements of his paradox in a creative relationship that gave rise to a richly new religious expression. An Indian scholar describes Kabīr's special theological position against the Hindu background:

> He whom the yogis worship in the form of Saccidanand is not Brahma, nor is he Vishnu, nor is he Indra, nor is he earth, water, air, fire or the atmosphere. He is neither Veda nor the [Vedic] sacrifice, neither sun nor moon, neither Space or Time—he is dissimilar from . . . every existing form. The mode of Kabirdās' Ram is flawlessly apart from everything else. Brahmā contains flaws, Viṣṇu contains flaws, Śiva also, the Gopīs also, the Purāṇas also, knowledge also, worship also, the gods also, almsgiving also, apparel also, the holy also, asceticism also, places of pilgrimage also. The flawless Rām is unique, different from everything else and free from everything else.[60]

Stated thus, it is the most emphatic kind of monotheistic affirmative, clearly linking Kabīr much more closely to Islam than to the great majority of all ancient Hindu writers. There has always been an effort to minimize that connection, however.

Mahāmati Prānnāth

The mystery behind Kabīr's personal religious commitment and even the authentication of the verses that are attributed to him will perhaps remain as long as scholarship continues to investigate.[61] The theme of Muslim-Hindu reconciliation is taken up very directly in the work of a later poet and religious reformer much revered in the Kāyastha caste that was mentioned earlier. Indeed, the impact of Indian universalism can be found in explicitly Muslim sectarianism in India from the Middle Ages onward, but a special emphasis is presented by the Hindu saint Mahāmati Prānnāth, whose dates are 1618 to 1694. As a modern writer about him says,

> Illumined by the integral knowledge (Tartamya-Jnana) he actually saw and realised the hierarchy of the entire Divine Plan within his inner divine vision. In the illumination of the Divine Plan he discovered the relevance not only of the hundreds of the Hindu scriptures but also thousands [of] others of all the other religions originated in Semitic families such as the Quran, the Bible and the religious writings of the Jews. He therefore took upon himself the responsibility of presenting the synthetic form of the Divine Plan of creation and showing the relevance of the various conflicting texts of the manifold scriptures.[62]

Prānnāth's family had risen to very high status in Jannagar State, where his father was the prime minister. Prānnāth grew up in a religious household and eventually came under the influence of his father's guru, Śrī Devācandra Nijānand Swāmī. The guru, recognizing Prānnāth's special qualities, chose him to continue the task of bringing unity to the great diversity of religions and particularly to resolve the destructive conflict between the Muslim overlords and the Hindu subjects. Prānnāth, whose name previously was Śrī Mehrāj, acquired his spiritual name in the following manner:

> In the beginning, with a view to serve the fellow-companions gathered round his Guru, financially and otherwise, Shri Mehraj accepted the office of the Chief Ministership of Jannagar. But soon he found that his administrative job came in the way of disseminating his spiritual experiences. One other companion known as Sundersath also prompted him to complete his Guru's mission. Shri Devachandra called God his Prannath, i.e., master of his life. Shri Mehraj called his Guru his Prannath. Now Sundersath saw both God and Guru in him so they addressed him as Prannath. . . . Mahamati means the wisdom of God which brings His fellow beings towards Him. From Shri Prannath's spiritual ecstasy started flowing verses in the name of Mahamati. All those verses have been written down by the disciples around him. The verses number more than eighteen thousand. . . . The collection of those verses is now known a "Tartanya-Vani" and also as "Kulzan-Swarup" compiled in nearly two thousand pages.[63]

Srī Prānnāth wandered through Rajasthan and gathered a large following, which traveled with him. Evidently a crucial turn in his mission came in the following manner:

> One day while going through the market in Merta [Rajasthan] Mahamati heard the call for prayer (*Azan*) from the tower of a mosque. The Mullah was reciting the sacred Mantra of the Quran, "La-llah-Lilillah." At once it was revealed to Mahamati that those were the words akin to the "Tartamya Mantra", and they have similarity in meaning with the words of the Gita. *La* means "not existing" (*Kshara*), *llah* means that which exists (*Akshara*) and *Lilillah* means beyond the indestructible existence (*Aksharatita*), the Supreme Uttan Purusha of the Gita. . . . This was a moment of overwhelming joy for Mahamati. Those were the days of Aurangzeb the Mughal emperor of India. The people were distressed all over the country. The Hindus were bound by rituals and Islam became the religion of torturing others. At this odd time, Mahamati set before himself the task of expounding the tenets of true

> religion and bringing about a revolution in the world through religious awakening.[64]

Inspired by this vision and provoked by the problem, Prānnāth went to Delhi, where he attempted to gain an interview with Aurangzeb to discuss the new views he had developed on Muslim-Hindu relations. Although he did not succeed in meeting the Moghul emperor, he was allowed to leave Delhi unmolested, and thereafter he sought to enlist the interest of various Hindu kings but was unsuccessful until he met Shri Chatrasal of Bundelkhand. The latter was "crowned" by Mahamati and took up the cause of the Hindus against the Muslims, ironically choosing Prānnāth as his guru and establishing the new sect as the primary focus of religious life in his state with its headquarters in Panna, a district of Madhya Pradesh.

Prānnāth continued his efforts at organization and solidifying his teaching until his death on 29 June 1694. In the ranks of the Hindu saints of the time Mahāmati Prānnāth remains obscure, but his enormous scriptural creativity deserves further attention, as do the basic ideas of his creed, which remind us of the teachings of Nānak, Kabīr, and some of the Sūfīs.[65] The contribution of Mahāmati Prānnāth seems to be a milestone on that road of influence and creativity that brings Hinduism in the modern period into its special light as offering through its religious, saintly leadership numerous alternative perspectives on the human condition whether at home or abroad (but first and foremost in India itself) and with a deliberate attempt to enunciate a panreligious universalism, the latter a characteristic of developments in the early modern period of Hinduism.

THE MODERN PERIOD

Perhaps the greatest crisis faced by the religious traditions of world prominence was that provoked by the transition to modernity. Obviously different areas of the world came to this crisis in differing manners and adjusted to it in highly individual ways. An extreme example might be that of Japan, which was sequestered from European influences after the sixteenth century until the middle of the nineteenth century. Thereafter Japan embarked upon a wholesale transformation in the direction of modernization with significant impact upon Japanese religious traditions as well.

India, conversely, was not afforded the luxury of independence from outside domination during the critical period from the late Middle Ages to the present. European powers had begun their inroads into India in the sixteenth century with the advent of the age of exploration. By the mid-eighteenth century India was under siege from abroad and internally sundered by Muslim-Hindu military conflict. The British emerged as victors in the European conquest of India and for nearly a century and a half provided a government for a unified India that came to be defined as the British Rāj. In looking at the evidence respecting the saintly vocation in this period, therefore, we may say that the crisis of Indian religious history in the colonial period required adaptation of the presentation of Hinduism to the fact of European domination and the high status accorded to yet another religious tradition of foreign origin: the Christian. Of course there is considerable difference in the impact of Christianity upon India as contrasted with that of Islam, for the latter involved the conquest of India in the name of a religion; whereas in the case of the British, the Western world was already well on the way toward developing the compartmentalized secular state. Nevertheless the Christian rulers of India added cachet to the doctrines and way of life of Christianity. Moreover the whole baggage of Western ideas became available to the literate Indian public, which of necessity learned to cope and some even to excel in yet another language medium, the English of the conquerors.

In this setting, therefore, the Hindu saint took on a new and, if anything, more important function even than in Hinduism's past, for the saints of the modern period fight in the vanguard of preserving Hindu values not only against the claims of rival creeds—or more often through assimilating such claims to the already existing Hindu system—but also against the general modern trend toward materialism and skepticism in the area of religious belief.[66] The converse of this is the adaptation, as in the West, of the positions of science and contemporary philosophy to the life of religious faith. An additional feature of modern India's experience was that of coping with being a colonial dependency of a foreign power, so that Hinduism and its saintly leadership could provide stimulus to the development of political and nationalistic positions and contribute to what is called "the independence movement."[67]

It is my impression that the modern period of Hinduism in its typical expression begins in the early nineteenth century with the appearance of quasi-saintly personalities, such as those connected with the Brahmo

Samāj, matures through the outstanding mystical genius of Srī Rāmakrishna,[68] and develops more or less climatically toward the achievement of independence properly speaking, under the direct impact of Mahātmā Gandhi, a "saint" in a very special category in light of the fact that his vocation lay almost exclusively in the realm of politics and social reform.[69]

POSTINDEPENDENCE

Since attaining independence in 1947, India's attempt to survive as a secular democracy has not excluded further evolution in the functions of the saintly leadership. The crisis of modernity takes on a global aspect. An enhancement in the appeal of Hinduism through its living saints has registered around the world, so that in the post-Independence period Hindu religious movements have found increasing support among a foreign clientele. This, of course, has adduced not only admiration for Hinduism but criticism from entrenched viewpoints in the West. Some of the new Hindu religious movements have been thought to be "cults" as this term is understood, particularly in America. Efforts have been made to "rescue our youth" from brainwashing, and so on.[70] In the popular Western religious outlook, therefore, the saintly leadership of Hinduism has been equated with the "cult leadership" of America's own religious tradition. This has led to misunderstanding as well as a peculiar kind of negative reaction within Hinduism itself that regards the flocking of Western adherents to the feet of its teachers as a mixed blessing.

At home because of the politicizing of the Indian public in the natural development of representative democracy in India, the need for direct intervention of the saints, à la Gandhi, in the political process has been less evident since Independence. Yet Vinoba Bhave, certainly of saintly reputation in the Gandhian mold, the leader of the Sarvodaya movement, continued his efforts at land distribution well into the Independence period. Indeed, the mantle of Mahātmā Gandhi in a sense fell upon the first prime minister, Jawaharlal Nehru, and his daughter Indira Gandhi and her family, whom the Indian masses have regarded with some of the reverence reserved for India's religious leadership.

The Śaṅkarācāryas survive in the modern period as an ultimate authority and are often called upon to rally the masses to social and political issues of religious import, such as communal harmony or matters involving cow slaughter. Their integrity, ascetic life, and reputed paranormal insight, if not powers, still stir the masses with profound feelings of awe and reverence. Very often the religious leadership seems caught between the need to vouch for the traditional values and way of life and the effect that modern technology has on the way of life of prominent individuals. The use of automobiles, jet air travel, and the mass communication media of journals and newspapers and, recently, television are particular instances. Of concern to many of the pronouncements of the modern religious leadership is the preservation of a traditional way of life while meeting the obvious challenges of surviving economically in the modern world. A statement long on the lips of the saintly leaders of India is that "work is worship," authority for which can be found as anciently rooted as in the *Bhagavad Gītā*.[71]

Another feature of the organization of new Hindu religious movements under contemporary saintly leadership is their tendency to take on a pan-Indian following with the saints themselves appearing in person before a widely scattered constituency whose ethnic background in the Indian context may be quite diverse.[72] In some instances such flexibility may be linked to a community that provides, because of its way of life—for example, being of a merchant caste that has adapted to living in more than one region of India—a widely dispersed base from which local people may be influenced.[73] The problems and crises of the world at large are also influential in varying degrees upon the contemporary saintly leadership. The achievements of the superpowers in space exploration or questions having to do with armaments and the quest for peace figure in the sermons and other expressed concerns of the saints.

The Brahmā-Kumārīs

Many facets of the anxious world, addressed by the modern saint in India, are brought together in an apocalyptic Hindu sect, founded by a retired Sindhi jewel merchant whose former name was Dada Lekh Raj but who came to be called Prajāpitā Brahmā, as though to say that he was the creator of creatures in the new age. He is the founder of the movement identified under the title Brahmā-Kumārīs Ishwariya Vishwa-Vidyalaya, or simply Brahmā-Kumārīs. Prajāpitā Brahmā died on 18 January 1969 after founding a religious movement meant to prepare humanity for the imminent destruction of the world, which has been interpreted as being simultaneously the natural cataclysm at the end of the Kālī or fourth period of the Hindu cycle and the inevitable holocaust resulting from the proliferation of nuclear weapons.[74] The Brahma-Kumārīs, or "maidens of Brahma," have opened centers, the Vishwa-Vidyalaya, throughout India in larger cities. There they appeal to as wide a constituency as they can reach to abandon the materialism and irreligion of the current age and to adopt a strict regimen of meditation and yoga practice ultimately leading to heavenly rest at the end of the Kālī age and subsequent rebirth in deity form at the beginning of the next cosmic cycle. Their sense of urgency in the task of preaching the truth about the human condition and providing the means for salvation is symbolized in one of the dramatic paintings with which they illustrate their theology. It is called *Śṛṣṭi Cakra* and, as the Sanskrit words indicate, depicts the "cycle of creation" as a kind of clock with the hands of the clock pointing nearly to midnight or the end of the age. According to this new interpretation of venerable Indian theories, the cycle of creation and destruction has a limit of five thousand years. This time period is now nearly exhausted.

Dada Lekh Raj

Dada Lekh Raj was born in the city of Hyderabad, Sindh in what is now Pakistan. His father was the headmaster of a school, but Dada Lekh Raj entered business and became an expert in grading and evaluating jewels. He established his business headquarters in Calcutta and, according to his biography, became a multimillionaire. Even in spite of his business way of life, however, he was noted for his integrity and exemplary moral life. He also apparently had an unusually robust physique and a commanding physical presence. His biography describes him as follows:

> Dada was indeed a powerful personality. Besides a lofty forehead, well-formed body and a bright countenance, he had always a smile on his lips. Even at the age of 90, he would sit straight, his eyesight was keen and long, his hearing was sharp, he climbed hills with ease, played badminton vigorously, and, what is most remarkable, walked without any aid, human or otherwise. One can easily imagine how well-ordered and healthy his life and ways were. Neither lethargy nor despair could ever touch him.[75]

After the age of fifty-five he turned more and more toward a life of religious absorption and began to have visions.

> Without an effort on his part, one day, he suddenly got a vision of the four-armed Vishnu, who said, "Thou art that." [Tat Tvam

> Asi] In other words, he felt as if he had been clearly told that he was indeed himself Shri Narayan in his essential form. Later, when he happened to be deep in contemplation in the garden of a friend in Varanasi, he had a vision of the self-luminous orb of Light, i.e., of Shiva, the Supreme Soul, Supreme Father. Also he saw in advance, in another Vision, the forthcoming destruction of this Iron-aged world being caused by atomic and hydrogen bombs, civil wars and natural calamities. (Dada had those visions long before the Americans and the Russians invented these bombs.) At the sight of these dreadful visions, he found in the depth of his being, a strong desire to have done with his business which had absorbed so many years of his precious life. He soon went to Calcutta, acquainted his partner with his firm resolve and from there . . . dissolved his partnership.[76]

It was shortly thereafter that the revelatory moment arrived and it became clear that the final savior of the age had appeared on the scene:

> While a *Satsang* at Dada's place was going on, he left all of a sudden and entered his room where he went straightway into a state of concentration. It was at this time that the greatest event of his life took place. His wife and daughter-in-law went after him to his room, only to find that his eyes were red as if red bulbs were lighted in them. His countenance too was glowing red, and the whole room was suffused with light. A voice was heard, coming from Dada's mouth as if it came from above. This divine voice said:—"I am the Blissful self, I am Shiva, I am Shiva. I am the knowledgeful self, I am Shiva, I am Shiva. I am the luminous self, I am Shiva, I am Shiva." And when this had been heard, Dada's eyes opened, he looked around with wonder. On being asked what he was looking for, the following words came from him: "Who was he? It was a light. It was some Might. A new beautiful, righteous world it was. Far, far up beyond the sky were visible some spiritual entities having shape like the stars. And when these stars descended, one out of these would be seen to become a divine prince, another a divine princess. That Light and Might: A Light indeed."[77]

Theory and Practice

Subsequent to this Prajāpitā Brahmā was substituted for his former name, and the work of spiritual renewal began. The events just recounted occurred in 1937, and it was at that time that Prajāpitā Brahmā founded the Brahāmā-Kumārīs-Ishwarīya-Vishwa-Vidyalāya. The implication of the title is that universities (Vishwa-Vidyalāya) having to do with knowledge of God (Ishwariya) are under the direction of the nuns or maidens of Brahmā (Brahmā-Kumārīs). One of the rather special teachings of Prajāpitā Brahmā was that in the Age of Confluence at the end of the cosmic cycle men have become so corrupted that it is necessary for women to take over the leadership of the religious community and to act as missionaries to promulgate the truth about salvation and preparation for the destruction and recreation of the world. Men are admitted into the community as "Kumāra"—roughly speaking, "monks"—but they fulfill an auxiliary role to that of the Kumārīs.

I visited the Brahmā-Kumārī center on the Ring Road in New Delhi on various occasions and can briefly describe how they operate. When Prajāpitā Brahmā began his mission, his preaching attracted a number of followers, whom he organized into the community described earlier. For a period of about fourteen years following 1937 the movement was rather inward-looking. Thereafter it turned to very active missionary endeavor. The headquarters was established eventually on Mount Abu in Rajasthan and among its works succeeded in producing a number of "mystically inspired" paintings of the basic teachings. These illustrations are presented in published texts and can be shown in slide format, but most typically one sees them first in the main room of the spiritual "museum" that is present in many Brahmā Kumārī centers.

The visitor enters the room and is guided by one of the Kumārīs from large-size illustration to illustration while she explains meanings and the overall theological interpretation of the present and future ages. One learns that it is the destiny of the human soul to reincarnate eternally and that there is the possibility of enjoying eighty-four births in a single cosmic cycle. I use the word "enjoy" deliberately because it is the contention that the soul does enjoy constant rebirth. However, for those souls which are not prepared for the end of the age—that is, who do not accept the teaching of Prajāpitā Brahmā and observe the pure way of life—rebirth in the next age will be delayed to the second half of the cosmic cycle. Thus they will not have the opportunity to enjoy the "deity" status of those born in the golden age of the first phase of the cosmic cycle, which continues to be blissful into the second or silver age but which turns into "hell" in the third, the copper, and the fourth, the iron age of the cycle. It is likely that nonbelievers will be reborn in the hell half of the next cosmic cycle.

For one who appears sincerely attracted to the first presentation of the doctrine, he or she will be invited to enroll in a course that lasts a week and in which a more elaborate presentation of the Brahma-Kumārī viewpoint is given. A longer period of instruction may then follow. One who finally accepts membership in the movement, if single, may become a Kumārī or Kumār and work full-time in the missionary activity of the group or, if married or otherwise encumbered, may continue in a secular occupation but must attend daily classes in the early morning at the Vishwa-Vidyalāya, where the doctrine is expounded and one learns the special meditation technique of the group. The four pillars of the teaching, which are regarded as essential for all who wish to make rapid progress toward perfection in the Confluence Age, whether married or single, are (1) celibacy; (2) cultivating the divine virtues; (3) Sat Sang, or meeting with other aspirants for meditation and instruction; and (4) eating only *sattvic* food, which excludes all types of animal flesh and certain vegetables, such as onions.

The Brahma-Kumārīs have attempted to exert a direct influence upon the moral quality of public life in India. They have organized parades and demonstrations in support of purity of life and integrity in government positions. They regularly visit government officials to remind them of the need to maintain the highest standards in public life. Through their approximately three hundred centers spread over India they have been able to bring the special viewpoint of Prajāpitā Brahmā to a wide audience. They have also begun to establish branches overseas.

Although many might regard the Brahmā-Kumārī movement, and Prajāpitā Brahmā in particular, as eccentric within the framework of Hinduism's mainline traditions, there is certainly a great variety of interesting material in the teaching and methodology of the movement. I have spoken about the adaptation of Hinduism to crisis through the special insight and work of the saints who seem in each period of India's history to have found the resources to counteract what had almost been, or might be, a dire threat to the very survival of Hinduism. Of course I did not mean to suggest that the crisis aspect of the functioning of the Indian saints completely precluded other aspects of their achievements. The very complexity of Indian civilization and of the various modes of Hinduism itself must deny any one-dimensional answer. However, the crisis reference role is one of the most significant characteristics of the functioning of the Indian saint.

In this light it may be seen that Hindus, together with the rest of the world's adherents of the living religions of mankind, must now grapple with the most compelling crisis to date. It is a multidimensional problem, potentially of catastrophic proportions. On the one side the integrity of cultural isolation and specific religious uniqueness appear now to have been irrevocably compromised throughout the world. This produces a relativism that can be accommodated only with difficulty to most religious systems. Political ideology and *Realpolitik* demand changes in human attitude and behavior—products of worldwide industrialization, economic interaction, and military/political confrontation—that may involve religious persons in compromises previously unexperienced. At the heart of much of the world's agony today lies the simmering confrontation between the Soviet Union and the United States, who together hold the world hostage to the threat of an apocalyptic destruction in nuclear war.

In one of the vivid paintings one sees in the Brahmā Kumārīs' spiritual museum one sees the *World Genealogical Tree*. It grows from the roots of the previous Age of Confluence when Brahmā and his spiritual consort Saraswatī had prepared the inauguration of the new age. The painting shows the emergence of the Golden Age and the Silver Age in the lower part of the tree's trunk. And at last, as the Copper Age came into existence, the tree put out the branches that we recognize today as the religions and cultures of the world, including the Jewish, Buddhist, Hindu, Christian, Muslim, and others. Now with the reappearance of Prajāpitā Brahmā—so to speak, the final fruit as well, of the "World Genealogical Tree"—we see poised just above his head a world globe bathed in flame and two repulsive-looking animals, America and Russia, holding the military implements that have caused the conflagration. There is a logic and integrity in this vision of the followers of the erstwhile Sindhi jewelry magnate that evokes a familiar, if sometimes unpleasant, vista for Westerners. We have only to compare such a vision of the apocalypse with the urgent appeal of radical Christian fundamentalism to dominate all areas of American life with a vision of the end of the age and consummation of the world in the fiery advent of the Christian Savior (possibly with America at his side) to defeat the forces of Antichrist, often identified in such circles with the actual adversaries of American global power.

With the special finesse of Indian religious inspiration, the Brahmā Kumārīs present us with an alternative to an exclusive Christian apocalypticism. In their vision the salvation of the world has been prepared for in Hindu terms. Accepting Prajāpitā Brahmā as the guide to the next golden age, one can wait out the endemic global crisis with the knowledge that what is going on is all according to plan. The basic Hindu vision of the world will stand the test under the apparent contradictions of the internationalization and relativizing of all human values in the arena of economics and *Realpolitik* and under the threat of nuclear holocaust.

NOTES

1. The Puruṣa Sukta, R.V. X. 90.
2. I.e., "the human priest who is . . . a god among men," from Thomas J. Hopkins, *The Hindu Religious Tradition* (Encino, Calif.: Dickenson Publishing Co., 1971), p. 25.
3. See Sir John Marshall, *Mohenjo-daro and the Indus Civilization,* 3 vols. (London: Arthur Protstain, 1931).
4. Referred to, for instance, in "The Code of Manu," X.45, mentioned in S. Radhakrishnan and C. A. Moore, *A Sourcebook in Indian Philosophy* (Princeton: Princeton University Press, 1973), p. 176.
5. The discussion of proto-Śiva has recently assumed the character of a controversy. The original thesis was set forward by *Mohenjo-daro and the Indus Civilization.* Contrasting and contentious reinterpretations appear in Alfred Hiltebeitel, "The Indus Valley Proto-Śiva Reexamined through Reflections on the Goddess, the Buffalo and the Vahanas," *Anthropos* 75 (1978): 767–797; H. P. Sullivan, "The Indus Valley Civilization," in *The Abingdon Dictionary of Living Religions* (Nashville: Abingdon, 1981), pp. 340–342.
6. Benjamin Walker, *The Hindu World* (London: George Allen & Unwin, 1968), II: 297 ff.
7. Ibid., p. 299.
8. Charles S. J. White, "The Sāī Bāba Movement: Approaches to the Study of Indian Saints," *Journal of Asian Studies* XXXI, no. 4 (August 1972).
9. Walker, *The Hindu World,* I: 78.
10. Richard H. Robinson, *The Buddhist Religion* (Belmont, Calif.: Dickenson Publishing Co., 1970), p. 13; Edward J. Thomas, *The History of Buddhist Thought* (London: Routledge & Kegan Paul, 1967), p. 73.
11. Charles S. J. White, *Bhakti as a Religious Structure in the Context of Medieval Hinduism in the Hindi Speaking Area of North India* (doctoral dissertation, University of Chicago, 1964), p. 192. The example is Kabīr.
12. Information from the research of my former student, Professor J. Daniel White of the University of North Carolina.
13. Charles S. J. White, "Swami Muktānanda and the Enlightenment through Śakti Pāt," *History of Religions* 13, no. 4 (May 1974).
14. Edward J. Thomas, *The Life of Buddha as Legend and History* (London: Routledge & Kegan Paul, 1960); essential details of Mahāvīra's life are given in P. Thomas, *Epics, Myths and Legends of India* (Bombay: D. B. Tavaporevala Sons, 1961), chap. XVI.
15. E. J. Thomas, *The Life of Buddha* and *History of Buddhist Thought.*

Also see Robinson, *The Buddhist Religion*; H. T. Francis and E. J. Thomas, *Jātaka Tales* (Bombay: Jaico Publishing House, 1957).

16. However, the Sikh religion and the sects of Kṛṣṇites are spreading abroad in a manner that might one day rival the achievements of the ancient Buddhists.

17. See E. J. Thomas, *History of Buddhist Thought.*

18. Swami Ghanananda, ed., *Women Saints of East and West* (London: The Ramakrishna Vedanta Centre, 1955), p. 3.

19. Ibid., p. 5.

20. Ibid.

21. The system of stating the opponent's view (*pūrvapakṣa*) before one's own (*uttarapakṣa*) in classical philosophy is discussed in S. Chatterjee and D. Datta, *An Introduction to Indian Philosophy* (Calcutta: University of Calcutta, 1968), pp. 3–5.

22. Compare H. Kern. trans., *Saddharma Puṇḍarīka* (New York: Dover Publications, 1963).

23. Sukumari Bhattacharji, *The Indian Theogony* (Cambridge: Cambridge University Press, 1970), chap. 7.

24. Ibid., p. 201.

25. W. D. O'Flaherty, *Śiva the Erotic Ascetic* (New York: Oxford University Press, 1973).

26. T. M. P. Madadevan, *Ten Saints of India* (Bombay: Bharatiya Vidya Bhavan, 1961), p. 76.

27. Surendranath Dasgupta, *A History of Indian Philosophy* (Cambridge: Cambridge University Press, 1963), I: 437.

28. Walker, *The Hindu World,* II: 350 ff., bases his conclusion on a remark of Humayun Kabir.

29. See White, "Swami Muktānanda and the Enlightenment through Śakti Pāt."

30. Bhattacharji, *The Indian Theogony,* p. 178.

31. O'Flaherty, *Śiva the Erotic Ascetic.*

32. A Westerners' account of personal devotion to Shiva and Kālī is contained in Sister Nivedita's classic *Cradle Tales of Hinduism* (Calcutta, 1922).

33. Mahadevan, *Ten Saints of India,* and Walker, *The Hindu World.*

34. See S. Radhakrishnan, ed. and trans., *The Bhagavad Gītā* (New York: Harper & Row, 1973).

35. See Eliot Deutsch, *Advaita Vedānta: A Philosophical Reconstruction* (Honolulu: University Press of Hawaii, 1980).

36. Arthur Osborne, ed. *The Collected Works of Ramana Maharshi* (Tiruvannamali, India: Sri Ramanasramam, 1968), pp. i–iii.

37. Mahadevan, *Ten Saints of India.*

38. Walker, *The Hindu World,* II: 350.

39. See Mariasusai Dhavamony, *Love of God According to Śaiva Siddhanta* (Oxford: Clarendon Press, 1971); J. S. M. Hooper, *Hymns of the Āḻvārs* (Calcutta, 1929).

40. Chatterjee and Datta, *Introduction to Indian Philosophy,* pp. 412 ff.

41. Cf. V. S. Ghate, *The Vedānta* (Poona: The Bhandarkar Oriental Research

Institute, 1926). See R. C. Bhandarkar, *Vaiṣṇavism, Shaivism and Minor Religious Systems,* in *The Collected Works of R. G. Bhandarkar* (Poona: Bhandarkar Oriental Research Institute, 1929).

42. See B. N. K. Sharma, *History of the Dvaita School of Vedānta and Its Literature* (Bombay: Booksellers Publishing Co., 1960). Balaji Gopal, *The Srī-Kṛṣṇa Temple at Udipi* (master's thesis George Washington University, 1980).

43. Bhandarkar, *Vaiṣṇavism.*

44. Vijyendra Snatak, *Rādhā Vallabha Sampradāy Siddhānt aur Sāhitya* (Delhi: National Publishing House, 1968); Prabhudayal Mītal, *Braj ke Dharm-Sampradayoṁ kā Itihās* (Delhi: National Publishing House, 1958); Charles S. J. White, *The Caurāsi Pad of Śrī Hit Harivaṁas* (Honolulu: University Press of Hawaii, 1977).

45. Bhandarkar, *Vaiṣṇavism;* Surendranath Dasgupta, *History of Indian Philosophy,* III: 399 ff.

46. Bhandarkar, *Vaiṣṇavism,* p. 88.

47. M. S. Randhawa, *Kangra Paintings of the Gītā Govinda* (New Delhi: National Museum, 1963); Barbara Stoler Miller, *The Love Song of the Dark Lord* (New York: Columbia University Press, 1977).

48. Bhandarkar, *Vaiṣṇavism,* p. 89.

49. I returned to the Srījī Temple in the winter of 1983 and was able to make comparisons with my previous visit.

50. The Śaligrāma is a small fossil-bearing rock containing, for example, a mollusk in the shape of Viṣṇu's discus. But there are many other significant signs.

51. The female companions as a class are called Sakhī. The class of Sakhīs is divided into four groups: Sakhī, Sahacarī, Sahelī, and Mañjarī as these relate to sexual maturity. The Mañjarī is sexually immature and thus innocent in the role of observing companion of the divine lovers. The Sakhībhāva devotees may be classed accordingly. The Mañjarī is the most advanced devotee as his contemplations of divine eros are without sexual feelings, as, in a sense, is the experience of the divine lovers. For discussion of the Sakhī mode, see Vijyendra Snātak, *Rādhāvallabha Sampradāy Siddhānta aur Sāhitya* (Delhi: National Publishing House, 1968), pp. 211 ff. Cf. *Brajbhāsā Sūr-kos,* (Lucknow: Viśvaridyālaya Hindi Prakāśan, 5.2031), Dvitya Khaṁd, pp. 1331 and 1703.

52. See Dasgupta, *History of Indian Philosophy,* Ram Awad Dwivedi, *A Critical Survey of Hindi Literature* (Banaras: Motilal Banarsidas, 1966), pp. 125 ff. Dwivedi gives his year of birth as 1673.

53. Charles S. J. White, "Sufism in Medieval Hindi Literature," *History of Religions* 5, no. 1 (Summer 1965).

54. See G. A. Deleury, *The Cult of Viṭhobā* (Poona: Deccan College, 1960).

55. P. C. Bagchi, *The Adhyātmarāmāyana* (Calcutta, n.d., *The Calcutta Sanskrit Series,* Vol. XI).

56. For a recent work illustrating the interaction of Hindu and Sūfī spirituality in India, see Irina Tweedie, *Chasm of Fire* (London: Element Books, 1982).

57. See Niharranjan Ray, *The Sikh Gurus and the Sikh Society* (Patiala: Punjab University, 1970), and W. H. McLeod, *Early Sikh Traditions* (Oxford: Clarendon Press, 1980).

58. The most thorough discussion of the subject is in Charlotte Vaudeville, *Kabīr* (Oxford: Clarendon Press, 1974).

59. White, *Bhakti as a Religious Structure,* pp. 195 ff. from Charlotte Vaudeville, *Au Cabaret de l'amour* (Paris: Librairie Gallimard, 1959), p. 7. See also Charlotte Vaudeville, "Kabīr and Interior Religion," *History of Religions* 3, no. 2 (1964).

60. White, *Bhakti as a Religious Structure,* p. 185, from Hazariprasad Dvivedi, *Kabīr* (Bombay: Hindi-Granth-Ratnakar, 1960), p. 33.

61. See my review of Charlotte Vaudeville's *Kabīr* in the *Journal of the American Oriental Society,* 99, no. 1 (1979): 172 ff.

62. Anon., "The Concept of Universal Religion in the Philosophy of Mahamati Prannath," (New Delhi: Shri Prannath Mission), p. 1.

63. Ibid., p. 8.

64. Ibid., p. 9.

65. I have visited two Prānnāth temples in Delhi wherein devotional songs were sung in front of a symbol (not an image) of the deity.

66. See Charles S. J. White, "Hindu Holy Persons," in *The Abingdon Dictionary of Living Religions,* pp. 300 ff.

67. See Charles S. J. White et al., *The Religious Quest* (College Park, Md.: The National University Consortium, 1983), pp. 23 ff.

68. See Swami Nikhilananda, trans., *The Gospel of Śrī Ramakrishna* (New York: Ramakrishna-Vivekananda Center, 1952).

69. M. K. Gandhi, *The Story of My Experiments with Truth* (Boston: Beacon Press, 1957); Erik Erikson, *Gandhi's Truth* (New York: Norton, 1969).

70. See the report of an interview with Professor Harvey Cox, "The Mind-Control Controversy: Brains Awash," *Back to Godhead* (July 1983).

71. See *Bhagavad Gītā* IV: 20; IX: 27.

72. See White, "The Sāi Bābā Movement," and "Swāmi Muktānanda and the Enlightenment through Śakti-Pāt."

73. For example, the Sindhi saint "Dadaji" Sadhu T. L. Vaswani has a following in various parts of India where the Sindhi community has settled since partition. His shrine is in Poona.

74. For a brief sketch of his life, see "Brahma Baba . . . The Harbinger of New Age," a pamphlet published by Prajāpitā Brahmā Kumārī Ishwarīya Vishwa-Vidyalāya, Pandav Bhavan, Moun t Abu, India. Other works published under the same auspices are "How to Make Life Blissful and Worth Diamonds," "A Handbook of Godly Raja Yoga," "World Peace and Peace of Mind," and "One Week Course for Attainment of Complete Purity, Peace and Prosperity."

75. "Brahma Baba," p. 2.

76. Ibid., pp. 2 ff.

77. Ibid., pp. 3 ff.

5
The Arahant: Sainthood in Theravāda Buddhism

George D. Bond

From the nineteenth century to the present, many Western scholars have employed the terms "saint" and "sainthood" in discussions of the Buddhist tradition. Spiritually advanced individuals such as Bodhisattvas and *mahāsiddhas* have been referred to as saints. The *arahant,* the spiritual virtuoso in the Theravāda tradition, has commonly been termed a Buddhist "saint." Samuel Beal, writing in 1906, designated the *arahant* a "saint" having great "spiritual power."[1] Similarly, C. A. F. Rhys Davids wrote in 1913 of "the early Buddhist standard of saintship" and compared this "exceptional standard of values and of satisfactions for the arahants with that for 'saints in all ages.'"[2] Modern writers such as King,[3] Johansson,[4] and Conze,[5] have continued this practice, regularly translating the term *arahant* as "saint." In light of these interpretations, the purpose of this chapter is to inquire, what is an arahant, and in what sense can he be considered a saint? Does it distort or clarify the Buddhist religious system to refer to the arahant as a saint?

To be sure, as a general rule it is probably better to employ clearly defined Buddhist technical terms when explaining the Buddhist system than to introduce Western religious terms. This rule applies as well to the use of the terms *arahant* and "saint." A scholarly explanation of the Theravāda tradition has more precision if it uses and explicates the term *arahant* rather than referring vaguely to "Buddhist saints." This does not mean, however, that the religious concepts of the saint and sainthood have no value in assisting us to understand the nature and function of the arahant as a holy person in the Buddhist tradition.

In this volume we have defined the saint as a figure who (1) incorporates in his or her being two somewhat paradoxical qualities, shared humanity and otherness, and who (2) because of these two qualities serves as both a paradigm for imitation and an object of veneration. Defined in this way, the concept of sainthood corresponds very closely to the Theravāda conception of arahantship and helps us to understand the tension inherent in the nature of the arahant as Theravāda has depicted him.

For Theravāda the arahant has a dual nature: fully a human being yet qualitatively different from other men. Since he shares a common humanity, the arahant stands as a paradigm of the religious life; however, because he has transcended the ordinary human plane through his moral and spiritual perfection, the arahant can only be venerated, not imitated, by most Buddhists.

This paradoxical nature of the arahant has meaning in the context of the Theravāda worldview and religious system, for at the heart of the Theravāda worldview we find a basic dichotomy expressed in terms of a number of pairs of opposing but linked concepts. To describe these pairs of concepts, we might adapt Tambiah's term, "linked foci of religious action."[6] For Theravāda these linked foci include the following:

saṃsāra/nibbāna
dukkha/nirodha
lokiya/lokuttara
avijjā/paññā

Each pair of concepts represents the Theravāda view of (1) ordinary reality and ultimate reality, and (2) the human predicament and liberation or salvation.

The first pair, *saṃsāra/nibbāna,* relates the Theravāda understanding of an impersonal ultimate reality transcending ordinary reality. The human predicament vis-à-vis this ultimate reality is expressed by the term *saṃsāra,* the round of rebirths, and by the following term *dukkha,* suffering or dissatisfaction. Trapped in endless cycles of birth, old age, death, and rebirth, human beings experience profound *dukkha.* The good for man is to find the way to liberation (*nirodha, nibbāna*) from this predicament. The terms *lokiya/lokuttara* refer to the two realms open to human beings, the mundane, saṃsāric realm, called *lokiya,* and the supramundane, *nibbānic* realm, called *lokuttara.* Beings trapped in any of the many levels of *saṃsāra* are said to be in the *lokiya* path or realm; while beings who have made or are making the transition to *nibbāna* are said to be in the *lokuttara* path or realm. With this change of path or lineage the beings have attained liberation, or assurance of liberation, from the human predicament. The terms "ignorance"/"wisdom" (*avijjā/paññā*) denote the basic nature of the transition or liberation implied in all of these pairs of concepts. For Buddhism, as for Upanishadic Hinduism and other contemporaneous Indian traditions, wisdom represents the goal of the religious system, whereas ignorance represents the human predicament. Ignorance of the truth of *dhamma* separates one from *nibbāna.* By reinforcing one's *karma* and desires ignorance binds one to and constitutes *saṃsāra.* Because of ignorance beings experience *dukkha* in the *lokiya* realms.

Additional pairs of linked concepts might be used to fill in the picture of the Theravāda worldview and religious system. For example, the pair self-belief (*asmimāna*)/no-self (*anattā*) has an essential place in the system, as do concepts conveying a dichotomy we can refer to as mental unrest/mental tranquility. A number of different terms have been used by Theravādins to signify this latter dichotomy, and I shall consider some of them later in relation to the arahant, but the central pair might be the Pāli terms *āsava* and *anāsava,* influxes or cankers, and the absence of them. These concepts extend and specify the Theravāda notion of ignorance/wisdom.

The paradox or tension inherent in all these pairs of linked foci, and especially in the pair ignorance/wisdom, manifests an important distinction in the Buddhist worldview and religious system: the distinction between two levels of truth or reality, conventional truth (Pāli, *sammuti;* Sanskrit, *saṁvṛti*) and ultimate truth (Pāli, *paramattha;* Sanskrit, *paramārtha*). Although Nāgārjuna made this two-level distinction famous in his explanation of the notion of *śūnyatā,* Nāgārjuna himself indicated that the idea of two levels of truth and reality had deep roots in the Buddhist tradition. Nāgārjuna wrote, "Those who do not comprehend the distinction between these two truths, do not comprehend the deep reality in the Buddha's teachings."[7] From the outset Theravāda accepted this notion. According to Theravāda, the Buddha adjusted his teachings to the level of his hearers. To those on the *lokiya* path he taught in conventional terms; to those on the *lokuttara* path he related the higher truths. The Pāli canon distinguishes between *suttas* on these two levels.[8]

In some *suttas* the Buddha taught with indirect meaning (*nītattha*) as, for example, when he spoke about "selves" and "individuals." In other *suttas,* however, he taught with direct meaning (*neyyattha*), as when he discussed the doctrine of "no-self" and the aggregates underlying individual existence in the absolute sense.[9] The Pāli commentaries of the Theravāda tradition explicitly identified the distinction being made here as a distinction between conventional truth (*sammuti sacca*) and absolute truth (*paramatthasacca*). "Two-fold is the teaching of the Buddha, the Exalted One: conventional teaching and absolute teaching" (A.A.I. 94). Conventional teaching contains the truth of the world (*loka*), but absolute teaching conveys the truth of the *dhamma* (A.A.I. 95).

To understand these linked foci in the Theravāda system it is important to note that the relation between these two levels of truth and reality is not simply epistemological but also soteriological, and probably, in Theravāda, ontological as well.[10] Ultimate truth transcends conventional truth and is in itself ineffable and ultimately real. Conventional truth, however, has a provisional status; it is not sheer illusion or delusion, for only by means of conventional truth can ultimate truth be conveyed to ordinary persons. As Nāgārjuna said, "The highest truth cannot be taught without recourse to conventional language."[11] Bimal Matilal explains this relationship in its Mādhyāmika context by saying that "the phenomenal world (and phenomenal experience) is what should lead us to the realisation of the ultimate truth."[12] Sprung refers to this soteriological dimension in the two truths as a "transformational" rather than an explanatory relationship.[13] He writes, "The highest truth is not an explanation of the lower; it is what the lower becomes (hence the appropriateness of the word 'reality') under the conditions of freedom."[14]

This dynamic of "transformation" characterizes all of the linked foci we have considered, and the arahant participates in this same dynamic. The duality we have noted in the arahant's character can be explained by means of another pair of linked concepts; the ordinary person, *puthujjana*/the saint, arahant.[15] These two persons or types represent the two levels of truth and reality. They represent the human predicament and liberation from it. The *puthujjana,* characterized by ignorance, transmigrates in the saṃsāric, *lokiya* realm. His mind clouded by defilements and desires, he lives an anxious existence, surrounded by *dukkha,* unaware of any higher truth or reality. The arahant ordinarily has been regarded by scholars as the *puthujjana*'s opposite, but, consistent with our view of the two levels, it is better to see the arahant and the *puthuj-*

jana as standing in a relationship of transformation: the arahant represents what the *putthujjana* "becomes under the conditions of freedom."

THE ARAHANT'S COMMON HUMANITY

An arahant has reached the end of a long path of self-perfection, a path on which he or she began as a *puthujjana,* an ordinary person. As I. B. Horner wrote, "The whole arahan-theory is based upon the belief in the perfectibility of man, either here and now, or in some future state."[16] This goal of perfection is accessible to all in the Buddhist tradition, for all share a common humanity with the arahant.

Several important suttas in the Pāli canon depict a gradual path traversing the existential distance between the level of the *puthujjana* and that of the arahant[17] (e.g., D. I. 47 ff.; M.111.33 ff.; A.11.207 ff.; M.1.344 ff.). In these suttas the Buddha explains that those who become arahants originally must begin on this gradual path as ordinary ignorant householders (M.111.33). The *Samaññaphala Sutta* stresses that in the beginning the arahant can even be a person of the lowest standing in society (D.1.47 f.).

How does the ordinary householder begin to move toward the goal of sainthood? These path suttas all maintain that certain requisite conditions must be met in order for the transformation from *puthujjana* to arahant to begin. First, a Buddha must have appeared in the world, and, second, the householder must hear the *dhamma* from that enlightened being or from one of his disciples. Third, the most crucial step occurs when the householder, having gained confidence (*saddhā*) in the Buddha, renounces the household life for a life of homelessness.

The suttas clearly depict this break with the world as the first crucial step in the long process of transformation, and the emphasis they put upon renunciation raises the venerable question in the Buddhist tradition of whether a layperson can achieve arahantship. To be sure, we find scattered instances in the texts proclaiming the attainment of arahantship by some laypersons. For example, *Anguttara III.451 f.* lists some laymen who apparently reached the goal, and we also hear of ancient figures such as Yasa and the Buddha's father, Suddhodana, who became arahants while they were still laymen. But these clearly represent exceptional cases. The path suttas presuppose that one who seeks arahantship must renounce the world with all its desires and entanglements. The accounts telling of those exceptional persons who reached arahantship in the lay status in almost all cases go on to say that the person entered monastic life immediately afterward (e.g., Vin. I. 15–20). When forced to debate this question, the Theravādins held that it would be possible for a layman to attain arahantship only if the layperson actually had already renounced all those fetters that characterize ordinary lay life (Kvu. IV. 2). By definition, the Theravādins argued, worldly life and arahantship are incompatible.

THE ARAHANT'S TRANSCENDENT NATURE

Having begun as an ordinary person, the arahant has transcended the ordinary human level. By the dynamic of transformation central to the Buddhist tradition, the arahant has become qualitatively different from the common person, or *puthujjana.* Although one Western writer has suggested that we should not expect "very great differences between arahants and followers on other levels of development,"[18] the Theravāda tradition has maintained just the opposite. The arahants have been regarded as "further men," *uttarimanussā,* who stand on a totally different plane from ordinary men.[19]

The path suttas, referred to earlier, describe the ways that arahants attained perfection and the qualities that set them apart. By analyzing these suttas we can see what virtues defined the saintliness of the arahant.[20] Although the path suttas trace the development of the arahant in detail, Theravādins traditionally divided this development into three parts, called the "three trainings": training in higher morality, *adhisīla-sikkhā*; training in higher mentality or concentration, *adhicitta-sikkhā*; and training in higher wisdom, *adhipaññā-sikkhā.* These three trainings represent the three kinds of perfection attained by the arahant setting him apart from other beings.[21]

Perfection of moral conduct constitutes the first mark of the Theravāda saint.[22] The path suttas give prominence to the arahant's moral perfections. Although the path suttas simply list an extensive variety of moral perfections, we can categorize these under the four kinds of moral conduct given by Buddhaghosa in the *Visuddhimagga,* a text that essentially represents an exhaustive explication of the arahant's path. Buddhaghosa's first kind of *sīla* or moral conduct is *sīla* of *Patimokkha* restraint. In the explanations of the path suttas, this form of *sīla* amounts to the fulfillment of the Buddhist tradition's ethical precepts. The suttas tell us that the arahant lives by compassion and nonviolence, lives without stealing and dependent on gifts, practices chastity, and follows the rest of the major and minor precepts.[23] In these accounts two of the precepts seem to stand out: one because of the emphasis upon it, the other because of its omission from the list. The precept concerning truth-speaking receives the greatest emphasis and the lengthiest explanation. The arahant is said to be perfectly truthful in speech, avoiding all kinds of lying, slandering, gossipping, and all other forms of frivolous speech. It is not clear from the suttas why so much emphasis was placed upon this virtue of avoiding unnecessary and untruthful speech, although we know that the Jains and other contemporary religious movements also stressed this virtue. The one precept omitted from these lists of perfections is the precept concerning avoiding all intoxicants. The suttas skip from the fourth precept, truthfulness, to the sixth precept, eating only once a day, and omit the usual fifth precept about intoxicants.[24]

In addition to fulfilling these ethical precepts, as a second kind of virtue the arahant perfects what Buddhaghosa calls the "*sīla* of livelihood purification." All the path suttas tell us that the arahant "abstains from buying and selling . . . from bribery, fraud and deceit, . . . (and) from murdering (and) . . . highway robbery" (M.1.345 f.; 111.34; D.1.67; A.11.209f.). The *Sāmaññaphala Sutta* (and indeed all thirteen suttas in the first division of the *Dīgha Nikāya*) goes into great detail on many of these perfections and in its explanation of "purified livelihood" offers an interesting catalogue of vocations forbidden to monks and nuns (D.1.p. 67 f.). Because of his contentment with a simple life, the arahant has the freedom to wander "like a bird on the wing" and he experiences the "bliss of blamelessness," *anavajjasukha* (M.1.346, 111.34; A.11.209). The arahant's third kind of morality is closely related to this second, "livelihood purification," for the third kind consists of perfecting the *sīla* concerning requisites. The arahant lives content with his simple bowl and robe, the requisites of the monastic life, without accepting forbidden offerings.

According to the accounts in the path suttas, the arahant moves next to perfect his restraint of the sense faculties. The suttas seem to regard this as a separate perfection from that of the *sīlas* (M.1.346, III.35); however, Buddhaghosa counts restraint of sense faculties as another kind of *sīla* (the second in his classification, *Vism,* p. 16). The point of this perfection, however one counts it, is that the arahant develops control over his mental reactions to sensory impressions, thereby stemming the influx of impure thoughts. Controlling the senses rather than letting the senses control him, the arahant experiences the bliss of being "unaffected" or "unsullied" (M.1.346, 111.35; A.11.209 f.).

Next the suttas relate that the arahant perfects his mindfulness, *sati,* and clear comprehension, *sampajañña.* No matter what he is doing (walking, sitting, eating, etc.), the arahant is perfectly mindful. He lives fully in the present moment. The path suttas count this a separate perfection also (M.1.346, 111.35; A.11.209), but in the scheme of three trainings, this perfection of *sati* falls under the heading of *adhicitta* or the perfection of *samādhi.*

To develop *samādhi* the arahant, having this mindfulness, the suttas say, goes to a remote place and sits in meditation. The suttas describe this stage of mental purification by listing the mental hindrances, *nīvaranas,* eliminated by the arahant. This correlation of the perfection of *sati* with the elimination of the *nīvaranas* reflects teachings such as the *Kusalarāsi Sutta* (S.V.145), in which the four foundations of mindfulness are called "heaps of profit" and set against the five hindrances, called "heaps of unprofit."

The five hindrances, *nīvaranas,* represent one of the Buddhist tradition's many formulations of the negative mental states dominating the mind of the unenlightened, unperfected person (see D.1.246). Ordinary persons, *puthujjanas,* are characterized by sensual desire, ill-will, sloth and torpor, excitement and flurry, and, finally, doubt. The arahant, however, transcends the ordinary human level because he has eliminated these negative mental states (D.1.246). Although, as we shall see later, this list of negative states overlaps significantly with other classifications of mental defilements, such as the fetters or *saṃyojanas,* Theravādins associated the overcoming of this specific group of hindrances, *nīvaranas,* with the attainment of *samādhi,* concentration. Thus according to the path suttas, when the *nīvaranas* have been eliminated, the saint-to-be enters the successive *jhānas* or trance states of *samādhi* and attains the *jhānic* mental factors ending in pure mindfulness (*sati*) and equanimity (*upekkha*). These *jhānic* factors represent the positive mental states developed by the arahant after abandoning the hindrances of the ordinary mind. In some Pāli suttas the *nīvaranas* are said to be canceled out by the attainment of the positive mental states accompanying the *jhānas.* At this stage, although still on the mundane or *lokiya* plane, the meditator has moved far beyond the common person, for he now dwells with a mind composed, purified, clarified, without defilement, stable, and immovable (M.1.347, 111.36; D.1.77). The *Dīgha Nikāya* contrasts the saint at this point with the ordinary person by stating that the saint who attains this stage is as happy as a prisoner set free or as a man who finds his way out of the wilderness to safety (D.1.72 f.).

Interestingly, after having described in virtually identical terms the arahant's development up through the attainment of the *jhānas,* the path suttas now offer several different versions of the end of the path and the arahant's ultimate transformation by the attainment of wisdom. One group of suttas states that the arahant attains the "Threefold-Knowledge," *tevijja* (M.1.182, 1.347; compare M.1.22; Vin. III.5). Other suttas relate the arahant's developing the "six higher knowledges," *abhiññas* (D.I.77 ff.). Still other suttas depict the arahant moving directly from the *jhānas* to the destruction of the influxes or *āsavas* (M.111.33; A.11.210 f.).

These differing accounts raise the question of whether the Buddhist tradition held that all arahants had identical experiences of enlightenment and liberation. Did the tradition allow for differences in the content of a saint's perfection? Johansson supports this view, for he wrote, "We should also not expect great homogeneity among the arahants."[25] In the canon the descriptions of specific famous arahants, which we shall consider later, also tend to suggest that this was the case. Various *sutta* passages as well suggest a variety of religious experiences as the content of enlightenment; as, for example, the Saṃyutta text describing five hundred arahants, of whom sixty possessed the "threefold-knowledge," another sixty had the "six higher knowledges," while the rest were "liberated by wisdom alone," *paññāvimutti* (S.1.191). Despite this apparent variety, however, there is an underlying uniformity in the religious or liberating experiences of the arahants in these path suttas.

This underlying unity in the final attainments of the arahants manifests itself in the close relation between the "six higher knowledges," the "three knowledges," and the eradication of the *āsavas*. Taking the six *abhiññās* first, we can proceed from the numerically greatest to the least. The *abhiññās* have been translated as "roads to saintship,"[26] "higher spiritual powers,"[27] and "profound super-knowings."[28] A passage in the *Aṅguttara Nīkaya* explains the attainment of these "super-knowings" with a simile about gold (A.111.16 f.). Just as one must purify gold of its defilements before it will be fit for the best work, so, the text says, one must purify the mind of its defilements (*nīvaranas*) before it can attain wisdom. And when the defilements of the mind are removed, it shines with a natural brilliance and can be directed to the attainment of the *abhiññās* (A.111.17). This interesting simile is strangely reminiscent of the Jain conception of the mind or the *jiva* as being naturally omniscient once the impurities have been removed.

The six *abhiññās* represent powers more or less closely related to the goal and intention of arahantship. The first *abhiññā* is *iddhi-vidhā,* miraculous power or "psycho-kinetic activity."[29] Here the saint acquires the ability to do the miraculous deeds traditionally done by Indian holy men. For example, he can become invisible, travel through the air, walk on water, or travel to the moon (D.1.78; A.111.17). Horner observes that these miraculous powers constitute a central feature of the pre-Buddhist and non-Buddhist conception of an *arahant* or holy man in India. She writes, "the display of these (iddhi) would easily impress the many-folk (puthujjana), who are always more ready to compute worth by unusual physical prowess than by outstanding mental achievements."[30]

The second and third higher knowledges also have the quality of miraculous powers resembling the feats of the yogis and holy men in all ages of Indian history. The second, "divine ear," *dibba sota,* is the power to hear any sounds in the heavens or on earth (D.1.79; A.111.17). The third *abhiññā* enables the saint to penetrate and discern the minds of other people, to tell what mental state (e.g., calm, uncontrolled, lustful) a person has (*ceto-pariya-ñāṇa*).

The three remaining *abhiññās* compose also an independent group called the three wisdoms or knowledges, *tevijjā.* In several suttas the arahant's path concludes with these three knowledges, without any mention of the first three *abhiññās* (e.g., M.1.347 f.; M.1.182–184). These three knowledges (*tevijjā*) or the final three higher knowledges (*abhiññās*) are knowledge of one's own previous existences (*pubbenivāsānussati*), "divine eye" (*dibba cakkhu*), and knowledge of the destruction of the *āsavas* (*āsavakkhayañāṇa*).

The existence of these three knowledges as a group of attainments integral to arahantship has its roots in the accounts of the Buddha's own enlightenment. The suttas describe these three knowledges as the content of the Buddha's enlightenment experiences (e.g., M.1.22 f.; Vin. 111.5 f.). Given that both the Buddha and the arahants were said to reach the same—or virtually the same—enlightenment, the tradition established these three knowledges as the goals of the arahant's path. The term *tevijjā* arose partly as a reinterpretation of the Hindu ideal of wisdom. The Pāli texts tell us that the Buddha denied the traditional Brahmanic claim that a person who knew the three Vedas was *tevijjo,* "a three-fold knowledge person." Rather, the Buddha said that one who possessed these three knowledges was *tevijjo* in the only important sense of the term (S.1.166–167).

Although the first two of the three knowledges share something of the same character of miraculous power as the first three *abhiññās*, the Theravāda tradition seems to have regarded the three knowledges as more integral to sainthood than the first three *abhiññās*. K. N. Jayatilleke wrote that "of the six only three are necessary for the saving knowledge."[31] He reasoned that the first of these three forms of knowledge, "retrocognition," enabled the saint to verify "the fact of pre-existence." The second, "clairvoyance," gave the saint an understanding of the fact of karma. With the third knowledge, understanding the destruction of the *āsavas*, the arahant verified the essence of the *dhamma*.[32]

But if the six *abhiññās* can be reduced to and superseded by the three knowledges, the three knowledges can be reduced to and superseded by the final stage of knowledge, knowledge of the destruction of the *āsavas*. This attainment represents the lowest common denominator in all these descriptions of the arahant. It is the sine qua non of sainthood for the Theravāda tradition. According to Horner, "Indeed it seems certain that although the mastery of the threefold knowledge as a whole constitutes a man an arahan, only one branch of it—the knowledge of the destruction of the āsavas—has this power alone and apart from the other two branches."[33] Buddhaghosa clearly differentiates between the first five of these "super-knowledges" and the sixth. He interprets the five *abhiññās* as mundane (*lokiya*) benefits of *samādhi* or concentration (Vism. 373). Destruction of the *āsavas*, however, he describes as a supramundane (*lokūttara*) attainment, pertaining directly to wisdom, *paññā* (see Vism. chap. XXII).

Destroyer of the *āsavas* is the most common epithet of the arahant. The suttas show that this attainment more than any other sets the arahant apart from the *puthujjanas* (M.1.7 ff.), for in destroying the *āsavas* the arahant has eradicated the most fundamental negative states of mind. The term *āsava* has been translated as "canker," "influx," and "intoxicant" depending on which etymology of the Pāli term one accepts. Buddhaghosa suggests all of these meanings (Dhs. A.48). He tells us that the *āsavas* "flow from the senses and the mind" and that these influences keep beings within the saṃsaric realm (Dhs. A.48). The sense of the concept is somewhat similar to the Jaina use of the term *āśrava*, denoting the inflowing of karma.[34] For the Buddhists, the *āsavas* represent wrong mental states that bind one to karma and rebirth. The path suttas list three *āsavas* eradicated by the arahant: they are (1) *kāmāsava*, attachment to sensual desire; (2) *bhavāsava*, attachment to existence and rebirth (becoming); and (3) *avijjāsava*, ignorance of the ultimate truth (M.111.36; A.11.210 f.). A fourth *āsava, diṭṭhāsava,* attachment to views, seems to have been added later, although the commentaries maintained that *diṭṭhāsava* was implicit in *bhavāsava* even in texts where it was not mentioned (M.A.1.67).

Āsavas destroyed, the arahant attains the ultimate perfection and transformation. The stock description of the arahant in the Pāli canon bears out the central significance of the destruction of the *āsavas* and tells of the other perfections that follow upon this one. The description runs,

> The arahant who has destroyed the āsavas, who has fulfilled, who has done what was to be done, who has laid down the burden, who has attained his own goal, who has destroyed the fetters of becoming, and who having attained right knowledge is one who is liberated.[35]

The commentary explains that "what was to be done" meant understanding the four noble truths (D.A.863). The path suttas also make this association of the *āsavas* with the truths of *dukkha,* stating that the arahant realizes the reality, the origin, the cessation, and the path to the cessation of both *dukkha* and the *āsavas* (D.1.83 f.; M.1.348 f.; M.111.36; A.11.210f). The "burden" laid down by the arahant is said by the commentator to be either the burden of the aggregates or the burden of the defilements, *kilesas* (D.A.863). And the fetters of becoming that he has destroyed are said to be the bonds of desire, *taṇhā* (D.A.863).

Upon reaching this level, the arahant realizes his liberation and proclaims his attainment. Here again the Pāli canon has a stock passage for the arahant's proclamation: "Destroyed is rebirth, lived is the higher life, done is what had to be done, there is no further becoming for me."[36] The key item added here is the notion of liberation from the round of rebirth. For the Theravāda tradition, liberation from rebirth was conjoined with destruction of the *āsavas* and attainment of wisdom as the major transformations of the arahant or saint. In almost all descriptions of the arahant we find the "stopping of becoming" given emphasis (compare M.1.40; S.111.83 f.).[37] The arahant has delivered himself from the two-sided human predicament constituted by ignorance and the resulting karma and *saṃsāra.* In terms of our model of linked foci, the arahant has destroyed the lower member of each pair of terms and attained the liberation expressed by the higher member.[38]

LEGENDS OF THE ARAHANTS

The picture of the arahant we have been considering thus far, drawn from suttas attributed to the Buddha, represents the rule or the *dhamma* about the way arahants develop and the qualities they perfect.[39] That is, the path suttas' description of the arahant was not regarded by Buddhists as an abstract ideal but, rather, as a normative pattern realized in one of its forms by every valid saint. Supplementing and, to some extent, complementing this view of the arahant, however, are the Theravāda accounts of specific figures regarded as arahants. These hagiographic writings depict further the dual nature of the arahant and the process of transformation from *puthujjana* to *arahant*.

Theravāda possesses a rich hagiographic literature. At the canonical level the tradition has preserved the reputed proclamations of male and female arahants in the *Theragāthā* and the *Therīgāthā*.[40] Also in the canon is the *Apadāna* setting forth the stories of the major arahants of the Buddha's time.[41] The richest vein of hagiography, however, is to be found in the commentarial literature, where more complete accounts of the saints' lives occur.[42] The saints remembered in these writings were the disciples of the Buddha and the early pioneers of the tradition.

Although usually attributed to the arahants themselves, these accounts in the canon and the commentaries often seem to have been done according to a formula, so similar do the saints appear. In some cases the same descriptions and sayings have been assigned to different arahants in different stories.[43] Yet the accounts of the saints retain enough variation and individuality to remove the suspicion that these accounts are pure fiction. They are pious legends many of which probably at some now distant point were based upon remembrances of actual arahants. But that stratum is in the background—where it was ever present at all—for these legends primarily represent the beliefs of the community about the great saints of the tradition.

For our purposes in understanding the role of the saint in the Theravāda tradition, this hagiography has considerable significance. These legends of the arahants supplement the picture of arahantship in the path suttas in three important ways: (1.) by their emphasis upon the previous lives of the arahant; (2.) by their account of the variety of attainments resulting in enlightenment; and (3.) by their colorful descriptions of the virtues and qualities distinguishing the saints from ordinary folk.

1. A new note concerning the arahant's path of development is

sounded in these legends when they recount the previous lives of each arahant. Whereas the path suttas say nothing about the process of transformation extending over many lifetimes of an individual, these legends now presuppose that it must. The commentaries to the *Theragāthā* and *Therīgāthā,* for example, put each arahant's proclamation of enlightenment in context by detailing the story of his or her previous lives. The arahants still are held to have begun on the path as ordinary people but to have done so countless rebirths ago.

Extending the path of perfection over vast aeons, these legends assume that the great arahants of the tradition attained the goal in this life by virtue of their past perfections. The commentator relates, for example, that Sīhā, a female arahant, attained wisdom because of the "cumulative effect of her former efforts" (Thig. A.79). Similarly, Sāriputta, the Buddha's chief disciple, is said to have become a "stream-enterer" in this life after hearing only the first two lines of a stanza of the *dhamma,* so sharp had his intuition been honed in his previous lives (Dh. A.1.73 ff.; Thag. A.111.93 f.). Other accounts abound of arahants on the brink of enlightenment when they were born in this Buddha-age, such as the Therī Sujātā, who is said to have already "consolidated the essential conditions for liberation" when she was born at Sāketa (Thig. A.136 f.), and the Therī Subhā, who attained release in this life because she had in previous lives "perfected the conditions of liberation" and "ripened her wisdom" (Thig. A.245 f.). Similar to the story of Sāriputta is the story of Bhaddā Kuṇḍalakesa, an ex-Jaina who because of her previous lives reached arahantship upon hearing the Buddha recite one of the verses in the *Dhammapada* (Thig. A.99 ff.).

The accounts of the arahants' previous lives include several standard and interesting features. First, the arahant-to-be almost always is said to have met a previous Buddha in the remote past and, because of this influence, to have made a vow to become an arahant. This vow or resolve is found in almost all the legends and seems to represent a late development in the Theravāda tradition. C. A. F. Rhys Davids notes that it was more fully developed in Mahāyāna.[44] In the legends of the arahants these vows frequently are quite specific. Rather than vowing just to be an arahant, the men and women vowed to become arahants who excelled in particular ways. For example, Kisā Gotamī made a very specific vow to become the arahant foremost in the wearing of rough garments (Thig. A.174 ff.). For the later Theravāda community the arahants' vows seem to have served as explanations for the individual differences among the arahants. A sutta in the *Anguttara-Nikāya* lists forty-one male arahants and thirteen female arahants who were "foremost in various qualities such as wisdom, miraculous powers, logical analysis and interpretation" (A.1.23 f.). The commentarial legends of these arahants explain all these outstanding abilities to be the result of vows made by the arahants in previous lives.

Following the vow, the arahants are said to have performed great works of merit to ensure that the vow would be realized. This acquisition of merit thus represents a second standard feature of the legends. Khemā, who made her vow to an exalted Thera rather than to a Buddha, gave the Elder sweet cakes and her hair as gifts to advance her vow to become great in wisdom. In her subsequent lives Khemā, born as a queen among gods and humans, donated land and monasteries to the Sangha (Thig. A.126 ff.). Mahā Kassapa, who vowed to become the arahant foremost in ascetic practices, in his previous lives fed five hundred Paccekabuddhas and earned immense merit by decorating shrines with rich cloth and golden lotuses (Thag. A.III.121 f.). Likewise, the Therī Uppalavaṇṇa, having heard the Buddha Padumuttara designate a female disciple chief among those who have miraculous powers (*iddhi*), vowed to attain that rank someday and to that end held a week-long almsgiving for the Buddha and the Sangha (Thig. A.190 f.).

The third regular feature of these accounts is the long sequence of fortunate rebirths and bountiful acts of merit that preceded the arahant's rebirth in Gotama's time. Often this sequence is abbreviated in the legends by a phrase such as "heaping up merit of age-enduring efficacy in this and that rebirth." But in many cases the legends recount the sequence of previous Buddhas met by the arahant-to-be and the generosity of the arahant toward the Buddhas and the Sangha.[45] These legends at times would seem to tax the credulity of even the most pious Buddhists, as when the seven most prominent female arahants are all said to have been sisters, daughters of King Kiki of Kāsī in the time of Kassapa Buddha (see J.IV.481, Thig. A.17). Their brother at that time was the future Rāhula, who had already vowed to be the son of a future Buddha (A.A.1.257 ff.). These seven sisters "heaped up merit" by building seven monasteries for the Buddha, but Rāhula, surpassing them, probably out of his desire to be born as the future Buddha's son, built five hundred monasteries (A.A.1.257 ff.).

Finally, then, as a result of their vows and their meritorious and virtuous lives, the arahants-to-be attained extremely favorable rebirths in this life. Most of the women were born into this age with beauty, high-caste status, wealth, and luxury. Most of the men were born with high-caste status, athletic prowess, and all the luxuries the world had to offer. The stories of these arahants thus frequently resemble that of Gotama's having yet renouncing the highest worldly pleasures.

The Theravādins seem to have subscribed to the general Indian conception that an individual could gradually elevate himself or herself in caste and worldly wealth through acts of merit, but the Theravādins held these attainments to be more or less by-products of a deeper spiritual evolution. Because of this spiritual evolution the arahants-to-be were not infatuated with their wealth and status but rather saw through it to the higher truths of the *dhamma*. Although technically they were born into this life still in the state of *puthujjanas,* they had reached the brink of the supramundane path and the higher spiritual life. Perhaps the best example of this is given in the legends of Sāriputta and Moggallāna. Born in this age as wealthy and privileged Brahmins, the two boys went one day to a fair in Rājagaha, where, instead of seeing the attractions and delights, because "their insight had reached maturity," they saw all the people as already dead. This vision prompted them to renounce their wealth and seek liberation.

2. The legends of the arahants depict their attainment of wisdom in ways that conform to the norm set out in the path suttas. Just as those suttas indicate some variations in the states attained, so these legends also portray some individual variations in the enlightenment attainments of the arahants.[46] Some arahants such as Ānanda are said to have received liberation upon attaining the six super-knowings, *abhiññās* (Thag. A.II.113). Other arahants, among them Anuruddha, declare that they have attained the threefold knowledge, *tevijjā* (Thag. 903). Extinction of the *āsavas* and freedom from rebirth, however, rank as two of the most frequent attainments mentioned in the legends. Rāhula and Ānanda are among the many arahants who proclaim their enlightenment in terms of the extinguishing of the *āsavas* and the end of rebirth (Thag. 296, 1022).

Individual variation appears also in the legends in the methods or meditation subjects employed by the arahants to reach these attainments. We have already noted the legends of the female arahants who attained the goal when the Buddha, puncturing their vanity, made them see the truth of the foulness and impermanence of the body. Other arahants used their experiences of suffering as meditation subjects to reach enlightenment. Sīvali, for example, understood the truth of suffering by meditating on the seven days of labor he underwent at his birth (Thag. A.I.146 f.).

The methods of meditation were almost as numerous as the arahants themselves, as each person had to overcome his or her own distinctive set of mental hindrances. The legends even relate that the Buddha's two chief disciples, who had been associated for aeons of rebirths, attained the goal by different means. Moggallāna overcame his sloth and torpor by meditating on the elements; Sāriputta won arahantship a week later while listening to a particular discourse taught by the Buddha.[47]

3. The third way in which the legends of the arahants complement the path suttas lies in their vivid accounts of outstanding incidents in the lives of the saints. Bringing to life the Buddhist norm of arahantship, these stories depict the great deeds of the arahants while they were on the path and after they had reached their enlightenment. Here we see not only the distinctive qualities for which each of the famous arahants has been remembered but also concrete examples of the ways that, according to Theravādins, arahants transcend both the values and the existential orientations of ordinary people, *puthujjanas*. Because of these qualities, the tradition says, these arahants were greater than the gods.[48]

Although almost all the distinctive Buddhist values are exemplified in these stories, several themes seem to predominate. Of these themes, the most frequently repeated one by far is the arahants' conquest of desire for and attachment to the world. Free from the snares of desire, arahants lived in but not of the world. The classic example of this quality is found in the story of a female arahant, Subhā of Jīvakaś mango grove (Thig. 366–399). Although she had great beauty and came from an eminent Brahmin family, Subhā renounced the world to seek enlightenment as a Buddhist nun, or *bhikkhunī*. While she was striving for enlightenment, having completely extinguished all sensual desire, she encountered in the forest a man who accosted her. He urged her to abandon the monastic life in order to seek pleasure with him while she was yet young and beautiful. Fearful, she inquired what he found so beautiful about a body she now regarded as foul and impermanent. When he replied that her deerlike eyes inflamed his passions, Subhā tore out her eye and gave it to him. The story concludes, anticlimactically, that after this she went to the Buddha, whereupon seeing him her eye was restored and she reached the highest liberation.

Such total aversion to the pleasures of the senses, especially sexual pleasures, represents a popular theme in numerous other stories of the arahants. For example, the *bhikkhunī* arahant Khemā, who had attained arahantship when the Buddha revealed to her the emptiness of her vanity and the impermanence of the body, defeated Māra in his sexual advances.[49] She responded to Māra's overtures by declaring that the lusts of the body do not provide pleasure but instead cut like daggers. She continued,

> Slain completely is the love of pleasure.
> Rent asunder the gloom of ignorance. (Thig. 142)

Similarly, the Thera Anuruddha rebuffed a goddess who sought to entice him into seeking rebirth with her in the heavens. Anuruddha proclaimed that he had no interest in rebirth with her either in the heavens or on earth since he had destroyed all desire (Thag. 908).

Arahants rose above not only sexual desire but also the pernicious entanglements of home, family, wealth, and society. The epitome of this nonattachment was Mahā Kassapa. Legend tells that his parents arranged his marriage to the most beautiful woman to be found in all India. But both Kassapa and his bride-to-be desired arahantship rather than marital pleasures. So although the wedding took place as planned, the couple never consummated the marriage and in later life went forth from home to homelessness. At first they traveled together in their monastic quest for enlightenment. But then, lest anyone misunderstand their relationship and incur bad karma from criticizing them falsely, they parted company forever. The commentary adds that the earth quaked under the weight of such virtue (Ap. 11.583, M.A.1.347 f.).

Of the female arahants, both Dhammadinnā and Soṇā are remembered as examples of the virtue of renouncing the household life. When Dhammadinnā's husband went forth to seek liberation, he offered her all his wealth; but rejecting this, she chose to leave the world also (Thig. A.15 f.). Sonā left her sons and daughters when she was old to seek the path (Thig. 102). Sounding the same note, the female arahant Sakulā declared that when she heard the *dhamma* preached, she left her children, her treasures, and her house for the homeless life (Thig. 98). This motif of rejection of the worldly pleasures of home and marriage occurs most frequently in the legends of the female arahants, in which time and again the women renounce immense wealth, dowries, royal suitors, or thrones to follow the path to sainthood.[50]

A significant variation on the same theme is found in several stories about arahants who arrived at the state of desirelessness and nonattachment not from having experienced the best that the world had to offer but from having experienced the worst. These arahants seem to stand as examples of beings who conquered the evils of existence that defeat most people. The primary examples here are the female arahants Paṭācārā and Kisā-Gotamī. Paṭācārā experienced a Job-like tragedy of having her entire family die in a succession of disasters, after which she finally wandered about madly in her grief. In time, however, she encountered the Buddha, who taught her that life in the round of rebirth is characterized by suffering. From this teaching she attained enlightenment, her desire and attachment to life disappearing along with her grief (Thig. A.47, 117, 122). Kisā-Gotamī's experience was similar. Upon losing her only child, she went to the Buddha requesting him to bring the child back to life. The Buddha said such a cure could be done only if she obtained a mustard seed from a household where no one had ever died. In quest of this nonexistent mustard seed she realized the truth of death and life (Thig. A.174 ff.; Dh. A.11.270; A.A.1.378).

As a result of these experiences, the great arahants attained the ideals of equanimity and nonattachment. The descriptions of the arahants stress their peace and insight. Anuruddha, the *Theragāthā* tells us, having forsaken mother, father, sister, brother, and all his kin, sat rapt in reverie. Having left all things behind, devoted only to the Buddha's *dhamma,* Anuruddha passed over the mighty flood and sat in peace (Thag. 892–894). And the wise Sāriputta, also embodying this quality, proclaimed that he had a desire neither to die nor to live but simply existed in serenity and mindfulness (Thag. 1002–1008).

A second dominant theme in these legends deals with the wisdom of the arahants, which was the source of their serenity and nonattachment. Although wisdom does not receive quite as much attention as these secondary virtues, it is never forgotten. The arahants are remembered in these stories as profound sages. Revata exemplifies in the legends the arahants who delighted in solitary meditation in the forests, where they devoted their lives to the practice of meditation (M.1.213). The venerable Anuruddha is depicted as a champion of meditation upon the four foundations of mindfulness (S.V.294 ff.). Through meditation the arahants attained wisdom of the *dhamma* and in their lives they radiated this salvific wisdom to people lost in ignorance.

Chief among the arahants in wisdom was the venerable Sāriputta. He stood second only to the Buddha in his wisdom. Because of his wisdom he came to be regarded as the Buddha's chief disciple. Frequently only Sāriputta could answer the questions asked by the Buddha. Sāriputta employed his wisdom to aid humanity for he frequently delivered sermons on topics suggested by the Buddha.[51] This is an important point in the legends. Arahants are depicted not as silent, self-centered sages but as beings interested in liberating humanity from its predicament. The arahants Aññā-Koṇḍañña, Mahā Kappina, and Puṇṇā, among others, were also revered for their ability to teach the *dhamma* to others. Another arahant praised for his exceptional wisdom was Mahā Kassapa. He is praised for having attained the three wisdoms, *tevijjā,* so that he stood thrice wise among gods and men (Thag. A.III.121 ff.).

A somewhat different view of wisdom emerges in the legends of Ānanda, the Buddha's attendant for twenty-five years. Ānanda did not become an arahant until after the Buddha died, so he is not said to have possessed intuitive wisdom of the *dhamma* as did Sāriputta. But Ānanda is celebrated as a model of learning. Traveling with the Buddha, he learned eighty-four thousand texts or discourses by heart (Thag. 1024). Because of this knowledge of the Buddha's teachings, he was able to teach the *Sutta Pitaka* to the monks at the First Council after the Buddha's death. Ānanda praised learning as the "root of holy life" (Thag. 1027). Without learning the *dhamma* one could not attain the realization of the truth in meditation.[52] Because for the Sangha learning the texts of the *Tipiṭaka* represented a central duty, it is not surprising to find many arahants in addition to Ānanda praised for this scholarly virtue.[53]

Finally, two further qualities of the arahants, the power to perform miracles, *iddhi,* and a dedication to asceticism, constitute another frequent theme in these legends. It is interesting to find these two qualities assigned to Buddhist arahants because these constitute central features in the lives of non-Buddhist Indian holy men and yogis. Down through history, and even to the present day, yogis have claimed the power to perform miracles such as flying through the air, traveling out of their bodies, creating things out of thin air, and reading the minds of others. The *Yoga Sutra,* which formalized a portion of this tradition, states that yogis attain powers to become as light as air, to roam through space, and to see into the past and future.[54]

Horner has shown that in pre-Buddhist India the term *arahant,* denoting a saintly person in general, was closely associated with these two qualities, miraculous powers and asceticism.[55] Holy men in pre-Buddhist times seem to have been regarded as arahants, or "worthy ones," because they demonstrated that they possessed these powers. This usage raises an interesting question. Given that yogis and pre-Buddhist holy men—termed *arahants*—were said to possess these qualities, did the Buddhists view their arahants, whom they said also possessed these powers, as coequal with these non-Buddhist saints? The short answer to this question, of course, is no. Buddhists drew a sharp distinction between their arahants and Indian holy men in general. Although the Buddhists may have taken over the word *arahant* from pre-Buddhist usage, as Horner has shown, they poured new meaning into the term.[56] While Buddhism continued to regard miraculous powers and asceticism as qualities of the arahants, it did not view these qualities as definitive. These powers were not central either to the arahant's identity or to his mission.[57]

The Buddhist attitude toward miraculous powers is illustrated in a celebrated incident in the *Vinaya* (V.II.109–111). A rich merchant of Rājagaha placed a costly sandalwood begging bowl on top of a high post. He challenged any holy man who was an arahant possessed of miraculous power to remove the bowl through the use of that power. All the great sages of the time, the Buddha's chief rivals, assembled to try for the prize. Two Buddhist arahants, Mahā Moggallāna and Piṇḍola Bhāradvāja, also heard of the contest, and Piṇḍola went there. The arahant Piṇḍola won the prize. He not only removed the bowl by rising in the air, but then proceeded to fly around Rājagaha three times. Hearing of this event, the Buddha summoned Piṇḍola. Instead of congratulating him for defeating his rivals, however, the Buddha rebuked him for displaying these powers before householders. Because of this incident the Buddha is said to have promulgated a rule prohibiting exhibitions of miraculous power by monks.

We should note in the foregoing story that the Buddha never denied these miraculous powers. In fact, the story refers to Piṇḍola's powers as the *dhamma* or qualities of a "further man" (Vin. II.111). But the Buddha opposed displaying them to attract the attention of ordinary people.

The Buddhist attitude toward these powers is stated more clearly in the *Kevaddha Sutta* (D.1.211 ff.). In that sutta a young layman tells the Buddha that he should command one of his monks to perform a miracle in order that the Buddhists might get more attention from the townspeople. If they saw, he argues, that the Buddhists had the powers of "further men," it would be well. The Buddha, however, explains that he can perform three kinds of miracles. The first kind includes physical miracles, such as walking on water, and the second kind includes telepathic powers, such as discerning the mind of another. The Buddha states that although he can do these two kinds of miracles he disapproves of them and clearly has no desire to gain attention by them. He approves only of the third kind of miracle, the miracle of instructing others in the *dhamma.* Whereupon he proceeds to outline the way to arahantship as in the path suttas.

Nevertheless the legends still depict many of the arahants as workers of miracles of the first two kinds. These legends do not exactly contradict the official Buddhist view of miracles, however, for they do not claim that miracles make one an arahant. These legends seem to have arisen for two basic reasons: first, to satisfy the demands of popular piety; and, second, to show that when miracles were performed they were done in order to promote the Buddha's *dhamma.*

Buddhists believed that their arahants possessed these powers, even if the powers were not the most important qualities. They told legends about the great arahants such as Anuruddha, who spent much of his time in meditation surveying a thousand worlds with his divine sight, *dibba cakkhu* (Thag. 907–909). In another story four arahants, Mahā Moggallāna, Mahā Kassapa, Mahā Kappina, and Anuruddha, travel magically to the heaven of Brahmā to hear the Buddha debate Brahmā (S.1.144 f.). The point of this story is revealed in the introduction to the sutta that says that Brahmā had believed "no monk or brahmin can come here" (S.1.144). The arahants proved their superiority to the Hindu deity.

In other stories arahants use their *iddhi* powers to serve the Buddha. The female arahant Uppalavaṇṇā miraculously created a chariot and four horses in order to travel to worship the Buddha (Thig. 229). Mahā Kaccāna, although he had become the head of the order of monks in the distant province of Ujjeni, used to return regularly by flying to hear the Buddha preach (Dhp. A.11.176).

With regard to asceticism, the legends follow much the same approach. Although it is not regarded as the sine qua non of the arahant, the legends proclaim that Buddhist arahants were superior to any other holy men in their abilities in this area. The legends justify the practice of asceticism by showing that it was done as an aid to meditation and to attaining the goal. This emphasis is made in spite of the Buddha's canonical rejection of asceticism in his own struggle for enlightenment.[58]

Mahā Kassapa was remembered by the tradition as the foremost ascetic.[59] He observed all the ascetic practices listed in the *Path of Purification* such as forest-dwelling, living at the foot of trees, dwelling in the burial ground, and various kinds of food restrictions (Vism. chap.

II). Legend tells that Mahā Kassapa, who inherited the Buddha's cast-off rag robe, did not lie down to sleep for one hundred and twenty years. The legends about Mahā Kassapa depict an arahant living a solitary life of asceticism, meditation, and study. The Chinese pilgrims reported that Buddhists in their time believed Mahā Kassapa had never died but continued to live in the remote hills of India.

Other arahants practiced similar kinds of asceticism. The *bhikkhunī* Kisā Gotamī wore rough robes all her life. Anuruddha Thera slept only a few hours a night for thirty years, and then for the remaining thirty-five years of his life shunned sleep entirely (Thag. 904; Thag. A.III.72).

Many other virtues and qualities are ascribed to the arahants in the canonical and commentarial legends. Taken together, the legends depict the arahants as beings who, fulfilling *sīla, samādhi,* and *paññā,* attained the goal. Sāriputta exemplifies the fulfillment of *sīla.* It is said that he was meticulous in his observance of the moral precepts, doing nothing without the Buddha's permission. On one occasion when he was suffering from an illness the only cure for which was a preparation containing garlic, a food forbidden to the monks by the Buddha, he chose to suffer until someone obtained the Buddha's approval of the use of garlic as medicine (Vin. 11.140). So great was the force of his virtue, *sīla,* that it warded off the demons who sought to harm him (Ud. IV.4). Because of such virtue, and all the other qualities brought out in the legends of the arahants, the Theravāda tradition held that the arahants stood on the supramundane plane (*lokuttara*), far above the mundane plane (*lokiya*) of ordinary *putthujanas.*

IMITATION AND VENERATION OF THE ARAHANT

At the outset we said that the arahant, because of his dual nature, serves as both a paradigm for imitation and an object for veneration. Now we must examine this statement. How does the arahant fulfill these two roles in the tradition? How do Buddhists involved in the world both venerate and imitate the arahant?

Clearly the arahant stands as a paradigm for all Buddhists in the Theravāda tradition. The arahant represents the goal of the tradition, and his accomplishments must be duplicated by those who would achieve liberation and *nibbāna.* In the logic of the linked foci, as we have seen, he represents what the ordinary person, *puthujjana,* can become. Numerous suttas lift up the arahants as examples for imitation. Buddhists are instructed to follow the moral precepts by remembering that just as the arahants kept the precepts, so must all who wish to advance (A.1.211; IV.248). Other texts exalt the arahants Sāriputta and Moggallana as role models for monks and the arahants Khemā and Uppalavaṇṇā as models for nuns (S.11.235; A.1.88 f.).

Although there can be no doubt that arahants and arahantship represent the norm for the Buddhist tradition, yet because the arahant stands on the lofty plane depicted in the legends and path suttas, ordinary people, both monks and householders, traditionally have found veneration of the arahant to be a more appropriate response. *Puthujjanas* existing on the ordinary level of existence with all the entanglements of desire and attachment simply cannot imitate the desirelessness of the perfected arahant. Although they admire the arahant's wisdom and liberation, this admiration more readily translates into veneration than emulation.

The canonical texts encourage the laity to venerate the arahants. In one sutta the Buddha (S.1.177 f.) answers a Brahmin's question about whom one should respect and venerate. He tells the Brahmin to respect mother, father, and eldest brother but, above all, accord the arahants the highest veneration. In another sutta Brahmadeva, a monk who attained arahantship, returning home, instructed his mother to abandon the worship of the gods for the worship of the arahants. Arahants, he assured her, surpass the gods and the worship of them yields greater merit and happiness (S.1.140–142). Similarly the monk Upavāna taught the Brahmin Devahita that arahants deserve worship and honor by laypeople. Gifts given in veneration to arahants, Upavāna said, bear much fruit for the giver (S.1.174 f.).

For the laity, then, and probably for most monks as well, the arahant fulfills two roles: object of veneration and model for imitation. Just as the *puthujjana* and the arahant constitute linked foci in the Theravāda tradition, so veneration and imitation do also: these two attitudes also stand in a relationship of transformation. But the link between veneration and imitation is perhaps more difficult to see than the connection between some of the other linked foci because the laity seem capable only of veneration. Even the texts appear at times not to encourage laity to try to imitate the arahants. In the sutta cited earlier in which two male arahants are upheld as examples for monks and two female arahants upheld as examples for nuns, two householders are upheld as examples for laypersons (S.11.235). How can ordinary folk, especially laymen who have not "gone forth," make the transformation from veneration to imitation?

It seems possible that the arahant may have represented a more imitable ideal in the early days of the Buddhist tradition and that early on veneration more readily translated into imitation. But gradually the arahant came to be regarded as a distant norm, radically set apart from ordinary persons. For example, numerous suttas tell of the Buddha's preaching to people such as the first five disciples who became arahants quickly upon hearing his *dhamma* (Vin. 1.8 f.; S.111.66 f.). These stories indicate at least a belief that at an early period arahantship was easily accessible in this very life (*diṭṭhe va dhamme*). Contrasted with these stories of many people quickly becoming arahants is the sutta in which Mahā Kassapa asks the Buddha, toward the end of his life, why there were then more precepts and fewer arahants (S.11.223 f.). Mahā Kassapa laments that formerly there were fewer precepts, and more monks became arahants, but now the situation has reversed. The Buddha tells Mahā Kassapa that this latter situation prevails when the true *dhamma* is obscured by laxity in study and practice on the part of the Sangha.

This conversation between Mahā Kassapa and the Buddha represents a remarkable text, for it indicates that arahantship had become a remote norm fairly early. To be sure, this text may not reflect conditions in the Buddha's time but probably stems from a period early in the development of the tradition. This trend for arahantship to become more remote seems to have increased in the commentarial period. The *Visuddhimagga,* for example, regards arahantship as a very distant goal indeed. Buddhaghosa, author of the *Visuddhimagga,* spelled out the requirements for arahantship in minute detail, showing that the path was long and arduous. At one point Buddhaghosa says that only one in a thousand people is capable of reaching even a fairly low stage on the path. And, he continues, of those who reach that stage, only one in a thousand succeeds in reaching the next stage, and so on.[60]

The distance of arahantship from the ordinary person's plane of existence and the difficulty of its attainment are also reflected in the fact that arahants do not abound in the history of the Theravāda tradition. Once past the Buddha's time and the age of his great disciples, arahants are few and far between in the history of Theravāda. In modern times traditional Theravādins have held that there have been no arahants for centuries.[61]

Now the question recurs compounded: if arahantship is so distant, how can the *puthujjana* possibly imitate the arahant? What is the link between veneration and imitation for the laity? Where is the logic of transformation? The Theravāda tradition's answer to this question was given in several different ways. First, an answer was given in the path suttas considered earlier. By explicating the gradual process of the arahant's development, the path suttas provided a link between veneration and imitation. The path suttas show that although an ordinary person cannot imitate the arahant perfected, he can imitate the developing arahant. Veneration of the arahant—especially of the supreme arahant, Gotama—is shown to be a stage on the path; it leads one to have the faith (*saddhā*) necessary to renounce the world and begin on the long path (compare S.V.67).

A further answer to the question is found in the commentarial legends of the arahants. These legends both complicate and simplify for the *puthujjana* the matter of imitation of the saint. They complicate the picture because by introducing the notion of arahants perfecting themselves in previous lives, the legends greatly increase the distance between the ordinary person and the arahant. Arahantship in these legends represents a very remote goal virtually impossible to attain in one lifetime. As we have seen, the legends say that those who became arahants in this life did so because of countless lives of preparation.

At the same time, however, the commentarial legends simplify the matter of imitating the arahant. They do this by relating the activities of the arahants in previous lives, thereby establishing those activities as part of the paradigm for the laity. In prior births the saints lived on the mundane plane in the world, where they began the process of transformation with acts such as vows, merit-making, and almsgiving. In other words, the legends show that the arahants began as good householders; thus householders can imitate the arahants when they perform the same actions and fulfill the *dhamma* of householders.

Merit-making practiced by householders in this way, however, represents more than merely a simple form of imitation; it constitutes a definite link with the path of meditation necessary for the attainment of arahantship. When householders venerate the arahants with offerings of food, flowers, robes, or other gifts, they are said to accrue merit. Merit is a shorthand explanation for good karma that produces fruit in the future. But there is more to merit than simply this mechanical process of retribution. For Theravāda, merit produces its effects because the meritorious actions purify the mind of the actor. So laypersons are encouraged to venerate Mahā Kassapa and other arahants because doing so will "gratify the mind" (Thag. 1173). That is, the merit-making involved in venerating arahants represents a form of meditation. This meditation, although quite basic, functions more or less in the same way as advanced forms to elevate the mind from lower truths to higher truths. The layperson venerating an arahant is exposed to the values and truths of the *dhamma,* which now begin to ferment in his mind.[62]

We might suggest that merit-making and meditation represent a further pair of linked foci, standing in close relation to the pair veneration/imitation. The connection between merit-making and meditation clarifies the transformation from veneration to imitation.

Still another facet of Theravāda's solution to the problem entailed by the remoteness of the arahant and the difficulty of imitating him is to be found in the doctrine of the four paths or four ways, *maggas.* We have seen that the Theravāda tradition divided the path into two parts—the worldly path, *lokiya,* and the transcendent path called *lokuttara.* The *puthujjanas* occupy the worldly path; the arahants fulfill the transcendent path. But the transcendent path itself was held to have stages or gradations.

The *lokuttara* path was segmented into four parts or four paths, *maggas.* In addition each of these paths led to a fruition, *phala,* upon mastery of its conditions. The first path, the path of stream-attainment (*sotāpatti-magga*), marks the transition from the *lokiya* plane to the *lokuttara* plane. Upon completion of this path one attains the fruit of stream entry and is assured attaining enlightenment in a future birth. The *Visuddhimagga* says that no matter how "negligent he may be," the stream enterer is bound to attain *nibbāna* when he has undergone seven rebirths among gods and men (Vism. 677). The second path is the path of once-returning (*sakadāgāmi-magga*), the fruit of which assures one of returning only once to this world before attaining the goal. Third comes the path of nonreturning, (*anāgāmi-magga*), wherein one attains assurance of transcending this world forever to reach arahantship in the "Pure Abodes" of the heavens. Arahantship itself constitutes the final path, with fulfillment of the arahant ideal being the fruition of the entire system.

The occupants of these paths are called the "four noble persons," and the criteria distinguishing their levels of attainment are clearly delineated in the Pāli canon and commentaries. The paths are divided according to the gradual levels of perfection attained by the four kinds of noble persons. Horner terms these four paths "a cathartic process, arahantship not being possible until all the moral faults and obstructions, which are to be got rid of by progressing along the lower Ways, are truly eliminated as these ways are mastered."[63]

The most commonly given description of the catharsis of these noble persons explains how on each path the noble person must eliminate certain mental fetters, *saṁyojanas* (e.g., D.1.156 f.; M.1.34–36). These fetters resemble and overlap with the negative mental states we considered earlier, the hindrances (*nīvaraṇas*) and the intoxicants (*āsavas*). Buddhaghosa explains that these mental states are called fetters because they bind people to the wheel of rebirth. A person attains the fruit of stream entry by eliminating the first three fetters: delusion of self, *sakkāya-diṭṭhi*; doubt, *vicikicchā*; and belief in good works and ceremonies, *sīlabbataparāmāsa*. At the second level the once-returner, having destroyed these fetters, reduces lust, ill will, and delusion to a minimum. The third noble person completes the destruction of the first five fetters by destroying sensual desire (*kāma-rāga*) and ill will (*vyāpāda*). To become an arahant one must proceed to eliminate the five remaining fetters, called higher fetters: desire for material existence (*rūpa-rāga*), desire for immaterial existence (*arūpa-rāga*), conceit (*māna*), restlessness (*uddhacca*), and ignorance (*avijjā*). The texts make it clear that this elimination of the fetters does not supplant but goes along with the destruction of the *āsavas* (D.1.156 f.).

The perfection of the noble persons occasionally is described in terms of the wisdom they have to attain. For example, the stream enterer must understand the five aggregates of existence and the arahant must see these for himself intuitively (S.111.191). Similarly to enter the stream one must begin to understand the six sense faculties and their working, and to attain arahantship one must understand these completely.[64] The *Visuddhimagga* describes the process of moving from one path to the next as being based on a comprehensive, gradual attainment of wisdom and elimination of negative states (Vism. chap. XXII).

This doctrine of the four paths further develops the possibilities for the imitation of the arahants. Whereas the commentarial legends extended the mundane, *lokiya,* path and the opportunities for spiritual development there, this doctrine extends the supramundane path, *lokuttara.* By doing this it offers hope to those Buddhists who have surpassed the ordinary person in spiritual attainments but who still have not been able to imitate fully the arahant's perfections. As Horner wrote, "These who have progressed well are not ranked merely as non-arahans" but are given a definite place on the supramundane path.[65]

CONCLUSION

We can summarize this investigation of the nature and role of the arahant in the Theravāda Buddhist tradition by drawing together some of our findings. The Theravāda conception of the arahant seems compatible with an understanding of the dual nature of a saint, fully human and yet transcendent. For the Buddhist tradition this dual nature of the arahant is grounded in a basic dichotomy expressed by pairs of contrary but linked concepts. These "linked foci" are governed by a dynamic of transformation, a move from bondage to liberation that is at the heart of the Theravāda tradition. Linked with the arahant in this dynamic is the *puthujjana,* the ordinary person.

Because of the dynamic of transformation, the arahant fulfills a dual role in the tradition as both an object of veneration and a paradigm for imitation. While holding the arahants in high esteem as saints embodying the ideals of the Buddhist tradition, Theravādins have maintained that all beings can aspire to and imitate the perfections of the arahants. The Theravāda tradition balanced and conjoined the goals of veneration and imitation of the arahants by setting out a gradual path to arahantship. This gradual path, stretching over countless lives of an individual on both the mundane and supramundane planes, constitutes the essence and genius of the tradition as well as the solution to the problem of the veneration and imitation of the arahant. Shown by the texts to have been followed by all the arahants, the gradual path provides a multiplicity of models imitable by ordinary people at various stages of development. In keeping with its belief that religion must take account of the variations in individual temperaments, the Buddhist tradition held that no single role model could serve the spiritual needs of all people. But all people could imitate some aspect of the arahant's path of spiritual development, either on the mundane level, as illustrated in the legends of the arahants' previous lives, or on the supramundane level, as illustrated in the four ways of the four noble persons. Veneration of the perfected arahant by persons at various levels of the path both leads to and is in itself imitation of the arahant's development. Thus through its gradual path, the Theravāda tradition offers a range of goals and rewards for all persons on their way to eventual sainthood.

NOTES

1. Samuel Beal, *Buddhist Records of the Western World* (London: Kegan Paul, Trench, Trubner and Co., 1906), 1: 134.

2. *Psalms of the Early Buddhists,* Vol. II, *The Brethren,* trans. C. A. F. Rhys Davids (London: Pali Text Society, 1937), p. xliv.

3. Winston L. King, *Buddhism and Christianity: Some Bridges of Understanding* (London, Allen and Unwin, 1963), p. 222.

4. Rune E. A. Johansson, *The Psychology of Nirvana* (New York: Anchor Books/Doubleday, 1970), p. 114.

5. Edward Conze, *Buddhist Thought in India* (Ann Arbor: University of Michigan Press, 1970), p. 26.

6. S. J. Tambiah, *Buddhism and the Spirit Cults in Northeast Thailand* (New York: Cambridge University Press, 1970), p. 346.

7. Mādhyamika-Kārikā XXIV. 8, 9.

8. K. N. Jayatilleke, *Early Buddhist Theory of Knowledge* (London: George Allen and Unwin, 1963), pp. 361 f.

9. Ibid., p. 362.

10. Conze, *Buddhist Thought in India,* p. 25.

11. MK. XXIV.10.

12. Bimal K. Matilal, "A Critique of the Mādhyamika Position," in *The Problem of Two Truths in Buddhism and Vedanta,* ed. Mervyn Sprung. (Boston: D. Reidel, 1973), p. 59.

13. Mervyn Sprung, "Introduction," in *The Problem of Two Truths in Buddhism and Vedanta,* p. 3.

14. Ibid.

15. This distinction occurs throughout the canon; for example, *Kathāvatthu* II.2 and *Anguttara Nikāya* IV.67 f.

16. I. B. Horner, *The Early Buddhist Theory of Man Perfected: A Study of the Arahan* (London: Williams and Norgate Ltd., 1936), p. 42.

17. In this chapter we refer to these suttas as "path suttas." This group of suttas includes D.1.47 ff.; M.1.163 ff., 1.339 ff., 111.33 ff.; and A.11.207 ff.

18. Johansson, *Psychology of Nirvana,* p. 116.

19. See Horner, *Early Buddhist Theory of Man Perfected,* pp. 112 f. and Vin. 1.209, 111.90, D.1.211 f., etc.

20. The Buddhist tradition has analyzed the process of enlightenment in great detail. Our purpose in this chapter, however, is not so much to examine all the technical terms pertaining to the Buddhist philosophy of mind as to examine some of the major suttas and formulae describing the perfections of the arahant and the path to arahantship. These latter descriptions, although dealing with the same phenomenon, are usually less technical than the philosophical, abhidharmic analysis of the mind. A detailed treatment of the Theravāda philosophy of mind lies beyond the scope of this chapter and must be reserved for a future work.

21. Although, as we shall see, the path suttas actually divide the perfections of the arahant into five categories, these can be subsumed under these three headings.

22. See A.1.102, which says, "Wisdom shines forth in one's conduct."

23. See, for example, D.1.63 ff., M.1.33 f., and A.11.208 f.

24. Curiously, in the texts at the place where the precept about intoxicants would be expected to stand, there is the statement that the arahant "abstains from that which causes destruction to seed growth and plant growth" (e.g.,

M.1.345). Was this some kind of veiled reference to the production of alcohol? Or did the authors feel the need to put in the place normally occupied by the fifth precept a reference to complete nonviolence toward living things?

25. Johansson, *Psychology of Nirvana,* p. 116.

26. *Dialogues of the Buddha (Dīgha Nikāya),* trans. T. W. and C. A. F. Rhys Davids (London: Pali Text Society, 1910), p. 129. Nathan Katz has a good discussion of these *abhiññās* in his *The Concept of the Arahant in the Sutta Pitaka, with reference to the Bodhisattva and the Mahāsiddha* (unpublished dissertation, Temple University, 1979). Katz's admirable study should be consulted for more information about all aspects of the *arahant* ideal.

27. Nyanatiloka Thera, *Buddhist Dictionary* (Colombo: Frewin and Co., 1956), pp. 2–3.

28. Horner, *Early Buddhist Theory of Man Perfected,* p. 122.

29. Jayatilleke *Early Buddhist Theory of Knowledge,* p. 422.

30. Horner, *Early Buddhist Theory of Man Perfected,* p. 83. We shall discuss these powers in more detail later.

31. Jayatilleke, *Early Buddhist Theory of Knowledge,* p. 466.

32. Ibid.

33. Horner, *Early Buddhist Theory of Man Perfected,* p. 122.

34. Har Dayal, *The Bodhisattva Doctrine in Buddhist Sanskrit Literature* (London: Kegan Paul, Trench, Trubner and Co., 1932), p. 118.

35. This description occurs throughout the canon, e.g., D.111.83, 97; M.1.4 f.; S.1.71; A.1.144.

36. This formula, too, recurs frequently, e.g., S.1.140, M.1.139, D.1.84, Vin. 1.14.

37. In Mahāyāna this notion of ending rebirth underwent transformation along with the doctrine of *Nirvāna.* But Dayal notes that early Mahayana shared the view of Theravāda. See Dayal, *The Bodhisattva Doctrine,* p. 121.

38. See M.1.139, S.111.83, Dhp. 89–99.

39. See M.11.33, where it says that an arahant's description of his enlightenment would be in accordance with *dhamma,* and thus acceptable, if it conformed to the pattern of the path suttas. This is similar to the use of the term *dhammatā* in suttas such as the *Mahāpadāna Sutta* (D.11 ff.), where it means the natural order of things in the world.

40. *Thera-therī-gāthā,* ed. H. Oldenberg and R. Pischel (London: Pali Text Society, reprint 1966). Two English translations have been made of these texts: *Psalms of the Early Buddhists,* 2 vols., trans. C. A. F. Rhys Davids (London: Pali Text Society, 1909, 1937). Also see *The Elder's Verses,* Vols. I and II, trans. K. R. Norman (London: Pali Text Society, 1969).

41. *Apadāna,* Vols. I and II, ed. M. E. Lilley (London: Pali Text Society, 1925).

42. *Theragāthā Commentary,* 3 vols., ed. F. L. Woodward (London: Pali Text Society, 1940–1959). *Therīgāthā Commentary,* ed. E. Muller (London: Pali Text Society, 1893). *Apadāna Commentary,* ed. C. E. Godakumbura (London: Pali Text Society, 1954). In addition, many other Pali commentaries contain hagiography.

43. See for example, *Therīgāthā,* verses 59, 62, 188, 195, 203, and 235. A

common story running through the *Therīgāthā* tells of a beautiful woman who was extremely vain until the Buddha revealed to her the impermanence of the body, e.g., the stories of Sundarī-Nandā, Abhirūpa-Nandā, and Khemā.

44. *Psalms of the Early Buddhists, The Sisters,* p. xix.

45. For example, see the legend of Sundarī Therī: Thig. A. 228 f.

46. Mrs. Rhys Davids has tabulated the attainments of arahants in the *Theragāthā* and *Therīgāthā*. For her lists, see *Psalms of the Bretheren,* pp. 420–422, and *Psalms of the Sisters,* pp. xxxvii f.

47. See Thag. A.III.90–96, 162 f.

48. Compare S.1.140 f.

49. Māra is the Buddhist equivalent of Satan. As ruler of the kingdom of death, *saṃsāra,* he does his best to keep mortals bound up in the desires that lead to rebirth.

50. See the legends of Uppalavaṇṇā, Anopamā, Sundarī, and others.

51. See, for example, M.III.46, 55, 249, and other suttas.

52. See M.1.213.

53. Compare the legend of Mahā Cunda, Thag. 141–142.

54. Patañjali's *Yoga Sutra,* chap. III.

55. Horner, *Early Buddhist Theory of Man Perfected,* p. 83.

56. Ibid., chaps. II–IV.

57. Ibid., p. 83.

58. See Majjhima Nikāya, suttas 36, 85, and 100, wherein the Buddha tells of how he tried and rejected extreme austerities as the way to *nibbāna.* Nevertheless the Theravāda tradition included ascetic practices as an optional stage of the path. See *Vism.* chap. II.

59. A.1.24; M.1.213. f.

60. *Vism.* 375.

61. Richard Gombrich, *Precept and Practice* (Oxford: Clarendon Press, 1971), p. 285, notes that Sinhalese Buddhists believe the last arahant lived in the first century B.C. On the Burmese Buddhists holding a similar view, see R. L. Slater, *Paradox and Nirvana* (Chicago: University of Chicago Press, 1951), p. 49.

62. In another article ("The Sinhalese Idea of Ultimate Reality and Meaning" co-authored with G. Gamburd, *Journal of Ultimate Reality and Meaning* 3, no. 3 [1980]: 214) I have written about the explanation of merit that I received from modern Theravāda monks. They told me that merit is "any activity that purifies the mind and leads to *vimutti,* liberation." On this point see also Gombrich, *Precept and Practice,* p. 244.

63. I. B. Horner, "The Four Ways and the Four Fruits in Pali Buddhism," *Indian Historical Quarterly* 10 (1934): 789.

64. For a more complete discussion of these four ways, see Horner, *Early Buddhist Theory of Man Perfected,* chap. VI.

65. Horner, "The Four Ways and the Four Fruits," p. 786.

6
Sanctification on the Bodhisattva Path

Donald S. Lopez, Jr.

For you must know, beloved, that each one of us is beyond all question responsible for all men and all things on earth, not only because of the individual transgressions of the world, but each one individually for all men and every single man on this earth. This realization is the crown of a monk's way of life, and, indeed of every man on earth. For a monk is not a different kind of man, but merely such as all men on earth ought to be.

—Father Zossima in *The Brothers Karamazov*[1]

What the Russian father says of the monk is for Mahāyāna Buddhism also true of the Bodhisattva, that person who vows to take upon himself or herself the responsibility of freeing all beings in the universe from suffering and leading them to the bliss of enlightenment. Such an aspiration is noble—indeed, saintly. But is the Bodhisattva a saint? Joachim Wach thought so. He wrote in the *Sociology of Religion* that Mahāyāna Buddhism provides "a detailed classification of the various stages of sainthood, as in the famous treatise called *Bodhisattvacarya* written by the celebrated Śāntideva."[2] In the pages that follow we will have occasion to consider Śāntideva's famous treatise as well as a number of other Mahāyāna texts in an effort to determine whether Wach is correct in implying that the components of the Bodhisattva path are "stages of sainthood." In describing the Bodhisattva's aspiration and his path, reference will be made from time to time to the qualities of the saint in the Roman Catholic tradition, for it is here that our preunderstanding of the meaning of sainthood has its root. Once we have followed the Bodhisattva from the creation of his aspiration (*cittotpāda*) through the five paths (*mārga*) and ten grounds (*bhūmi*) to his achievement of Buddhahood, it will then be necessary to assess the Bodhisattva to determine in what ways, if any, the Bodhisattva can properly be termed a saint.

The greater part of this chapter will provide a general presentation of how the Bodhisattva is portrayed in the major Indian Mahāyāna *sūtras* and *śāstras*. It will not attempt to survey the historical development of the Bodhisattva ideal in India,[3] nor will it deal with the Bodhisattva in East Asian Buddhism.[4] Space limitations also do not provide the opportunity to discuss the *mahāsiddha*, the Bodhisattva of Vajrayāna Buddhism, who provides a rich and, for the most part, untapped source for examining our notion of sainthood and the role of hagiography.

THE MEANING OF THE WORD "BODHISATTVA"

The Sanskrit term *bodhisattva* is made up of two words, *bodhi* and *sattva*. *Bodhi* is derived from the verbal root *budh*, "to wake," so that *bodhi* means the state of being awake—that is, enlightenment. The second component of the term is more troublesome. In his classic study, *The Bodhisattva Doctrine in Buddhist Sanskrit Literature*, Har Dayal lists seven possible interpretations of the word *sattva*,[5] three of which warrant mention here. The first meaning of *sattva* is "sentient being," in which case the compound *bodhisattva* would be read as "a being seeking enlightenment." A second meaning of *sattva* is "mind" (*citta*) or "intention" (*abhiprāya*), so that a *bodhisattva* would be "one whose mind or intention is directed toward enlightenment." Third, *sattva* has the sense of strength or courage, making the compound *bodhisattva* mean "one whose strength is directed toward enlightenment."

To gain some sense of how the term was understood by late (circa eighth century) Mahāyāna Buddhist *paṇḍitas* in India, it is useful to consider the Tibetan translation of *bodhisattva*, *byang chub sems dpa'*. *Byang chub* is the translation of *bodhi*, enlightenment. *Sems* means "mind" or "intention," and *dpa'* can serve as either a noun meaning "strength" or "courage" or as an adjective meaning "courageous" or "heroic." This suggests that the Indian and Tibetan scholars who coined the term *byang chub sems dpa'* to translate *bodhisattva* were aware of both the second and third meanings of *sattva* mentioned earlier and believed that both should be incorporated into the Tibetan translation, with the resulting meaning being "one who is heroic in his or her intention to achieve enlightenment."[6]

An important etymology of *bodhisattva* is provided by the influential Svātantrika master Haribhadra (eighth century):

> He is enlightenment (*bodhi*) because he observes enlightenment with the power of wisdom and he is a sentient being (*sattva*) because he observes sentient beings with great mercy. Thus, he is called a Bodhisattva, just as meditation observing the ugly is called the ugly.[7]

Haribhadra's point is that the Bodhisattva is called *bodhi* or enlightenment not because he is enlightened but because he seeks enlightenment through the cultivation of wisdom; wisdom is his object. He is called *sattva* not because he is a sentient being (although he is) but because through his great compassion he seeks the welfare of sentient beings; that is his object. This is a case of giving the name of the object to the subject, as in the case of designating the famous meditation on the ugly or foul (*aśubha*) with the term "the ugly": the meditation itself is not ugly; it is the ugly that is contemplated.

Haribhadra makes two important points in his etymology—first that the Bodhisattva has two objects or aims, his own achievement of enlightenment and the welfare of sentient beings and, second, that those two aims are pursued with wisdom and compassion, respectively. These points will be discussed in detail later.

THE BODHISATTVA IN THE HĪNAYĀNA

The earliest use of the term *bodhisattva* in Buddhist literature seems to be that which occurs in the Pāli *Nikāyas,* where the Buddha speaks of himself in statements such as this: "in the days before my enlightenment when I was still only a Bodhisatta."[8] That is, the Buddha uses the title Bodhisattva (Pāli: *bodhisatta*) to refer to himself when he speaks of the time before he achieved Buddhahood at the age of thirty-five. In the *Suttapiṭaka* he uses the term not only to refer to the early years of his life as Prince Siddhārtha but also to refer to his previous lives. The Buddha seems to have sometimes recounted events from his past lifetimes to illustrate a point of doctrine. These *Jātaka Tales* were later compiled and expanded with apocryphal elements into a massive collection of 547 stories that have functioned in Buddhist history as a combination of Butler's *Lives of the Saints* and Aesop's *Fables*.[9] It is in the introduction to the *Jātakas* that we find the fullest articulation of the Bodhisattva doctrine as understood by the Hīnayāna, presented in the story of Sumedha.

Four countless aeons and one hundred thousand aeons ago there lived a *brahman* named Sumedha who, realizing that beings are subject to birth, aging, sickness, and death, sought a deathless state. He retired into the mountains, where he lived the life of a renunciate and gained yogic powers. One day as he was flying through the air, he looked down to see a gathering of people listening to a teacher. Sumedha descended and asked who this teacher might be and was told that he was the Buddha Dīpaṃkara. When he heard the word "Buddha" he was overcome with joy. As Dīpaṃkara approached, Sumedha loosened his matted locks and laid down in the mud so that the Buddha would not soil his feet. As he lay there waiting for Dīpaṃkara to arrive, Sumedha reflected that he had the capacity to achieve freedom from rebirth in that very lifetime, if he were to practice Dīpaṃkara's teaching. Yet he thought:

> But why should thus in an unknown guise
> Should I the Doctrine's fruit secure?
> Omniscience first I will achieve,
> And be a Buddha in the world.
>
> Or why should I, a valorous man,
> The ocean seek to cross alone?
> Omniscience first I will achieve,
> And gods and men convey across.[10]

Dīpaṃkara came to a halt before Sumedha's prone form and announced to the crowd:

> Behold ye now this monk austere,
> His matted locks, his penance fierce!
> Lo! he, unnumbered cycles hence,
> A Buddha in the world shall be.[11]

Dīpaṃkara went on to prophesy the details of the lifetime in which Sumedha would attain Buddhahood, who his parents would be, and who his disciples. He told of the tree under which he would sit on the evening when he achieved enlightenment. And as the story goes, four countless aeons and one hundred thousand aeons later, the prophecy came true when Prince Siddhārtha became a Buddha.

The commentary to this story enumerates the qualifications Sumedha fulfilled to become a Bodhisattva, qualifications which, by implication, anyone who wishes to become a Bodhisattva must meet according to the Theravāda school. In the lifetime in which the vow to become a Buddha is initially made, the aspirant must fulfill eight conditions:

1. He must be a human.
2. He must be a male.
3. He must be able to achieve liberation in that lifetime.
4. He must make the vow in the presence of a living Buddha.
5. He must be a renunciate.
6. He must possess the five powers and eight attainments. The five powers are: the power to perform physical miracles (the ability to create manifold forms, to appear and disappear, to walk through walls and mountains, to dive in and out of the earth, to walk on water, to fly in the lotus posture, to touch the sun and moon with one's hands, to physically go to the realm of the gods), the power to hear at a distance, the power to know others' minds, the power to remember past lifetimes, the power to see how beings fare according to their deeds. The eight attainments are: the attainment of the eight levels of the form realm (*rūpadhātu*) and the formless realm (*ārūpyadhātu*).
7. He must be an individual capable of sacrificing his life.
8. He must have great zeal.[12]

The extraordinary person endowed with such qualities, having made his vow to achieve Buddhahood for the sake of others and whose destiny has been confirmed by the prophecy of a Buddha, sets out on the long and arduous path of thousands of lifetimes during which he perfects himself by practicing a set of virtues called the perfections (*pāramitā*/*pāramī*). In the Pāli list there are ten, consisting of giving (*dāna*), ethics (*sīla*), renunciation (*nekkhamma*), wisdom (*paññā*), effort (*viriya*), patience (*khanti*), truthfulness (*sacca*), resolution (*adhiṭṭhāna*), love (*mettā*), and equanimity (*upekkhā*).[13] Instances of the Bodhisattva's dedication to these virtues provide the subject matter for many of the *Jātaka* stories.

One such story is that of the sage Khantivādi (Sanskrit, Kṣāntivādin), the preacher of patience. The king of Benares became drunk one day and went to a park with a company of female dancers and musicians. During their performance he fell asleep, at which point the women began to wander through the park. They came upon a sage sitting under a tree and sat in a circle around him to hear his teaching. The king awoke, enraged to find his harem had deserted him, and, sword in hand, went off in search of them. He found them listening to the sage. The king demanded to know what doctrine he was preaching, to which the sage replied that he taught the doctrine of patience. When the king asked what patience is, the sage replied that it is not becoming angry when struck, abused, or reviled. To test the sage's commitment to his teaching, the king had his executioner give the sage two thousand lashes with a whip of thorns, after which the king again asked him, "What doctrine do you teach?" The sage replied that he taught the doctrine of patience and that it was not skin-deep but lay within. The king then had his executioner cut off the sage's hands, and then his feet, and then his nose and ears, each time asking the sage what doctrine he taught. Each time the sage replied that he taught patience and that it was not to be found in his amputated extremities. The sage, who was in fact the Bodhisattva, never became angry and before he died wished the king a long life.[14]

The long list of extraordinary qualifications for the Bodhisattva and the story of the Bodhisattva's devotion to the practice of patience raise two important issues in the consideration of the Bodhisattva as saint: miracles and martyrdom. According to the procedures for canonization set down by Urban VIII in 1642, candidates for sainthood (with the exception of martyrs) must fulfill three general criteria: doctrinal purity, heroic virtue, and miraculous intercession after death.[15] Even when it is clear that the candidate was doctrinally pure and practiced the Christian virtues heroically, the Church demands confirmation in the form of miracles. Although the hagiographies are filled with stories of miraculous cures and resuscitation of the dead, it is miraculous intercession after the death of the candidate that is considered crucial as proof that he or she is both in heaven and is a powerful intercessor before God; it is God who performs the miracle at the request of the saint who has interceded at the throne of God in response to the prayer of the faithful.[16] It is common for the miracle to take place at or somehow be associated with the tomb of the candidate; "Heaven and Earth joined at the grave of a dead human being."[17] Thus for the Church the essential miracles are those that occur after the death of the candidate, serving as a sign from God that he or she is in heaven and is an intercessor for the living and for souls in purgatory.

In contrast we find that the various forms of thaumaturgy listed among the eight conditions that must be fulfilled by the Bodhisattva are *prerequisites,* required before even beginning the path to Buddhahood, which will last four countless aeons. The ability to walk on water, fly, disappear, and so forth are not signs of sanctity but are merely the results of yogic practice. They imply no particular level of insight and are obtainable by the Buddhist and non-Buddhist alike. Although miraculous feats occur in the Pāli canon, the attitude expressed toward them is much more casual than that found in the lives of the saints. Supernatural powers are considered somewhat commonplace, an incidental side effect of spiritual exercises. In the *Kevaddhasutta* the Buddha says that there are three kinds of marvels (*pāṭihāriya*): magical powers (*iddhi*) such as flying in the lotus position, walking through walls, and walking on water; the marvel of mind reading (*ādesanā*); and the marvel of teaching (*anusāsanī*). He says that he is distressed by and abhors the first two types of marvels because the power to perform them can be obtained through the use of charms and thus cannot be judged as infallible signs of spiritual attainment. The marvel of teaching is not open to such suspicion.[18] A further indication of this attitude toward miracles is to be found in the famous story of Kisā Gotamī, who took her dead son to the Buddha and asked for medicine to bring him back to life. The Buddha instructed her to bring him a mustard seed from every house in which no one had ever died. Upon hearing tales of sorrow at each house, she came to understand the universality of death and joined the order of nuns.[19]

Martyrs were accorded a special place in the decrees of Urban VIII; the fact that they died witnessing their faith in Christ at the hands of persecutors of the Church was the only proof needed of their sanctity.[20] Because technically the martyr must die defending his faith, at least in word, there are few true martyrs in Buddhist literature because there are few persecutions recorded in the scriptures. As E. J. Thomas has noted,[21] if Buddhism has a martyrology, it is to be found in the *Jātaka,* where the Bodhisattva suffers death again and again in his practice of the perfections, especially those of giving and patience. Buddhism has its share of gruesome deaths and self-mutilations for the sake of virtue,[22] although few match the excesses of the more grisly Christian tales such as the martyrdom of St. Clement of Ancyra and St. Clement of Anathangelus.[23] Even in the *Jātaka* it can rarely be said that the Bodhisattva dies in witness of his faith; Khantivādi died not so much because he taught patience as because a drunken king found him surrounded by the king's harem. It should also be pointed out that in Buddhism the gravity of sacrificing one's life is lightened somewhat by the fact that this is not the only life the Bodhisattva has to give; he will be reborn thousands of times before he achieves enlightenment. His "martyrdom" for the sake of virtue does not, therefore, confer any final reward in the celestial realms; it merely ensures an auspicious rebirth in the next life.

To bring this digression to a close, then, it can be said that although the ability to perform miracles is a prerequisite for undertaking the Bodhisattva path in the Theravāda, the ability to perform miracles does not a Bodhisattva make. Also, although stories of personal sacrifice, including that of one's life, abound in the *Jātaka* stories, martyrdom does not carry the weight in Buddhism that one finds in the Roman Catholic tradition. This difference can be attributed most obviously to the striking dissimilarity of the historical circumstances out of which the two traditions arose. But the relative insignificance of miracles and martyrdom in Buddhism can also be traced to a fundamental difference from Christianity in its soteriological perspective. This is suggested by the Buddha's preference for the "marvel of teaching" and will be more evident in the Mahāyāna.

An assessment of the eight conditions that the potential Bodhisattva must fulfill quickly leads one to the conclusion that he is a most rare individual. Doctrinally the Theravāda saw no need for a multiplicity of Buddhas at any one time in history because its goal was to become an Arhat rather than a Buddha. The primary function of the Buddha is to teach the path to enlightenment. So long as that teaching is available, there is no need for another Buddha to appear. Hence the Theravāda conceived of one Buddha for each age who functioned as a teacher far more than as an exemplar. Sumedha had the capacity to achieve nirvana in the lifetime when he met Dīpaṃkara, but he looked forward to a time when the teaching of the buddhas of the past would disappear from the world. Out of concern for those beings in the future who would not have access to the path to liberation, he vowed to achieve Buddhahood when all memory of the teaching had disappeared from the world. Thus the main difference between the Bodhisattva and the Arhat in the Theravāda is that the Bodhisattva discovers nirvana on his own whereas the Arhat must rely on the directions of a Buddha. The Bodhisattva in the Theravāda is the extraordinarily rare individual who embarks on the long path to Buddhahood out of compassion for others, thus postponing by aeons his own entry into nirvana.

THE BODHISATTVA IN THE MAHĀYĀNA SUTRAS

In *The Structure of Scientific Revolutions,* Thomas Kuhn writes that a new theory,

> however special its range of application, is seldom or never just an increment to what is already known. Its assimilation requires the reconstruction of prior theory and the re-evaluation of prior fact, an intrinsically revolutionary process that is seldom completed by a single man and never overnight.[24]

If Kuhn's theory of paradigm change can be successfully applied to the history of religions,[25] then such a change occurred in Buddhism with the appearance of the Mahāyāna *sūtras,* roughly four hundred years after the Buddha's final nirvana. In those *sūtras* we find a revolutionary shift in ideal. The goal is no longer to follow the teachings of the Buddha and become an Arhat but, rather, to follow the Bodhisattva path and become a Buddha oneself. As in the case of scientific revolutions, this change in paradigm necessitated the reassessment and redefinition of a constellation of issues involving worldview, values, and praxis. The Mahāyāna *sūtras,* composed over a period of several centuries, do not present an entirely systematic treatment of these issues.[26] Nonetheless they do provide the scriptural bases for later delineations of Mahāyāna doctrine, to be considered in a subsequent section. In this section our purpose is to identify a few of the more important reassessments of Buddhist doctrine that occurred in the Mahāyāna *sūtras,* especially as they relate to the Bodhisattva.

A recurrent theme in the Mahāyāna *sūtras* is the exaltation of the Bodhisattva above the Hīnayāna practitioners; his compassion for all sentient beings and his willingness to forgo his own welfare in an effort to ensure theirs make him the most laudable of the Buddha's disciples. The Mahāyāna *sūtras* thus articulate two ways of practice, that of the *śrāvaka* and *pratyekabuddha,* those who seek nirvana in order to find liberation from suffering and rebirth for themselves alone, and the path of the Bodhisattva, who vows to free all beings in the universe from suffering. In the *Pañcaviṃśatisāhasrikāprajñāpāramitāsūtra* the Buddha says to Śāriputra:

> A glowworm, being a mere insect, does not think that its light could illuminate the Continent of Jambudvīpa, or shine over it. Just so, the Disciples (*śrāvaka*) and Pratyekabuddhas do not think, not even one of them, that they should, after winning full en-

> lightenment, lead all beings to Nirvana. But the sun, when it has risen, sheds its light over the whole of Jambudvīpa. Just so a Bodhisattva, after he has accomplished the practices which end in full enlightenment, leads countless beings to Nirvana.[27]

The reluctance of the *śrāvaka* and *pratyekabuddha* to lead all beings into nirvana is not construed to arise from some selfishness on their part, for it is through the destruction of the conception of self (*ātmagraha*) that their liberation is attained; it is not that they are not compassionate. Rather, it is from their perceived inability to take upon themselves the responsibility of freeing all beings from suffering that their reluctance arises. As the *Sāgaramatiparipṛcchāsūtra* says:

> For example, Sāgaramati, a merchant or householder had an only son who was lovable, beautiful, affectionate, pleasant, and agreeable to see. That son, being a child, was dancing and fell into a pit of filth. The boy's mother and relatives then saw that he had fallen into the pit of filth and, having seen it, they lamented, grieved, and wailed; they did not enter the pit of filth and take the boy out. Then the boy's father arrived and saw that his only son had fallen into a pit of filth. Seeing it, he was seized by the wish to rescue his only son quickly and, without disgust, descended into the pit of filth and pulled out his only son.[28]

The *sūtra* goes on to explain that the pit of filth is the cycle of rebirth (*saṃsāra*). The only son is sentient beings. The mother and relatives are the *śrāvakas* and *pratyekabuddhas* who, though deeply moved by the plight of sentient beings, are unable to rescue them. The merchant or householder is the Bodhisattva who regards sentient beings as a father does his own child and who takes rebirth in the world in order to extirpate sentient beings from suffering.[29]

What distinguishes the Bodhisattva from the *śrāvaka* and *pratyekabuddha* is his great compassion (*mahākaruṇā*). The compassion of the followers of the Hīnayāna manifests itself only in their lamentation at the pitiful plight of sentient beings. The great compassion of the Bodhisattva motivates him to action on their behalf; it is essential at the outset of the path. As the *Akṣayamatinirdeśasūtra* says:

> Furthermore, venerable Śāriputra, the great compassion of Bodhisattvas is essential. Why? Because it is a prerequisite. Venerable Śāriputra, it is thus: the inhalation of breath is the prerequisite of the life force of a human. In the same way, the great compassion of a Bodhisattva is the prerequisite of the complete achievement of the Mahāyāna.[30]

Thus great compassion is praised again and again in the Mahāyāna *sūtras* as the key to the achievement of Buddhahood and the alleviation of the sorrows of the world. The *Dharmasaṃgītisūtra* says:

> Transcendent Victor (*Bhagavan*[31]), a Bodhisattva should not learn many doctrines. Transcendent Victor, if a Bodhisattva thoroughly upholds and thoroughly understands one doctrine, all the qualities of a Buddha are in the palm of his hand. What is the one doctrine? It is great compassion.[32]

The Mahāyāna thus drastically reduces the qualifications for becoming a Bodhisattva. The path is open to everyone, monks and laypersons alike. In contrast to the Hīnayāna *sūtras,* which counseled renunciation of life in the world as a necessary condition for becoming an Arhat,[33] we find important Mahāyāna *sūtras,* such as the *Ugraparipṛcchā,* extolling the virtues of the householder Bodhisattva. The most famous of the lay Bodhisattvas is, of course, Vimalakīrti, to whom Arhats such as Śāriputra and Bodhisattvas of the stature of Mañjuśrī came for instruction. Vimalakīrti was a householder, but a most unusual householder:

> He wore the white clothes of the layman, yet lived impeccably like a religious devotee. He lived at home, but remained aloof from the realm of desire, the realm of pure matter, and the immaterial realm. He had a son, a wife, and female attendants, yet always maintained continence. He appeared to be surrounded by servants, yet lived in solitude. He appeared to be adorned with ornaments, yet always was endowed with the auspicious signs and marks. He seemed to eat and drink, but always took nourishment from the taste of meditation. He made his appearance at the fields of sports and in the casinos, but his aim was always to mature those people who were attached to games and gambling. He visited the fashionable heterodox teachers, yet always kept unswerving loyalty to the Buddha. He understood the mundane and transcendental sciences and exoteric practices, yet always took pleasure in the delights of the Dharma. He mixed in all crowds, yet was respected as the foremost of all.[34]

Thus the Mahāyāna path was open to any and all who were capable of feeling the great compassion that motivates one to take on the sufferings of the world. In sharp contrast to the Hīnayāna, which said that there need be only one person who vows to achieve Buddhahood and undergo the long path in order to revive the teaching when it has disappeared from the world, the Mahāyāna seemed to say that the world needs as many Buddhas as possible and as quickly as possible, and thus it is right to set out on the long path to Buddhahood. It was the view of the Mahāyāna *sūtras* in general that ideally everyone should become a Bodhisattva, that this was the superior path. It was also the view of certain Mahāyāna *sūtras,* most notably the *Saddharmapuṇḍarīkasūtra* (the *Lotus Sūtra*), that everyone eventually would become a Bodhisattva, that there was, in reality, only one vehicle (*ekayāna*), the Buddha vehicle, and that the other paths that the Buddha had taught were only expedient devices to lead his disciples to the true path:

> O, Śāriputra!
> For the beings' sake, I,
> By resort to this parable,
> Preach the One Buddha Vehicle;
> All of you, if you can
> Believe and accept these words,
> Shall without exception
> Completely attain to the Buddha Path.[35]

There are many other philosophical and soteriological innovations of the Mahāyāna *sūtras* that cannot be considered here, doctrines such as the eternal nature of Buddhahood, the three bodies (*trikāya*) of the Buddha, and the Buddha nature (*tathāgatagarbha*) that abides in all beings. We also have not considered another type of Bodhisattva apart from those who, as sentient beings, feel deep empathy for others and strive to achieve Buddhahood for their sake. These are the so-called celestial Bodhisattvas, such as Avalokiteśvara, Mañjuśrī, and Vajrapāṇi, who are not considered to be historical but are instead physical manifestations of various qualities; Avalokiteśvara is, for example, said to be all the compassion of all the Buddhas appearing in the form of a Bodhisattva. These Bodhisattvas developed their own cults with the devotees ascribing salvific functions to them. The twenty-fifth chapter of the *Saddharmapuṇḍarīkasūtra* ends with a list of the various calamities from which one may be saved by invoking Avalokiteśvara. Indeed, it is Avalokiteśvara (especially in China as Kuan-yin) and Amitābha (who is a Buddha rather than a Bodhisattva) who provide the closest parallels in Buddhism to the intercessors in heaven of the Roman Catholic church. Despite this parallel, the celestial Bodhisattvas are not being considered here in the inquiry into the question of whether the Bodhisattva is a saint because the celestial Bodhisattvas, though they have hagiographies,[36] are not conceived as beings who struggled long to overcome the obstacles of mundane existence to reach their exalted position.

What concerns us here is, instead, the Bodhisattva who is set forth as the ideal of the Mahāyāna, the person who is unwilling to pursue his or her own salvation while others remain deluded by ignorance and beset by the afflictions (*kleśa*) that follow in its wake. The vow that such a person makes is set forth over and over again in the Mahāyāna *sūtras* but perhaps nowhere more powerfully than in one of the earlier *sūtras*,[37] the *Vajracchedikā,* where the vow articulates the apparent paradox of the compatibility of compassion for persons and the doctrine that persons do not ultimately exist. The Buddha says:

> Regarding this, Subhūti, one who has entered correctly into the Bodhisattva vehicle should create the aspiration, thinking: "As many [beings] as are included in the class of sentient beings—those born from an egg, born from a womb, born from heat and moisture, born spontaneously, with form, without form, with discrimination, without discrimination, with neither discrimination nor nondiscrimination—as many types of sentient beings are designated by the designation 'sentient being,' all of them will I lead to complete quiescence in the realm of the nirvana without remainder." Yet, although countless sentient beings have entered nirvana, there are no sentient beings whatsoever who have entered nirvana. Why? Subhūti, if a Bodhisattva discerns sentient beings, he is not to be called a Bodhisattva. Why? Subhūti, he who discerns a self, or discerns a sentient being, or a living being, or a person is not to be called a Bodhisattva.[38]

THE BODHISATTVA IN THE MAHĀYĀNA ŚĀSTRAS

In *The Structure of Scientific Revolutions,* Kuhn asserts that the famous classics of science served to define the problems and methods of a field of research for generations because of two essential characteristics:

> Their achievement was sufficiently unprecedented to attract an enduring group of adherents away from competing modes of scientific activity. Simultaneously, it was sufficiently open-ended to leave all sorts of problems for the redefined group of practitioners.[39]

The achievement that Kuhn perceives in such works as Aristotle's *Physica* and Lyell's *Geology* can also be ascribed to the major Mahāyāna *sūtras*. They certainly won the allegiance of a wide group away from the Hīnayāna perspective.[40] At the same time, their expositions were sufficiently varied and, at times, contradictory to require tomes of commentary. The commentaries themselves were by no means monolithic, although they intended to be consistent within the various schools and subschools of the Mahāyāna. For our purposes it is useful to concentrate attention on the delineations of the Bodhisattva path composed in the last centuries of the Mahāyāna in India, notably those found in the works of Śāntideva, Kamalaśīla, Haribhadra, and Atīśa. Their works are particularly helpful for two reasons. First, they were written after the important Mahāyāna *sūtras* and thus represent doctrinal positions that take account of the range of viewpoints represented in those texts. Second—and this is particularly true of Kamalaśīla and Haribhadra, who were proponents of the Yogācāra-Svātantrika-Mādhyamika school—their writings represent the last synthesis of Mahāyāna thought in India, integrating the positions of the Yogācāra and Mādhyamika schools into a single system of practice.

Before turning to their works, it is important to say something about the men themselves. In comparing the Roman Catholic and Mahāyāna traditions on the problem of sainthood, it is notable that Buddhism lacks a genre of literature directly parallel to the "lives of the saints." There are the *Jātaka Tales,* but these represent didactic accounts of diverse origin which purport to provide details of the past lives of the Buddha, the historical documentation of which is difficult, to say the least. The protagonists of the Mahāyāna *sūtras* are rarely fully developed characters, functioning mainly as interlocutors with the Buddha. Even those whose stories are told in some detail, such as Vimalakīrti and Sadāprarudita, tend to be of a character more literary than historical. In the case of the Christian saint, although there are often layers of legend that encrust the biography, there is usually some historical person to be discovered within.[41] This is seldom the case with the great Bodhisattvas of the Mahāyāna *sūtras*. The extent to which historical validity or the lack of same is important in the case of the Mahāyāna Bodhisattva is another question.[42]

If the Mahāyāna has a genre of literature concerning the lives of the saints, it is to be found in the biographies of the savants, the "doctors of the Church." It is significant to note that the Mahāyāna tradition considers the *paṇḍitas,* who in their works delineated the path of the Bodhisattva, to have themselves been Bodhisattvas. Their stories are collected in the Tibetan histories of Indian Buddhism, where often, as in the case with Nāgārjuna and Asaṅga, the author will close his account with a statement of what level of the Bodhisattva path the master achieved.[43] These biographies are filled with miraculous events—Candrakīrti milks a picture of a cow to feed the monks, Śāntideva rises into the sky as he recites the *Bodhicaryāvatāra,* Candragomin receives instruction from a statue of Avalokiteśvara—and, indeed, they seem to fulfill Delehaye's definition of hagiography.[44] Still, as is often the case with the magical in the *sūtras,* the miraculous deeds seem commonplace, even secondary, with the biographer/hagiographer choosing to concentrate more on the master's philosophical lineage, the works he wrote, and how he defeated non-Buddhist logicians in debate. Thus the lives of historical Bodhisattvas for the Mahāyāna are the lives of those who explained how one becomes a Bodhisattva and, having done so, how one follows the long path to Buddhahood, the implication being that the path they described was one they had followed themselves.

One becomes a Bodhisattva through developing the aspiration to enlightenment (*bodhicitta*). The content of this aspiration was expressed by Asaṅga in his *Bodhisattvabhūmi*:

> May I become completely purified into unsurpassed, perfect, complete enlightenment. May I achieve the welfare of all sentient beings and establish them in final nirvana and the wisdom of the Tathāgatha.[45]

As the inspiration for the entire Bodhisattva path, *bodhicitta* receives abundant praise. Śāntideva says in his *Bodhicaryāvatāra*:

> Those who wish to destroy hundreds of sufferings in
> mundane existence,
> And those who wish to clear away the unhappiness of
> sentient beings,
> And those who wish to experience hundreds of joys
> Should never forsake the aspiration to enlightenment.
>
> All other virtues are like a plaintain tree;
> They produce fruit and then they die.
> The tree of the aspiration to enlightenment bears
> fruit eternally;
> It continues to grow unceasingly.[46]

This aspiration to enlightenment, however, is not said to arise spontaneously; the tree described by Śāntideva requires a seed and that seed is said to be compassion. Candrakīrti says in his *Madhyamakāvatāra:*

> Just mercy is held to be like the seed of this
> marvelous harvest of the Conqueror,
> Like water for growth,
> Like ripening to a state of long enjoyment.
> Therefore, at the beginning I praise compassion.[47]

Everyone should become a Bodhisattva; therefore everyone should feel this compassion which inspires one to seek Buddhahood for the welfare of others. Yet this compassion is not something with which all are naturally endowed. To remedy this the authors of the *śāstras* formulated arguments as to why one must feel compassion for others and why one must take on the responsibility of freeing them from suffering. Later Tibetan commentators, such as Tsong-kha-pa (1357–1419), identified two techniques for the generation of compassion and the aspiration to Buddhahood, one set forth by Śāntideva in the *Bodhicaryāvatāra,* the other traced to Atīśa in his *Bodhipathapradīpa* but which relies heavily on arguments presented by Kamalaśīla in his first two *Bhāvanākrama.* As each technique provides a somewhat different perspective on the motivation of the Bodhisattva, both deserve consideration here.

Śāntideva's method is called the equalizing of self and other (*parātmasamatā*) and the exchange of self and other (*parātmaparivartana*) and is delineated in the eighth chapter of the *Bodhicaryāvatāra.* The reason why self and other are equal is rather straightforward (VII:95–96):

> When both myself and others
> Are alike in wishing for happiness,
> What is special about me?
> Why do I strive for happiness for myself alone?
>
> When both myself and others
> Are alike in not wishing suffering,
> What is special about me?
> Why do I protect myself and not others?[48]

That is, all beings are equal in wanting happiness and not wanting suffering. Once it has been understood that self and other are essentially equal, one must set about the more difficult task of exchanging self and other. By this Śāntideva means that the cherishing attitude that one has felt for oneself for so long should be directed to and felt for others and that the neglectful attitude felt so long for others should be directed to oneself. Śāntideva's argument for altruism is based, at least in part, on self-interest (VII:120, 129–130):

> Whoever wishes to protect quickly
> Oneself and others
> Should practice the most excellent of secrets:
> The exchange of self and other.
>
> Whatever happiness there is in the world
> All arises from the wish for others' happiness.
> Whatever suffering there is in the world,
> All arises from the wish for one's own happiness.
>
> What need is there to say more?
> The childish act for their own welfare.
> The Subduer (*muni*) acts for the welfare of others.
> Look at the difference between the two!

Śāntideva's rather bold assertion that all happiness arises from the attitude of cherishing others is firmly rooted in the doctrine of karma, for deeds motivated by the wish to avoiding harming others—deeds such as sustaining life, giving, and speaking truthfully—are virtues that serve as causes for the future happiness of their agent. Deeds motivated by self-interest, such as killing, stealing, and lying, serve as the causes of future suffering. With this in mind, then, it is in one's best interests to cherish others, as Śāntideva states so succinctly in the third stanza of the foregoing quotation: Childish beings (*bāla*) are common worldly beings in the cycle of rebirth (*saṃsāra*). Their activities are motivated by a concern for their own welfare, the self-cherishing attitude. Consequently they continue to cycle in the realms of suffering. Although they seek happiness, their motivation has proved grossly counterproductive; not only have they not found the happiness they so desperately seek, they have continued to encounter suffering in birth after birth.

The Buddha, in contrast, is utterly free from the fetters of rebirth, is omniscient, and constantly enjoys the bliss of highest enlightenment. He was once a childish being himself. But at some point long ago he decided to cherish others rather than himself. As Śāntideva says, "Look at the difference between the two!" For him, the essential difference between an ordinary sentient being bound in cyclic existence and a Buddha is that a Buddha made the decision to give up the self-cherishing attitude and cherish others instead and has reaped the rewards of that decision. Śāntideva thus openly acknowledges that by seeking the welfare of others, the Bodhisattva guarantees his own welfare in a manner infinitely more effective than if he merely sought happiness for himself; self-cherishing benefits neither self nor other, whereas cherishing others benefits both. The exchange of self and other is, then, "the most excellent of secrets" because it serves as the cause for Buddhahood, which offers protection to both oneself and others.

Śāntideva's identification of the difference between a common being and a Buddha also points out a significant difference between the saint in the Roman Catholic tradition and the Bodhisattva, that of the means of sanctification. At least in the case of the martyr it is a single act, giving one's life in witness to faith in Christ, that ensured sainthood and the power to intercede after death. Although single deeds do indeed have power in Buddhism,[49] the path of the Bodhisattva comprises a vast collection of deeds—of body, speech, and mind—which serves as the means of taking one from the ordinary state of helplessness to oneself and others to the state of ultimate benefit, Buddhahood. The path is based upon a commitment to work for the welfare of others and a dedication to that commitment over many, many lifetimes. If the Bodhisattva is a saint, it is this constant commitment on all occasions that sanctifies him.

The second method for generating compassion for all sentient beings is one that is based on a sense of obligation and connection to all sentient beings and is set forth in Atīśa's *Bodhipathapradīpa* and Kamalaśīla's second *Bhāvanākrama*; Kamalaśīla's is the more detailed exposition. He argues that meditation on compassion must begin by engendering a feeling of equanimity toward all beings, recognizing that all equally want happiness and do not want suffering. He goes on to say that there is not a single being in the universe who has not been one's own friend hundreds of times in the past.[50] Atīśa makes the recognition that all sentient beings have been one's mother in the past, the starting point for the development of compassion. He writes:

> From the knowledge [that all sentient beings have been one's] mother arises the thought to repay [their] kindness; that is love. From the mind of love arises the mind of compassion. From the mind of compassion arises the aspiration to enlightenment.[51]

Based on the belief that the cycle of rebirth is beginningless, the conclusion is often drawn in Buddhist literature that everyone has, over the course of many lifetimes, been in every possible relationship to everyone else. From among all those relationships—friend, enemy, master, servant, teacher, student—Atīśa chooses the relationship of mother and child, perhaps because from among all the relationships it is the most universal, perhaps because the mother is the first "other" such that the relationship with her provides the basis for all future relationships, perhaps because the bond between mother and child is stronger than all others. To recognize that all sentient beings have at some time in the past been one's mother is to establish that strongest of bonds with each of them. Remembering their kindness, one feels a responsibility to repay that kindness and feels love for them. Love, according to Kamalaśīla, is the wish that others be happy. Having developed the feeling of love equally for all sentient beings, one should meditate on compassion, "the wish that all suffering sentient beings be free from that suffering."[52] Kamalaśīla counsels at this point that one contemplate the myriad sufferings that sentient beings undergo, the sufferings of beings in the hells and the sufferings of hungry ghosts (*preta*):

> Humans also seem to undergo limitless sufferings, such as lacking what they wish for and thus vying with and hurting one another, being separated from the beautiful, encountering the ugly, and becoming poor. The minds of some are entwined by a variety of snares due to the afflictions (*kleśa*) such as desire, and some are disturbed by a variety of wrong views. Because all of these are causes of suffering, [humans] are very miserable, like one standing at the edge of an abyss. . . . Therefore, one should view all transmigrators as being in the midst of a conflagration of suffering; one should think, "Just as I do not want suffering, so also are all others." One should at all times—in meditation and in all activities—cultivate the compassion for all sentient beings which makes [the sufferings of others] like one's own sufferings and wishes that they be free from them, [thinking,] "Alas, if these sentient beings who are so pleasing to me are suffering, how will I liberate them from that suffering?"[53]

The commitment to those beings who have been one's mother in the past is so great that one concludes that one must free all sentient beings from suffering; liberation is seen as the only suitable recompense for the kindness offered by these beings now tortured by the various sufferings of the world. As Bhāvaviveka (c. 500–570), founder of the Svātantrika school, wrote,

> What aid is there other than nirvana
> [To be given] in return to those
> Who, in other lifetimes,
> Helped me with love and respect.[54]

Having concluded that the best way to rescue these beings for whom one feels love and compassion is personally to lead them to nirvana, one realizes that the most effective way to accomplish this is to become a Buddha oneself. This realization is called the generation of the aspiration to enlightenment (*bodhicittotpāda*). It is defined in the *Abhisamayālaṃkāra*:

> The generation of the aspiration is the wish
> For perfect, complete enlightenment for
> others' welfare.[55]

The aspiration to enlightenment, then, has two objects: the welfare of others and one's own enlightenment, the latter being the means of achieving the former. It is this aspiration which makes one a Bodhisattva and marks the beginning of the long path to Buddhahood. This aspiration to enlightenment is highly praised in the Mahāyāna *śāstras*. The *Abhisamayālaṃkāra* (I:19–20) and *Mahāyānasūtrālaṃkāra* (IV:15–20) provide a list of twenty-two similes. It is like the earth because it is the basis of all auspicious qualities; it is like gold because it does not change until enlightenment; it is like the waxing moon because it increases all virtuous qualities; and so on.[56] Śāntideva says of it (III:30):

> It is the supreme medicine that
> Quells the sickness of transmigrators.
> It is the tree where transmigrators rest,
> Wandering and fatigued on the road of mundane
> existence.

Nāgārjuna says in his *Bodhicittavivaraṇa*:

> Thus far the Buddhas have seen
> No other means in the world
> For the achievement of one's own and others' welfare
> Than the aspiration to enlightenment.[57]

The wish to achieve Buddhahood for the sake of others, significant as it is, is not sufficient. Thus two types of the aspiration are distinguished: the wishful aspiration to enlightenment (*bodhipraṇidhicitta*) and the practical aspiration to enlightenment (*bodhiprasthānacitta*), which are compared to the wish to go someplace and actually setting out on the journey;[58] the wishful aspiration to enlightenment is the heartfelt wish: "May I become a Buddha in order to benefit all sentient beings."[59] The nature of that benefit is specified by Haribhadra in his version of the wishful aspiration: "Having become a complete and perfect Buddha, may I strive to teach the doctrine of the three vehicles for the welfare of others in accordance with [their] abilities."[60] Haribhadra thus emphasizes that the greatest benefit that a Buddha can bestow and the ability that a Bodhisattva seeks is that of teaching the path to freedom.

The practical mind of enlightenment begins with taking a formal vow to achieve Buddhahood for the sake of others,[61] after which the Bodhisattva begins the practices that will eventually fructify in his achievement of Buddhahood. Those practices, according to the Kamalaśīla,[62] are the six perfections (*pāramitā*), consisting of giving (*dāna*), ethics (*śīla*), patience (*kṣānti*), effort (*vīrya*), concentration (*dhyāna*), and wisdom (*prajñā*); the four immeasurables, consisting of equanimity (*upekṣā*), love (*maitrī*), compassion (*karuṇā*), and joy (*muditā*); and the four means of gathering students (*saṃgrahavastu*), consisting of giving gifts (*dāna*), speaking pleasantly (*priyavāditā*), teaching others to fulfill their aims (*arthacaryā*), and acting in accordance with one's own teaching (*samānārthatā*).[63]

Among these three sets of practices, the six perfections receive the most attention in the Mahāyāna *śāstras,* as they will here. The practice of the perfections is the means by which the Bodhisattva amasses the two collections: the collection of merit (*puṇyasaṃbhāra*) and the collection of wisdom (*jñānasaṃbhāra*), both of which are essential for the achievement of Buddhahood. Nāgārjuna says in his *Ratnāvalī*:

Thus, these two collections cause
Buddhahood to be attained.
So, in brief, always rely
On merit and wisdom.[64]

Within the range of opinion as to which of the perfections contributes to the collection of merit and which to the collection of wisdom, Kamalaśīla includes the first five perfections in the category of merit or method (*upāya*) and the sixth, wisdom, in the collection of wisdom.[65] He also cites the *Sarvadharmasaṃgrahasūtra* to the effect that each of the six perfections is practiced by the Bodhisattva for sixty aeons.[66] Elsewhere, in the *Abhisamayālaṃkāra,* it is explained that the Bodhisattva practices six types of each of the perfections. That is, he practices the giving of giving, the giving of ethics, the giving of patience, and so on, totaling thirty-six combinations.[67] The six perfections are thus what the Bodhisattva does to fulfill his promise to achieve enlightenment for the sake of others. They are the Bodhisattva deeds (*bodhisattvacaryā*).

In his *Madhyamakāvatāra,* Candrakīrti says that *pāramitā* (the word usually translated as "perfection") means "gone beyond," with the beyond referring to the far shore or the port in the ocean of cyclic existence—that is, Buddhahood—which is the state of having utterly abandoned all obstructions (*āvaraṇa*). Although that which goes beyond is specifically wisdom, virtues such as giving are called "perfections" when they are qualified by the dedication to go beyond to the state of Buddhahood.[68]

The perfection of giving (*dānapāramitā*) is the Bodhisattva's willingness to give away everything he possesses without regret. Śāntideva says (V:10):

The perfection of giving
Is said to be the thought to give
All beings all possessions and effects.
Therefore, it is an intention.

Despite this assertion that the perfection of giving is an intention or willingness to give away everything, it is not seen to be merely intentional; elsewhere Śāntideva promises to give up his body, his resources, and all his virtue collected in the past, present, and future in order to benefit all beings.[69] Sentient beings are the recipients of the Bodhisattva's giving.

Of the perfection of ethics (*śīlapāramitā*) Śāntideva says (V:11):

The killing of [such beings] as fish
Has not been abolished anywhere.
The perfection of ethics
Is the achievement of the wish to abandon
[such killing].

His point is not that the ethics of the Bodhisattva is merely a wish that need not be put into practice but, rather, that it should not be concluded that the Buddhas of the past did not perfect ethics based on the fact that unethical activities still take place, just as it should not be concluded that the Buddhas did not perfect giving because beggars still abound. The perfection of giving or ethics means the complete cultivation of the willingness to give or to act morally.

The ethics of the Bodhisattva encompasses a wide range of attitudes and activities; essentially he should not do anything that is not for the benefit of others.[70] The Bodhisattva should abstain from the ten nonvirtuous activities (*ākuśalāḥ karmapatāḥ*) of killing, stealing, sexual misconduct, lying, divisive speech, harsh speech, senseless speech, covetousness, harmful intent, and wrong view.[71] He should maintain a certain decorum in his activities, described at some length by Śāntideva in the fifth chapter of his *Bodhicaryāvatāra,* and should keep the Bodhisattva vows (*saṃvara*). The latter involve a long list of infractions to be avoided, set forth in the *Bodhisattvapratimokṣa,*[72] the most serious of which are praising oneself and belittling others, not giving one's wealth or the teaching to others, not accepting an apology, and abandoning the Mahāyāna. Although Śāntideva does not consider the Bodhisattva vows explicitly, he does speak of the gravest sin of the Bodhisattva, forsaking the aspiration to enlightenment (IV:8):

For the Bodhisattva
That is the heaviest of infractions.
If that should happen,
The welfare of all sentient beings suffers.

The perfection of ethics does not, however, consist entirely in keeping vows and avoiding nonvirtue. In the chapter on ethics in his *Bodhi-*

sattvabhūmi, Asaṅga provides a lengthy discussion of the Bodhisattva's services to others, services reminiscent of labors of charity for the needy and the sick performed by some of the medieval saints:

> Furthermore, the Bodhisattva attends the suffering. He nurses sentient beings beset by sickness. He leads the blind and shows them the way. He causes the deaf to understand using sign language by teaching them symbols for words. Those without arms or legs he carries himself or transports them by conveyance. . . .
>
> Furthermore, the Bodhisattva protects fearful sentient beings from fear. He protects sentient beings from fear of being harmed by beasts of prey. He protects them from fear of whirlpools and sea monsters, from fear of kings, from fear of robbers and thieves, from fear of foreign enemies, from fear of masters and lords, from fear of being without livelihood, from fear of insult, from fear of being timid in public, from fear of non-humans, and from fear of vampires. . . .
>
> Furthermore, the Bodhisattva takes away the grief of sentient beings who have suffered misfortune, beginning with misfortunes involving relatives and friends. That is, he takes away the grief at the death of parents. He takes away the grief at the death of a child or spouse, a male or female servant, an assistant or employee. [He takes away the grief upon] the death of a friend, a confidant, a kinsman, or a relative. [He takes away the grief at] the death of such people as masters, abbots, and teachers. . . .
>
> Furthermore, the Bodhisattva provides necessities for those who want necessities. He gives food to those who want food. He gives drink to those who want drink, transportation to those who want transportation, clothing to those who want clothing, ornaments to those who want ornaments, vessels to those who want vessels, perfumes, flower garlands, and creams to those who want perfumes, flower garlands, and creams, a place to stay for those who need a place to stay, and light for those who need light.[73]

The Bodhisattva is portrayed here as a cosmic social worker, not merely seeking the ultimate spiritual welfare of sentient beings but providing for their most immediate, existential needs as well.

The third perfection, that of patience, involves the willingness to endure hardship for the sake of the goal the Bodhisattva has set for himself. It also entails not responding to others in anger. The *locus classicus* for the treatment of the latter is found in the sixth chapter of the *Bodhicaryāvatāra,* where Śāntideva provides an intricate argument for patience and against anger, beginning with the assertion that the virtue amassed over a thousand aeons is destroyed by a moment of anger.[74] The rest of his argument is not quite so blunt; unfortunately his case for patience cannot be unfolded fully here. Near the end of the chapter he claims that not only should the angry person be forborne, he should be welcomed (VI:107–108):

> Therefore, like a treasure, effortlessly gained,
> Appearing in my house,
> The enemy should delight me
> Because he aids in the practice of enlightenment.
>
> Since I can practice on him,
> It is fitting that the fruit of patience
> Be given first to him;
> In this way, he is the cause of patience.

That is, the cultivation of patience by the Bodhisattva is contingent on his having enemies; if there is no one who is angry with him, it is impossible for him to practice patience.

This raises the important question of the relationship between the Bodhisattva and sentient beings. The Bodhisattva undertakes the long path to enlightenment out of compassion for their sufferings. He is seeking Buddhahood in order to place himself in the optimal position from which to bring about their happiness. Their ultimate welfare is his final goal. But over his long path to enlightenment, the Bodhisattva and sentient beings share a strangely symbiotic relationship. At least in the case of the "social" perfections of giving, ethics, and patience, sentient beings derive a dual benefit for the Bodhisattva, a long-term and short-term gain. Sentient beings will derive ultimate benefit when the Bodhisattva becomes a Buddha and teaches them the *dharma* as only a Buddha can. Meanwhile they are also the objects of the Bodhisattva's practice of the perfections; he gives them gifts, he nurses them to health, he responds to their acrimony with patience. Yet the sentient beings for whom the Bodhisattva is ultimately seeking Buddhahood are essential to him if he is to achieve his goal; he must rely on them to win enlightenment, for they are both for whom and through whom he achieves Buddhahood. Without them to serve as the objects of his giving, ethics, and patience, he cannot attain enlightenment for their sake. This point is not lost on Śāntideva (VI:113):

The qualities of a Buddha
Are gained from sentient beings and the Conquerors
alike.
Why do I not respect sentient beings
As I do the Conquerors?[75]

The importance of effort, the fourth perfection, is obvious. Śāntideva defines it as finding delight in virtue, adding that merit does not occur without it.[76] The perfection of concentration (*dhyānapāramitā*) involves the Bodhisattva's development of meditative stability (*samādhi*) by which he acquires the mental strength needed to penetrate beyond deceptive appearances and discern reality.[77]

If the perfection of concentration is the strong arm that wields the sword that cuts through the webs of ignorance, then the perfection of wisdom (*prajñāpāramitā*) is that sword. The perfection of wisdom is the Bodhisattva's understanding of the insubstantiality, the essencelessness, the selflessness (*nairātmya*) of persons and all other phenomena, the lack of inherent existence (*svabhāva*), the emptiness (*śūnyatā*) that, variously interpreted, is the nature of reality and the final mode of being for Mahāyāna Buddhism. It is a topic too profound to be treated adequately here. The essential point for our purposes is that the perfection of wisdom is essential for the achievement of Buddhahood. Speaking of all the practices he has discussed in the first eight chapters of the *Bodhicaryāvatāra,* Śāntideva begins the ninth chapter by saying (IX:1):

All of these branches
Were set forth by the Subduer for the sake of wisdom.
Therefore, those who wish to pacify sufferings
Should generate wisdom.

It is wisdom that cuts the root of suffering and ignorance and makes liberation possible. Without it the other perfections would serve merely as the causes of better rebirths for the Bodhisattva. Thus the Bodhisattva is counseled to practice the supramundane perfections[78] in which the virtuous practices are infused with wisdom. Candrakīrti says in his *Madhyamakāvatāra*:

Giving void of giver, gift, and recipient
Is called a supramundane perfection.

When attachment to these three is produced,
It is called a mundane perfection.[79]

That is, the Bodhisattva should practice giving without conceiving the gift, the giver, or the recipient to exist truly. In this way the understanding of emptiness is conjoined with the accumulation of merit. Candrakīrti makes similar statements concerning ethics and patience.

For the Bodhisattva method and wisdom are essential; Nāgārjuna calls them "the Bodhisattva's parents" because they produce and sustain him, with method the father and wisdom the mother.[80] The Bodhisattva must perfect those qualities associated with the heart and those associated with the head, must perfect the emotional and the cognitive, in order to achieve enlightenment. There is a synergy between compassion and wisdom that results in the attainment of Buddhahood, an attainment that neither can effect independently. Kamalaśīla quotes the *Vimalakīrtinirdeśasūtra,* which says: "Method without wisdom and wisdom without method are the Bodhisattva's bondage. Wisdom with method and method with wisdom are freedom."[81]

If the Bodhisattva is to be considered a saint in the Roman Catholic sense, his practice of the six perfections functions as his heroic virtue, a quality necessary for beatification and canonization. The nature of heroic virtue was delineated in the eighteenth century by Prospero Lambertini (who later became Pope Benedict XIV). Heroic virtues are the three theological virtues of faith, hope, and charity and the four cardinal virtues of prudence, justice, courage, and temperance practiced to a degree that exceeds the ordinary. The heroic degree is called the perfection of virtue. It does not differ in kind from ordinary virtue except in its excellence and intensity. For canonization, instances of heroic virtue must be numerous and there must be heroicity in a variety of virtues; the assumption is that the person who has one heroic virtue will have them all. The candidate for canonization must also have lived for an extended period in the state of heroic virtue.[82]

The parallels to the perfections are obvious. Ordinary virtues are perfected by the Bodhisattva through his performance of them as a means of achieving Buddhahood for the welfare of others. Because the Bodhisattva must practice all the perfections over thousands of aeons, the other qualifications are met. The significant difference lies in Lambertini's statement that heroic virtues do not differ in kind from ordinary virtues. It might be argued that this is true in the case of the mundane perfections, but it is clearly not true in the case of the supramundane perfections, conjoined with the wisdom of emptiness, which Candrakīrti describes. Furthermore according to Lambertini, the attainment of a heroic degree of the supernatural virtues was impossible without the aid of grace, and the attainment of even the natural virtues rarely occurred, if ever, without grace. This is obviously not true of the perfections, for Buddhism is a religion without a creator deity and thus without a doctrine of grace. Nonetheless an element of sanctification is infused into the virtues of giving, ethics, patience, effort, concentration, and wisdom from within by the Bodhisattva's compassionate aspiration to enlightenment, without which the practice of the perfections is impossible. Speaking of the Bodhisattva, Śāntarakṣita says in his *Madhyamakālaṃkāra*:

> Having first sought knowledge of reality,
> They ascertain the ultimate well
> And, having fully engendered compassion
> For the world lost in the darkness of wrong views,
>
> The wise, with minds directed toward enlightenment,
> Heroic in accomplishing the purposes of transmigrators,
> Train fully in the discipline of the Subduer,
> Adorned with wisdom and compassion.[83]

The Bodhisattva progresses to Buddhahood through five paths (*mārga*) and ten grounds (*bhūmi*). With his development of the wish to achieve Buddhahood for the sake of others, he has what is called the conventional mind of enlightenment[84] and begins the first of the five paths, the path of accumulation (*saṃbhāramārga*), so called because here he formally undertakes the accumulation of the merit and wisdom needed for the achievement of Buddhahood.[85] From here the Bodhisattva, still with the conventional aspiration to enlightenment, moves to the path of preparation (*prayogamārga*), where he prepares for the nonconceptual understanding of emptiness that will come with the next path. Here he passes through four levels[86] of increasing insight into the nature of reality until he comes to see emptiness directly with uncontaminated nonconceptual wisdom (*anāsravanirvikalpakajñāna*). This initial direct realization of emptiness marks (1) his attainment of the path of seeing (*darśanamārga*), (2) his attainment of the ultimate aspiration to enlightenment (*paramārthabodhicitta*), (3) his passage from the state of a common being (*pṛthagjana*) to that of a superior (*āryan*), and (4) his attainment of the first of the ten Bodhisattva grounds.[87] From this point on he will never be powerlessly reborn as an animal, hungry ghost (*preta*), or hell being again. Candrakīrti says in his *Madhyamakāvatāra*:

> He moves from ground to ground and ascends.
> At that time, all his paths to the bad realms end.
> At that time, all levels of common beings cease.[88]

The levels of the Bodhisattva path are called grounds because they provide the basis for an increasing number of marvelous qualities. Candrakīrti says:

> When the uncontaminated wisdom of Bodhisattvas, affected by compassion and so forth, is divided into parts, they receive the name "grounds" because of serving as the bases for good qualities.[89]

There is a considerable variety in the presentations of the grounds in the Mahāyāna *sūtras* and *śāstras*. Here we will follow that in the *Madhyamakāvatāra* by Candrakīrti, who bases his discussion on the *Daśabhūmikasūtra* and a brief treatment of the topic by Nāgārjuna in his *Ratnāvalī*.[90] Kamalaśīla's exposition in the first *Bhāvanākrama* does not differ significantly from that of Candrakīrti.[91]

The first ground is called the Joyous (*pramuditā*) because the Bodhisattva rejoices at having seen reality for the first time[92] or because he feels great joy seeing that he is close to enlightenment, whence he can achieve the aims of sentient beings.[93] On this ground he emphasizes the practice of the perfection of giving, although Kamalaśīla notes that it should not be inferred that the other perfections are ignored; all the perfections are practiced on all the grounds. Although the Bodhisattva has understood reality on this ground, as long as he is not aware of subtle ethical transgressions, he remains on the first ground.[94]

The remaining nine grounds occur on the fourth of the five paths, the path of meditation (*bhāvanāmārga*). The second ground is called the Stainless (*vimalā*) because there the Bodhisattva practices very pure ethics such that he is unstained by faulty behavior even in his dreams. He performs the ten virtues purified of the taints of the conception of self.[95] He remains on the second ground as long as he is unable to enter into all the worldly meditative states (*samādhi*) and as long as he is unable to remember the meaning of everything he has heard.[96]

The third ground is called the Luminous (*prabhākarī*). The light of his supramundane wisdom burns bright because of his attainment of the concentrations (*dhyāna*) and superknowledges (*abhijñā*).[97] He practices a superior form of the perfection of patience such that even if someone were to mutilate his body out of anger, he would respond with patience.[98] He remains on this ground as long as he cannot abide repeatedly in the qualities of the thirty-seven harmonies with enlightenment (*bodhipakṣa*).[99]

The fourth ground is called the Radiant (*arciṣmatī*) because here effort flames forth, surpassing the light of the prior stage, a result of the Bodhisattva's practice of the harmonies. He does not pass on to the next ground as long as he is unable to cultivate the harmonies to enlightenment in conjunction with method—that is, as long as he cannot meditate on the four truths while turning his mind away from cyclic existence and nirvana.[100]

The fifth ground is the Difficult to Overcome (*sudurjayā*) because demons find it impossible to conquer him. He practices the perfection of concentration and comes to understand the subtle nature of the four truths. As long as he cannot enter meditative equipoise (*samāhita*) on signlessness (*animitta*) because his mind is distressed by analyzing cyclic existence, he remains on this ground.[101]

The sixth is called the Approaching (*abhimukhī*). Through his practice of the perfection of wisdom and his understanding of dependent arising (*pratītyasamutpāda*), he approaches the qualities of a Buddha. He remains here as long as he cannot remain in meditative equipoise on signlessness uninterruptedly.[102] The famous six perfections having been exhausted on the first six grounds, the *Daśabhūmikasūtra* adds four more for the remaining grounds.

On the seventh ground, the Gone Afar (*dūraṃgamā*), the Bodhisattva practices the perfection of skillful means (*upāyakauśala*); he concentrates especially on the various techniques whereby he can best aid others to liberation. Although he realizes the signlessness of all signs, he does not negate the conventions that create signs, thus affirming the conventional nature of phenomena. The Bodhisattva has proceeded a long distance in order to reach the path of spontaneity whereby he can abide in the signless without effort. He remains on the seventh ground until he is able to do so.[103] According to Candrakīrti, on this ground the Bodhisattva can, in each moment, both enter into and rise from the absorption of cessation in which all elaborations (*prapañca*) cease.[104] It is the position of Candrakīrti that at the end of the seventh ground, the Bodhisattva achieves liberation from rebirth, having destroyed the afflictive obstructions (*kleśāvaraṇa*). He thus has completed the impure grounds—the first seven—which are tainted with the conception of self (*ātmagraha*)—and proceeds to the pure grounds, where he will work to overcome the obstructions to omniscience (*jñeyāvaraṇa*) that prevent the attainment of Buddhahood.[105]

The eighth ground is called the Immovable (*acalā*) because the Bodhisattva is unshakable in his nonconceptual understanding of the signless reality.[106] Here he practices the perfection of aspiration (*praṇidhānapāramitā*) because the thousands of aspirations made over the long course of the path are purified.[107] He remains on the eighth ground as long as he is unable to teach the doctrine in all its aspects.[108]

The ninth ground is called Good Intelligence (*sādhumatī*) for here the Bodhisattva has a special understanding of the doctrine, which allows him to teach unerringly. This special understanding comes from his attainment of four individual knowledges (*pratisaṃvid*). By means of the individual knowledge of phenomena (*dharmapratisaṃvid*) he gains a thorough knowledge of the specific characteristics of all phenomena. By means of the individual knowledge of meanings (*arthapartisaṃvid*) he gains a thorough knowledge of the categories of all phenomena. Through the individual knowledge of etymology (*niruktipratisaṃvid*) he knows how to teach without confusing doctrines. With the courageous individual knowledge (*pratibhānapratisaṃvid*) he is constantly aware of the causes contributing to the doctrine.[109] He practices the perfection of strength (*balapāramitā*). He remains on this ground as long as he is unable to display the land, retinue, and emanations of a Buddha, make full use of the qualities of a Buddha, and bring sentient beings to spiritual maturity.[110]

The tenth and final ground is called the Cloud of Doctrine (*dharmameghā*). Just as rain falls from a cloud, the excellent doctrine falls spontaneously from the Bodhisattva for the sake of increasing the harvest of virtue of transmigrators.[111] Here he practices the perfection of exalted wisdom (*jñānapāramitā*), whereby he is possessed of a special skill to ripen the minds of sentient beings.[112] When he has utterly eradicated the most subtle of the obstructions to omniscience, he gains an unimpeded understanding of all objects of knowledge.[113] Simultaneously he achieves Buddhahood, sometimes called the eleventh ground. This is the attainment of the fifth and final path, the path of no more learning (*aśaikṣamārga*), the culmination of a journey lasting three innumerable aeons (*asaṃkhyeyakalpa*).[114]

As the Bodhisattva ascends through the ten grounds, he acquires extraordinary powers, which are described by Candrakīrti in the eleventh chapter of his *Madhyamakāvatāra,* the chapter on the qualities (*guṇa*) of the Bodhisattva. On the first ground the Bodhisattva can *in one instant:*

1. see one hundred Buddhas
2. be blessed by one hundred Buddhas and understand their blessings
3. live for one hundred aeons
4. see with wisdom the past and future in those one hundred aeons
5. enter into and rise from one hundred meditative states (*samādhi*)
6. vibrate one hundred worlds
7. illuminate one hundred worlds
8. bring one hundred sentient beings to spiritual maturity using emanations
9. go to one hundred pure Buddha lands
10. open one hundred doors of doctrine
11. display one hundred versions of his own body
12. surround each of those bodies with one hundred Bodhisattvas.[115]

The Bodhisattva on the first ground thus has twelve sets of each involving one hundred qualities—he can see one hundred Buddhas, live for one hundred aeons, and so on. On the second ground, the number becomes one thousand—he vibrates one thousand worlds, displays one thousand versions of his body, and so forth. On the third ground one hundred thousand; on the fourth, one billion; on the fifth, ten billion; on the sixth, one trillion; on the seventh, a million trillion; on the eighth, a number equal to the particles of a billion worlds; on the ninth, a number equal to the particles of ten million billion worlds; on the tenth, a number equal to the particles of an inexpressible number of Buddha lands.[116]

Not only does the Bodhisattva gain these incredible powers that multiply as he moves from ground to ground, but his virtue impels him to higher and higher rebirths, ascending from earth to heaven and from one heaven to the next in the Buddhist cosmos, reigning as monarch in each. For example, on the first ground he is born as the king ruling the continent of Jambudvīpa; on the second ground he is reborn as the king of the four continents; on the third ground, as king of the Heaven of the Thirty-three (*trāyastriṃasa*); on the fourth, as king of Heaven without Combat (*yāma*); until on the tenth ground he is born as the great lord of the Highest Land (*akaniṣṭha*).[117]

The *Abhisamayālaṃkāra* presents it own list of the virtues possessed by the Bodhisattva on each ground, virtues that, although considerably less grand than the powers described by Candrakīrti, are particularly suggestive of the concerns of the Bodhisattva in his progress to enlightenment. These are the purifiers (*parikarmaṇā*) by which each ground is attained. There is a total of ninety-five purifiers over the first nine grounds; ten for the first, eight for the second, five for the third, and so on. These purifiers, conjoined with the aspiration to enlightenment and the realization of selflessness, purify the defilements of each ground and bring about the fulfillment of the particular qualities of each ground. The purifiers are too numerous to list here; examining the purifiers of three grounds will suffice. The *Abhisamayālaṃkāra* says:

> The first ground is attained
> Through ten purifiers.
> Thought, actual benefit,
> Equality of mind toward sentient beings,
>
> Giving, relying on a spiritual guide,
> Striving for the objects of the excellent doctrine,
> A mind of constant renunciation,
> Wishing for and liking the bodies of a Buddha,
>
> Teaching the doctrine, and teaching the truth
> Are asserted to be the ten.
> These are known as purifiers
> Because they are not seen to inherently exist.[118]

There are eight purifiers on the second ground:

> Ethics, repayment, patience,
> Joy, great compassion,
> Reverence, listening respectfully to teachers,
> And making effort in [the perfections] such as
> giving are the eight.[119]

By the time of the eighth ground, the Bodhisattva acquires special powers akin to some of those described by Candrakīrti:

Knowing the minds of all sentient beings,
Enjoying the superknowledges,
Achieving an auspicious Buddha land,
Relying on the Buddhas through analysis.

Clairvoyance, purifying lands of Conquerors,
Abiding like an illusion,
And taking rebirth according to his wish,
These are the eight aspects.[120]

The Bodhisattva ascends from heaven to heaven in his rebirths as he traverses the paths, but unlike the saint, he does not remain in heaven. The seventh of the eight purifications of the eighth ground listed earlier is "taking rebirth according to his wish" (*saṃcintya ca bhavādānam*), which Haribhadra describes as taking birth intentionally upon observing the welfare of all sentient beings.[121] It will be recalled that with his attainment of the first ground, the Bodhisattva destroys all causes for powerless rebirth as an animal, hungry ghost, or hell being. With the achievement of the eighth ground he is utterly free from rebirth. Yet out of his compassion he voluntarily descends into the world in order to be of service to sentient beings. His virtue is such that he would ordinarily be reborn as one of the kings mentioned by Nāgārjuna (*Ratnāvalī,* 442–460), yet he continues to return willingly to the world. The *Mahāyānasūtrālaṃkāra* notes that this return to the world of suffering is not a cause of fear or pain for the Bodhisattva but is an occasion for delight. Through his understanding that all phenomena are like illusions created by a magician and through his commitment to the welfare of others, voluntary birth in the world is his favorite place to be; even the most torturous hell is delightful. For the Bodhisattva rebirth is like a walk in the park.[122]

The grounds are thus very much levels of sanctification. As the Bodhisattva progresses from one to the next his wisdom deepens, his virtues become vast and pure, his miraculous powers multiply. These culminate in his attainment of Buddhahood, the ultimate source of benefit to others. Just as, as a Bodhisattva, he did not remain in the heavens that he won through his virtue, so as a Buddha, he does not remain in the nirvana described by the Hīnayāna where mind and body cease and from which he would be inaccessible to the world of suffering sentient beings. Rather, he abides in a nirvana that is both imminent and transcendent, the nonabiding nirvana (*apratiṣṭhitanirvāṇa*). Nāgārjuna says in his *Bodhicittavivaraṇa*:

> The great beings abide neither
> In cyclic existence nor nirvana.
> Thus, the Buddhas have explained this to be
> The non-abiding nirvana.[123]

Because of his compassion, a Buddha does not fear the cycle of birth and death; he therefore does not dwell in nirvana. Because of his wisdom, his understanding of reality, a Buddha is untainted by faults endemic in the world; he therefore does not dwell in cyclic existence as others do, for he sees it as it is, as empty of any essence.[124]

The Bodhisattva who becomes a Buddha thus abides in the nonabiding nirvana, remaining outside the extremes of cyclic existence and solitary peace. He is in neither heaven nor hell and always in both, understanding that ultimately there is not the slightest difference between the two, while devoting himself for eternity to leading sentient beings out of one and into the other.

CONCLUSION

After all this, then, is the Bodhisattva a saint? In the official procedures for canonization in the Roman Catholic church, the three general requirements for sainthood are doctrinal purity, heroic virtue, and miraculous intercession after death.[125] In the Buddhist context the first two criteria can be met by the Bodhisattva with minor modification. The requirement of miraculous intercession after death is less easily fulfilled, primarily because of the centrality of the doctrine of rebirth in Buddhism. Death carries with it little of the finality that it does for the saint because the Bodhisattva practices for three periods of countless aeons in birth after birth. As he progresses on the path, his accrual of merit and wisdom eventually fructifies in his ability to perform deeds that would commonly be considered miraculous. It can thus be said that the Bodhisattva performs miracles, but these do not occur after his death for, in a sense, he never dies. Those miracles, furthermore, are not seen as proof of his final attainment of his goal; he can vibrate one hundred worlds while still on the first ground. Rather, the miracles of the Bodhisattva represent his increasing ability to benefit others, resulting from his practice of the perfections of giving, of ethics, of patience, of effort, of concentration, and of wisdom in aeon after aeon. It is only with the completion of the path that he is able to perform what for

Buddhism is the greatest miracle, teaching the *dharma* as only a Buddha can. As it says in a *sūtra*:

> Buddhas neither wash sins away with water, nor remove the sufferings of beings with their hands. They transfer not their realizations to others. Beings are freed through the teaching of the truth, the nature of things.[126]

Apart from the official criteria, which were established relatively late, certain qualities were traditionally held as proof of sanctity in Christendom, qualities such as supernatural grace, asceticism, good works, worldly power, and evangelical activity.[127] Certainly all of these can be found in some form or another along the Bodhisattva path. But can there be sainthood without God and divine grace? For the Catholic tradition, a saint

> is a member of the Roman Catholic Church who hearing and unconditionally responding to God's call has led a life of ever-increasing union and conformity with Christ through the practice of charity and of all other Christian virtues, and who, because of his virtuous life, confirmed by subsequent miracles, has been proclaimed by the infallible teaching authority of the Church as being a person particularly pleasing to God.[128]

God, then, is at the very center of what it means to be a saint. The saint responds to God's call, he performs the virtues demanded by God, and, finally, his sanctity is confirmed by God. After his death the saint lives eternally with God. There, "in the light of celestial glory, he understands with greater clarity the spiritual needs of those on earth, and with love inflamed by the beatific vision longs to see Him glorified by those still on the road to eternal happiness."[129]

For the Bodhisattva there is no such God. In his place are sentient beings. He hears and responds to their call for freedom from suffering and undertakes the practice of virtue with their welfare as his object. As a result of his meritorious actions, purified and enhanced by his knowledge of emptiness, he gains the miracle of Buddhahood. As a Buddha, he lives eternally, not with God but for others, understanding with greater clarity the spiritual needs of those in the world and showing them the road to eternal happiness. The Bodhisattva and the Buddha live in eternal devotion, not to God but to others. If to give oneself freely and utterly to others is to be the Christ, then perhaps the Bodhisattva is closer to the Christ than to the saint.

In the foreword to this book the editors have noted two basic traits of the saint—his exemplariness and his otherness—as a result of which the saint serves both as a model to be emulated and a distant ideal to be revered. The tension between these two qualities is a significant one; as they write in the foreword, "the simple pious may try to be like him but know that ultimately they will not succeed; they may worship him but know that he was once like they are." This tension is recognized and ostensibly diminished in the Mahāyāna by the portrayal of two different kinds of Bodhisattvas, the so-called celestial Bodhisattvas, who are mythic manifestations of particular qualities such as wisdom or compassion, and the common Bodhisattva, who traverses the path described in this chapter. The celestial Bodhisattvas embody the quality of "otherness"; they are not considered to have been sentient beings in the past and, for "the pious," function effectively as gods. The common Bodhisattva, however, is depicted, as we have seen, as an ordinary person who is moved by the sufferings of others, vows to free them from their sufferings, and sets out on a long path in order to gain the capacity to do so.

Yet even in the case of the common Bodhisattva, the tension between otherness and exemplariness is felt. The person who sets on this long path is rare; rarer still are those who reach its end. In the *Aṣṭasāhasrikāprajñāpāramitāsūtra*, the Buddha says:

> Subhūti, it is thus. For example, there are few places on the great earth where there are no stones, where gold, bdellium, and silver are found. There are many more places in the great earth filled with salt water and swamps, by grass and many trees and various thorns. In the same way, Subhūti, among sentient beings, the Bodhisattvas, the Mahāsattvas who train in the perfection of wisdom, in omniscience are rare. Among sentient beings, there are many more who train in the practices of the *śrāvakas* and *pratyekabuddhas*.[130]

Referring to the two types of aspiration to enlightenment, the *Gaṇḍavyūhasūtra* says:

> Child of good lineage, even sentient beings who generate the wishful aspiration to unsurpassed, perfect, complete enlightenment are rare. Hence, those sentient beings who set out for unsurpassed, perfect, complete enlightenment are extremely rare.[131]

Thus on the one hand there is an imposing otherness about the Bodhisattva and his goal; those who even have the wish to begin the path are rare, and the journey takes aeons to complete. On the other hand, we have Śāntideva, acutely aware of his own failings but recognizing the rareness of the opportunity presented by the sudden appearance, like lightning, of the aspiration to Buddhahood and exhorting himself not to let it go (III:28, VII:18):

> Just as a blind man
> Finds a jewel in a rubbish heap,
> So, by some means,
> This aspiration to enlightenment has been born to me.
>
> Even those who are gnats, bees, mosquitoes,
> And worms will achieve enlightenment,
> Most difficult to attain,
> If they have the power of effort.

The path of Bodhisattva, according to Śāntideva, is the path that all can and should travel. To be a Bodhisattva is something venerable and something humble. To be a Bodhisattva authenticates one's being as a person, within the understanding that the person does not ultimately exist. It is an authenticity gained through a recognition of the other, an assent to the other, a commitment to the other. Despite the rarity of the aspiration and the difficulty of the path, it is Śāntideva's view that to be a Bodhisattva means, finally, to be fully human. As he says on the occasion of creating the aspiration to highest enlightenment for the sake of all beings:

> Today my life is fruitful;
> My life as a human has become auspicious.
> Today, I have been born in the family of Buddhas;
> A child of the Buddha I have now become.[132]

ACKNOWLEDGMENT

This article is dedicated to the memory of Geshe Wangyal, 1901–1983.

NOTES

1. Fyodor Dostoyevsky, *The Brothers Karamazov,* trans. David Magarshack, vol. 1 (Baltimore: Penguin Books, 1958), p. 190.

2. Joachim Wach, *The Sociology of Religion* (Chicago: University of Chicago Press, 1944), p. 359.

3. See Har Dayal, *The Bodhisattva Doctrine in Buddhist Sanskrit Literature* (Delhi, India: Motilal Banarsidass, 1970), pp. 30–49 and, for a more recent study, see Arthur L. Basham's "Evolution of the Concept of the Bodhisattva" in *The Bodhisattva Doctrine in Buddhism,* ed. Leslie S. Kawamura (Waterloo, Canada: Wilfrid Laurier University Press, 1981), pp. 19–60.

4. This topic has been dealt with in Yun-hua Jan's "The Bodhisattva Idea in Chinese Literature: Typology and Significance," Lewis R. Lancaster's "The Bodhisattva Concept: A Study of the Chinese Buddhist Canon," and Hisao Inagaki's "The Bodhisattva Doctrine as Conceived and Developed by the Founders of the New Sects of the Heian and Kamakura Periods," all of which appear in *The Bodhisattva Doctrine in Buddhism,* ed. Leslie S. Kawamura (Waterloo, Canada: Wilfrid Laurier University Press, 1981), pp. 125–192. See also Luis O. Gómez, "From the Extraordinary to the Ordinary: Images of the Bodhisattva in East Asia," in *The Christ and Bodhisattva,* ed. Donald S. Lopez, Jr. and Steven C. Rockefeller (Albany: SUNY Press, 1987), pp. 141–191.

5. Dayal, *The Bodhisattva Doctrine in Buddhist Sanskrit Literature,* pp. 4–9.

6. For an excellent analysis of Dayal's exegesis of *sattva,* see Yuichi Kajiyama's "On the Meanings of the Words *Bodhisattva* and *Mahāsattva* in the Prajñāpāramitā Literature" in *Indological and Buddhist Studies: Volume in Honour of Professor J. W. de Jong on his Sixtieth Birthday,* ed. L. A. Hercus et al. (Canberra, Australia: Faculty of Asian Studies, 1982), pp. 253–270. Kajiyama argues that the Tibetan term *sems dpa'* means "a brave mind" or "warrior." This is a possible translation given that *dpa'* can be used as an adjective and that the adjective normally follows the noun that it modifies in Tibetan. However, the Tibetan translation may simply be a case of the translators' seeking to convey two distinct denotations of the term, as was often their style. For example, in order to convey that the word *buddha* means both "awakened" and "opened" (in the sense of a blossoming flower), they rendered the term *buddha* as *sangs rgyas,* literally "awakened-spread." In this case, although *rgyas* is an adjective and follows *sangs,* it clearly does not modify *sangs. Sems dpa'* may be a similar case in which the translators were simply attempting to convey two important meanings of a single Sanskrit term. At any rate, Kajiyama's "one whose brave mind is fixed on *bodhi*" differs little from my "one who is heroic in his intention to achieve enlightenment."

7. Haribhadra, *Abhisamayālaṃkāra-ālokavyākhyā,* ed. P. L. Vaidya, Buddhist Sanskrit, Texts, No. 4 (Darbhanga, India: Mithila Institute, 1960), p. 287. Also cited by Kajiyama in the article cited in note 6.

8. See, for example, *The Collection of Middle Length Sayings (Majjhima-Nikāya),* vol. 1, trans. I. B. Horner (London: Pali Text Society, 1967), pp. 22, 120, 148, 207, 295.

9. These have been translated in three volumes under the editorship of E. B. Cowell as *The Jātaka or Stories of the Buddha's former Births* (London: Pali Text Society, 1957).

10. Henry Clarke Warren, trans., *Buddhism in Translations* (New York: Atheneum, 1969), p. 14.

11. Ibid., p. 15.
12. Ibid., pp. 14–15 (note 2).
13. Buddhaghosa, *The Path of Purification* (*Vissudhimagga*), 2d ed., trans. Bhikkhu Ñānamoli (Colombo, Ceylon: A. Semage, 1964), p. 353 (IX.124).
14. The *Khantivādi-Jātaka* is no. 313. See Cowell, *The Jātaka or Stories of the Buddha's Former Lives,* Vols. III and IV, pp. 26–29. The story is also found in an expanded version in Āryaśura's *Jātakamala.* See J. S. Speyer, trans., *The Jātakamala: Garland of Birth-Stories of Āryaśura* (Delhi, India: Motilal Banarsidass, 1971), pp. 253–268.
15. Donald Weinstein and Rudolph M. Bell, *Saints and Society: The Two Worlds of Western Christendom, 1000–1700* (Chicago: University of Chicago Press, 1982), p. 141.
16. Ibid., pp. 141–142.
17. Peter Brown, *The Cult of the Saints* (Chicago: University of Chicago Press, 1981), p. 1.
18. *Dialogues of the Buddha,* pt. I, trans. T. W. Rhys Davids (London: Luzac and Company, Ltd., 1969), pp. 276–284. *Dīghanikāya,* I.210–223.
19. The story appears in a number of sources. For one version, see *Psalms of the Early Buddhists: I. Psalms of the Sisters (Therīgāthā),* trans. Mrs. Rhys Davids (London: Pali Text Society, 1964), pp. 106–110.
20. Weinstein and Bell, *Saints and Society,* p. 160.
21. *Encyclopedia of Religion and Ethics,* s.v. "Saints and Martyrs (Buddhist)," by E. J. Thomas.
22. A number of such stories have been brought together by Dayal, *The Bodhisattva Doctrine in Buddhist Sanskrit Literature,* pp. 182–188. Others that come to mind include the story of Asaṅga cutting a piece of flesh from his body to feed maggots, and the story of Sadāprarudita sprinkling his blood on the ground to settle the dust around Dharmodgata. For an English translation of the former, see E. Obermiller, trans., *History of Buddhism by Bu-ston,* pt. II (Heidelberg, 1932), pp. 137–139. For the latter see Edward Conze, trans., *The Perfection of Wisdom in Eight Thousand Lines and Its Verse Summary* (Bolinas, Calif.: Four Seasons Foundation, 1973), pp. 277–298.
23. See Hippolyte Delehaye, *The Legends of the Saints,* trans. Donald Attwater (New York: Fordham University Press, 1962), pp. 71–72.
24. Thomas Kuhn, *The Structure of Scientific Revolutions,* 2d ed. (Chicago: University of Chicago Press, 1970), p. 7.
25. For a consideration of this question, see Ian Barbour's "Paradigms in Science and Religion" in *Paradigms and Revolutions: Appraisals and Applications of Thomas Kuhn's Philosophy of Science,* ed. Gary Cutting (Notre Dame, Ind.: Notre Dame University Press, 1980), pp. 223–245.
26. Variations on important points of doctrine are found even within a single genre. For example, see Nancy R. Lethcoe's "The Bodhisattva Ideal in the *Aṣṭa* and *Pañca Prajñāpāramitā Sūtras,*" in *Prajñāpāramitā and Related Systems: Studies in Honor of Edward Conze,* ed. Lewis Lancaster, (Berkeley: Berkeley Buddhist Studies Series, 1977), pp. 263–280.
27. Edward Conze, trans., *The Large Sutra on Perfect Wisdom* (Berkeley, Los Angeles, London: University of California Press, 1975), p. 59.
28. The *sūtra* is quoted by Tsong-kha-pa in his *Byang chub lam rim chen*

mo. Translated from a modern Tibetan blockprint of the text in the possession of the author; no place or date of publication appears, folio 193a6 to 193b3. The same passage is also cited in the *Uttaratantra.* For an English translation see Jikido Takasaki, *A Study on the Ratnagotravibhāga (Uttaratantra),* Serie Orientale Roma XXXIII (Rome: Istituto Italiano per il Medio ed Estremo Oriente, 1966), pp. 246–247.

29. Tsong-kha-pa, *Byang chub lam rim chen mo,* 193b3–5.

30. Ibid., 190b1–3.

31. *Bhagavan* is translated as "Transcendent Victor" based on the etymology provided by Vajrapāṇi in his *Bhagavatīprajñāpāramitāhṛdayaṭikārthapradīpa,* "Bcom ldan 'das ni nyon mongs pa dang shes bya'i sgrib pa ma lus pa bcom nas chos kyi sku mya ngan las 'das pa'o." This occurs in text no. 5219 of the Peking Edition of *The Tibetan Tripiṭaka* (Tokyo-Kyoto: Suzuki Research Foundation, 1956), Vol. 94, p. 288, folio 1, line 8.

32. Tsong-kha-pa, *Byang chub lam rim chen mo,* 191b3–4.

33. See George D. Bond's "The Problem of Sainthood in the Theravāda Buddhist Tradition" in this volume.

34. Robert A. F. Thurman, trans., *The Holy Teaching of Vimalakīrti* (University Park: Pennsylvania State University Press, 1976), pp. 20–21. For a more scholarly translation of the *Vimalakīrtinirdeśasūtra,* see Étienne Lamotte, trans., *L'Enseignement de Vimalakīrti,* Bibliothèque du Muséon, vol. 51 (Louvain: Publications Universitaires, 1962). Lamotte's authoritative translation and study have been translated into English by Sara Boin as *The Teaching of Vimalakīrti,* Sacred Books of the Buddhists, vol. 32 (London: Pali Text Society, 1976).

35. Leon Hurvitz, trans., *Scripture of the Lotus Blossom of the Fine Dharma* (New York: Columbia University Press, 1976), p. 73. For an analysis of the *ekayāna* doctrine, see David Seyfort Ruegg, *La Théorie du Tathāgatagarbha et du Gotra,* Publications de l'Ecole Française d'Extrême-Orient, No. 70 (Paris: Ecole Française d'Extrême-Orient, 1969), pp. 177–243. See also Ruegg's "The *gotra, ekayāna and tathāgatagarbha* theories of the Prajñāpāramitā according to Dharmamitra and Abhayākaragupta" and Arnold Kunst's "Some Aspects of the *Ekāyana,*" in Lancaster, *Prajñāpāramitā and Related Systems,* pp. 283–326.

36. For the hagiography of Avalokiteśvara, see the *Kāraṇḍavyūha.*

37. Nakamura places the origin of the *Vajracchedikā* between A.D. 150 and 200. See his *Indian Buddhism: A Survey with Bibliographical Notes* (Osaka, Japan: KUFS Publication, 1980), p. 160.

38. Translated from the Sanskrit edition of Edward Conze, *Vajracchedikā Prajñāpāramitā,* Serie Orientale Roma XIII (Rome: Is. M.E.O., 1957), pp. 28–29. Nāgārjuna echoes the *sūtra* in his *Bodhisaṃbhāra* (72): "Bodhisattvas benefit living beings (*sattva*) but do not see any living beings! This is indeed a very difficult point, exquisite, one cannot grasp it." Translated by Chr. Lindtner in his *Nagarjuniana: Studies in the Writings and Philosophy of Nāgārjuna* (Copenhagen: Akademisk Forlag, 1982), p. 236.

39. Kuhn, *The Structure of Scientific Revolutions,* p. 10.

40. Probably the most famous instance of conversion from the Hīnayāna

to the Mahāyāna camp is that of Vasubandhu. See Obermiller, trans., *History of Buddhism by Bu-ston,* pt. II, p. 143. The issue of conversion raises the important question of lineage (*gotra*), to which Asaṅga devotes an entire chapter in his *Bodhisattvabhūmi.* The wide range of opinion within the Mahāyāna on the nature of the Bodhisattva's lineage cannot be considered here. See the definitive study by David Seyfort Ruegg, *La Théorie du Tathāgatagarbha et du Gotra,* Publications de l'Ecole Française d'Extrême-Orient, No. 70 (Paris: Ecole Française d'Extrême-Orient, 1969).

41. See Delehaye, *The Legends of the Saints,* pp. 49–100.

42. On the magical nature of the Bodhisattva, see Thurman, *The Holy Teaching of Vimalakīrti,* pp. 8–9 and Luis O. Gómez, "The Bodhisattva as Wonderworker," in Lancaster, *Prajñāpāramitā and Related Systems,* pp. 221–261.

43. See Obermiller, *History of Buddhism by Bu-ston,* pt. II, pp. 130, 141.

44. Delehaye says in *The Legends of the Saints,* page 3, that "to be strictly hagiographical the document must be of religious character and aim at edification. The term then must be confined to writings inspired by religious devotion to the saints and intended to increase devotion."

45. Translated from the Tibetan translation of the *Bodhisattvabhūmi,* Derge edition, Tibetan Tripiṭaka (Tokyo, 1978), Toh. 4037, folio 7b1–2.

46. Here and throughout, translations from the *Bodhicaryāvatāra* have been made by consulting both the Sanskrit and the Tibetan. The Sanskrit edition used is P. L. Vaidya, ed., *Bodhicaryāvatāra of Śāntideva with the Commentary Pañjikā of Prajñākaramati,* Buddhist Sanskrit Texts, No. 12 (Darbhanga, India: Mithila Institute, 1960). The translation into Tibetan used is by Sumatikīrti and bLo-ldan-shes-rab, *Byang chub sems dpa'i spyod pa la 'jug pa* (Dharamsala, India: Tibetan Cultural Printing Press, n.d.). All future quotations are from these works and will be referred to by chapter and verse number in the body of the text.

47. Louis de La Vallée Poussin, ed., *Madhyamakāvatāra par Candrakīrti,* Bibliotheca Buddhica, IX (Osnabruck, West Germany: Biblio Verlag, 1970), p. 7. The first five chapters of the *kārikās* of Candrakīrti's text with Tsong-kha-pa's commentary have been translated into English by Jeffrey Hopkins in *Compassion in Tibetan Buddhism* (Ithaca, N.Y.: Snow Lion Press, 1980).

48. This stanza appears also as the first *kārikā* in Śāntideva's *Śikṣāsamuccaya.* See Cecil Bendall, ed. *Çikshāsamuccaya* (The Hague: Mouton and Co., 1957), p. 2.

49. For example, Asaṅga's moment of compassion for a wounded dog and the maggots feeding on her, mentioned in note 22, was more effective in bringing a vision of Maitreya than twelve years of meditation.

50. Kamalaśīla, *Bhāvanākrama II,* Derge edition, Tibetan Tripiṭaka (Tokyo, 1978), Toh. 3916, folio 43a1.

51. Translated from the Tibetan of Atiśa's *Bodhipathapradīpapañjikā* edited by Richard F. Sherburne in his "A Study of Atiśa's *Commentary*" on his *Lamp of the Enlightenment Path* (Ann Arbor: University Microfilms, 1976), p. 516. The passage occurs in the Peking edition at 285b8–287a1 and in the Derge edition at folio 249a.

52. Kamalaśīla, *Bhāvanākrama* II, folio 43a4.

53. Ibid., folios 43a7–43b5.

54. Cited by Tsong-kha-pa, *Byang chub lam rim chen mo,* 197a3–4.

55. T. Stcherbatsky and E. Obermiller, ed., *Abhisamayālaṃkāra-prajñā-pāramitā-upedeśa-śāstra,* Bibliotheca Buddhica XXII (Osnabruck, West Germany: Biblio Verlag, 1970), I.18a.

56. Haribhadra, *Abhisamayālaṃkāravṛtti-sphuṭārthā,* Bibliotheca Indo-Tibetica 2 (Sarnath, India, 1977), pp. 9–10 (Sanskrit section), p. 15 (Tibetan section).

57. *Bodhicittavivaraṇa,* 106. Edited by C. Lindtner in his *Nagarjuniana,* p. 214.

58. The two forms of the aspiration are mentioned in the *Gaṇḍavyūhasūtra* as cited by Kamalaśīla, *Bhāvanākrama* I, Derge edition, Tibetan Tripiṭaka (Tokyo, 1978), Toh. 3915, folio 25a2–3, and in Śāntideva's *Bodhicaryāvatāra,* I.15–19. Kamalaśīla's first *Bhāvanākrama* has been edited by Giuseppe Tucci as *First Bhāvanākrama of Kamalaśīla: Sanskrit and Tibetan Texts with Introduction and English Summary,* Minor Buddhist Texts, pt. II: Serie Orientale Roma IX.2 (Rome: Is. M.E.O., 1958). It has been translated into English by Stephan Beyer as "The Meditations of a Bodhisattva" in his *The Buddhist Experience: Sources and Interpretations* (Belmont, Calif.: Wadsworth Publishing Co., 1974), pp. 99–115. It has been partially translated into Spanish by Luis Gómez as "Primer Tratado de Cultivo Graduado," in *Dialogos: Revista del Departmento de Filosophie Universidad de Puerto Rico,* No. 29–30 (November 1977), pp. 177–244.

59. Kamalaśīla, *Bhāvanākrama* I, folio 25a3–4.

60. Haribhadra, *Abhisamayālaṃkāra-ālokavyākhyā,* p. 283, lines 15–16.

61. Kamalaśīla, *Bhāvanākrama* I, folio 25a4. Atīsá devotes the fourth chapter of his *Bodhipathapradīpa* to a discussion of from whom the Bodhisattva vow should be taken, the accompanying ritual, etc. See Sherburne, *Lamp of the Enlightenment Path,* pp. 251–311, 566–592.

62. Kamalaśīla, *Bhāvanākrama* I, folio 25b1.

63. For a discussion of the four means of gathering students (*saṃgrahavastu*), see Dayal, *The Bodhisattva Doctrine in Buddhist Sanskrit Literature,* pp. 251–259.

64. *Ratnāvalī,* 213. For a translation of the *Ratnāvalī,* see Nāgārjuna and Kaysang Gyatso, *The Precious Garland and the Song of the Four Mindfulnesses,* trans. Jeffrcy Hopkins and Lati Rimpoche (New York: Harper & Row, 1975).

65. Kamalaśīla, *Bhāvanākrama* I, folio 25b5–7.

66. Ibid., 27a6–7.

67. Obermiller and Stcherbatsky, *Abhisamayālaṃkāra,* I.43.

68. Poussin, *Madhyamakāvatāra,* I.16, pp. 30–31.

69. Śāntideva, III.11.

70. Ibid., V.101.

71. In fact, it is permissible for the Bodhisattva to commit physical and verbal nonvirtues if his motivation is one of compassion. Āryadeva says in his *Catuḥśataka* V.5: "Everything, whether virtuous or non-virtuous / Is auspicious for the Bodhisattva / Due to his intention / Because he has controlled his mind."

72. See *Encyclopedia of Buddhism,* s.v. "*Bodhisattva-Prātimokṣa,*" by Lung-lien.

73. Asaṅga, *Bodhisattva-bhūmi,* ed. Nalinaksha Dutt (Patna, India: Jayaswal Research Institute, 1966), pp. 100–102. For the Tibetan, see the Peking edition of *The Tibetan Tripiṭaka* (Tokyo-Kyoto: Tibetan Tripiṭaka Research Institute, 1957), text 5338, Vol. 110, p. 168, folio 1, line 3 to folio 3, line 8. For a summary of the ethics of the Bodhisattva as presented by Asaṅga, see *Encyclopedia of Religion and Ethics,* s.v. "Bodhisattva," by Louis de La Vallée Poussin.

74. Śāntideva, *Bodhicaryāvatāra,* VI.1.

75. "Conqueror" (*jina*) is an epithet for a Buddha.

76. Śāntideva, *Bodhicaryāvatāra,* VII.1–2.

77. The Bodhisattva thus seems to confound the categories of religious virtuosi put forth by Max Weber in *The Sociology of Religion* (Boston: Beacon Press, 1964), pp. 166–183. The Bodhisattva combines elements of the world-rejecting ascetic, the inner-worldly ascetic, and the world-fleeing contemplative mystic. Although Weber implies that as a Buddhist the Bodhisattva would belong to the last category, he in fact fits neatly into none.

78. Poussin, *Madhyamakāvatāra,* pp. 30–31.

79. Ibid.

80. See *Bodhisaṃbhāra,* 33. Translated by Lindtner in *Nagarjuniana,* p. 232.

81. Kamalaśīla, *Bhāvanākrama* I, folio 25b3–4.

82. See *New Catholic Encyclopedia,* s.v. "Virtue, Heroic," by K. V. Truhlar.

83. Peking edition of *The Tibetan Tripiṭaka,* text 5285, Vol. 101, p. 15, folio 1, line 3 to folio 2, line 1.

84. Kamalaśīla, *Bhāvanākrama* II, folio 44a2–3.

85. This etymology is provided by the eighteenth-century Tibetan scholar, dKon-mchog-'jigs-med-dbang-po (1728–1791) in his *Sa lam gyi rnam bzhag theg sum mdzes rgyan.* See *The Collected Works of dKon-mchog-'jigs-med-dbang-po* (New Delhi: Ngawang Gelek Demo, 1971), vol. 7, p. 428.6.

86. These four levels are called heat (*ūṣman*), peak (*mūrdhan*), forbearance (*kṣānti*), and supreme mundane quality (*laukikāgradharma*). They are described by Kamalaśīla in *Bhāvanākrama* I, folio 39a7–39b4.

87. Kamalaśīla, *Bhāvanākrama* I, folio 39b4–6.

88. Poussin, *Madhyamakāvatara,* I.7, p. 17.

89. Ibid., p. 12.

90. *Ratnāvalī,* 440–460.

91. They differ on one significant point. See note 105. For other discussions of the ten grounds (*bhūmi*) in English, see Dayal, *The Bodhisattva Doctrine in Buddhist Sanskrit Literature,* pp. 270–291, and *Encyclopedia of Buddhism,* s.v. "*Bhūmi,*" by S. K. Nanayakkara.

92. Kamalaśīla, *Bhāvanākrama* I, folio 39b6.

93. S. Bagchi, ed., *Mahāyānasūtrālaṃkāra,* Buddhist Sanskrit Texts 13 (Darbhanga, India: Mithila Institute, 1970), XX.32.

94. Kamalaśīla, *Bhāvanākrama* I, folio 40a1.

95. Poussin, *Madhyamakāvatāra,* II.1–2, pp. 32–37.
96. Kamalaśīla, *Bhāvanākrama* I, folio 40a3.
97. Ibid., folio 40a4–5.
98. Poussin, *Madhyamakāvatāra,* III.2, p. 47.
99. Kamalaśīla, *Bhāvanākrama* I, folio 40a5–6.
100. Ibid., folio 40a6–40b1.
101. Ibid., folio 40bl–4 and Poussin, *Madhyamakāvatāra,* V.1, p. 69.
102. Kamalaśīla, *Bhāvanākrama* I, folio 40b4–6.
103. Ibid., folio 40b6–41a1.
104. Poussin, *Madhyamakāvatāra,* pp. 342–343.
105. According to the Tibetan doxographers of the dGe-lugs-pa order, notably 'Jam-dbyangs-bshad-pa and lCang-skya, the Prāsaṅgikas assert that the afflictive obstructions (*kleśāvaraṇa*) are completely destroyed at the end of the seventh ground, whereas the Yogācāra-Svātantrikas, such as Kamalaśīla, hold that they are not completely abandoned until the end of the tenth ground. For a discussion of the two types of obstructions (*avaraṇa*), see Lamotte's "Passions and Impregnations of the Passions in Buddhism" in *Buddhist Studies in Honour of I. B. Horner,* ed. L. Cousins et al. (Dordrecht, Holland: D. Reidel, 1974), pp. 91–104.
106. Kamalaśīla, *Bhāvanākrama* I, folio 41a2.
107. Poussin, *Madhyamakāvatāra,* pp. 344–345.
108. Kamalaśīla, *Bhāvanākrama* I, folio 41a2–3.
109. Poussin, *Madhyamakāvatāra,* pp. 348–349. For a discussion of the individual knowledges (*pratisaṃvid*), see Dayal, *The Bodhisattva Doctrine in Buddhist Sanskrit Literature,* pp. 259–269.
110. Kamalaśīla, *Bhāvanākrama* I, folio 41a4–5.
111. Poussin, *Madhyamakāvatāra,* pp. 349–350.
112. Kamalaśīla, *Bhāvanākrama* I, folio 41a5–6.
113. Ibid., folio 41a7–41b1.
114. For a discussion of the length of the path, see Dayal, *The Bodhisattva Doctrine in Buddhist Sanskrit Literature,* pp. 76–79.
115. Poussin, *Madhyamakāvatāra,* XI.1–3, pp. 350–352.
116. Ibid., XI.4–8, pp. 352–354.
117. *Ratnāvalī,* 442–460.
118. Obermiller and Stcherbatsky, *Abhisamayālaṃkāra,* I.48–50.
119. Ibid., I.51.
120. Ibid., I.66–67.
121. Haribhadra, *Abhisamayālaṃkāravṛtti-sphuṭārthā,* p. 45.
122. Bagchi, *Mahāyānasūtrālaṃkāra,* IV.24–26. For a discussion of the doctrine of the intentional rebirth, see Gadjin M. Nagao's "The Bodhisattva Returns to This World," in Kawamura, *The Bodhisattva Doctrine in Buddhism,* pp. 61–79.
123. *Bodhicittavivaraṇa,* 102. See the version edited by Lindtner in his *Nagarjuniana,* p. 214. The fact that Nāgārjuna makes reference to the *apratiṣṭhitanirvāṇa* suggests that Alan Sponberg has overstated the case when he argues that it is a distinctively Yogācāra doctrine if one assumes, as Lindtner does, that the *Bodhicittavivaraṇa* is indeed the work of Nāgārjuna. For Spon-

berg's argument see "Dynamic Liberation in Yogācāra Buddhism," *Journal of the International Association of Buddhist Studies* 2, no. 1 (1978): 44–64.

124. See Nagao, "The Bodhisattva Returns to This World," p. 65.

125. Weinstein and Bell, *Saints and Society*, p. 141.

126. Cited in Tsong-ka-pa, Kensur Lekden, and Jeffrey Hopkins, *Compassion in Tibetan Buddhism* (Ithaca, N.Y.: Snow Lion Press, 1980), p. 79.

127. Weinstein and Bell, *Saints and Society*, p. 159.

128. *The New Catholic Encyclopedia*, s.v. "Saints, Intercession of," by P. Molinari.

129. Ibid.

130. Translated from the Tibetan. *'Phags pa shes rab kyi pha rol tu phyin pa brgyad stong pa* (Dharamsala, India: Tibetan Cultural Printing Press, 1978), folio 422a2–7.

131. Cited by Kamalaśīla in *Bhāvanākrama* I, folio 25a2–3.

132. Śāntideva, *Bodhicaryāvatāra*, III.25.

7
The Sage as Saint: The Confucian Tradition

Rodney L. Taylor

In an article on saints and martyrs in the 1922 edition of *Hasting's Encyclopedia of Religion and Ethics* it is suggested that the sage rather than the saint is paradigmatic of the Chinese religious tradition.[1] The inference is that sage and saint are quite separate categories in terms of a typology of religious functionaries; the saint is an obviously religious figure, the sage perhaps more of a wise man who may even preclude the question of religious dimension.

The focus of the present chapter is an analysis of the Confucian sage as a religious figure.[2] The approach is fundamentally historical and will analyze the term "sage" within its earliest context of Classical Confucian material. In turn I will focus upon the changing relevancy of the ideal as well as the image of the sage within the development of Neo-Confucianism. Whether the Confucian sage is compatible with the category of saint will depend in large part upon the salient characteristics that emerge in a typology of the figure.

In turn, however, the question rests as well with the nature of the figure known as the saint. If the term can be freed from its specific role in the history of Christianity, it may be a useful one to employ in describing a certain type of figure whose role can be defined within a number of different traditions. As a type of religious person, the saint suggests both characteristics of otherness or inimitability that have resulted in the veneration associated with the memory of the saint, if not his body itself. In addition there is an exemplariness or imitability about the saint that has resulted in the emulation of the saint by his followers.

The Confucian case is a fascinating one in this respect, for as a tradition Confucianism has consciously minimized the expression of "otherness" through miraculous and supernatural means. As a result hagiography takes on a very different content in the Confucian context. The Confucian tradition finds its religious dimension within the perimeters of humans perfecting their own moral nature. The sage is the exemplar of such perfection, but the record of his deeds suggests a certain degree of ordinariness rather than otherness. From the Confucian point of view it is being most human that is the measure of people's religious dimension. Does this particular form of religious dimension permit us to call the Confucian sage a saint?

ON THE WORD "SAGE"

The word "sage," *sheng* (archaic pronunciation **śiĕng,* ancient pronunciation, *śiäng*) is defined in the *Shuo-wen,* the basic Chinese etymological dictionary, as *t'ung* (archaic **t'ung,* ancient *t'ung*) meaning "to penetrate," "to pass through."[3] Schafer has suggested in his *Combined Supplements to Mathews* the extension "giving passage to."[4] This would indicate that the sage is one who penetrates or thoroughly understands, presumably the ways of Heaven (*T'ien*) and, if we take Schafer's rendering seriously, may also suggest the sense of the sage as one who "gives passage to" the ways of Heaven—that is, manifests the ways of Heaven through his own person for the benefit of man. Such an interpretation is reinforced by the philological structure of the character that is spoken of in the expanded commentaries of the *Shuo-wen* provided in the *Shuo-wen chieh-tzu ku-lin.* The character is composed of the radical or signific *er* (archaic **n'iəg,* ancient *nźi*), the character for ear, and the phonetic *ch'eng* (archaic **d'iĕng,* ancient *d'iäng*) glossed by Karlgren as "to manifest" and by extension "to reveal" or "to disclose."[5] With the role of the signific *er,* ear, the character sage suggests in part the one who hears. In this respect it is not surprising that there exists a close relation between the word "sage" and the word *t'ing* (archaic **t'ieng,* ancient *t'ieng*), to hear, to listen to, to acknowledge.[6] Thus the sage hears the ways of Heaven, suggesting his penetration and understanding. We also have to deal with the phonetic of the character *ch'eng,* which means to manifest. There may be a connection between the meaning of "sage," and the phonetic *ch'eng.* It seems likely that the phonetic in this case carries semantic significance. Thus the meaning of *ch'eng,* to manifest, may also have its relevance to the interpretation of the character. If this is the case, the sage is he who not only hears the ways of Heaven but manifests, reveals, or discloses them to man. In the *Shuo-wen chieh-tzu ku-lin* the sage is described in the following terms:

> There is nothing he does not penetrate. . . . Further, where there is a sage present, all things manifest *his* own feelings. The ear component does not mean simply to use the ear; it means instead that the mind penetrates the feelings of all things as the ear penetrates all sound. . . . It is said that the sage penetrates the feelings of Heaven and earth and understands the nature of man and the world."[7]

These inherent meanings of "sage" form an important foundation for the way the word is understood and used by Classical Confucians and Neo-Confucians alike.

Our main focus is an examination of the figure of the sage in major Confucian writings. A survey of this kind by its very nature must exclude important texts and figures from discussion. It is hoped, however, that in giving a detailed analysis of the concept of sage in the writings of Confucius (551–479 B.C.), and Mencius (372–289 B.C.), who for the later tradition became the primary interpreter of Confucius, as well as the later Neo-Confucian traditions, that the key elements in the concept of sage will be touched upon.

THE SAGE AND CONFUCIUS

The sage for Confucius is of the utmost importance and yet remains distant and ill-defined. If we turn to the use of the term "sage" in the Confucian *Analects* we find only eight occurrences, four as *sheng,* sage, and four as *sheng-jen,* sagely person. Let us look briefly at each of these to see how the terms are employed by Confucius. *Analects* book VI:28 is a reference to the ideal ruler. Confucius says that the person capable of transforming the state to order and peace would without doubt be a sage. The focus is upon the Confucian virtue *jen,* translated as "goodness," "humanity," or "humaneness" and the sage's ability to enact it and thereby transform the entire empire. Book VII:33 is a reference to the distance that separates Confucius and those whom he would regard as sages. Confucius claims for himself only an unwearying effort to pursue learning. Nothing is suggested of Confucius himself being a sage or, for that matter, anyone in the contemporary context of Confucius having the talents of a sage. Book IX:6 contains two references. A disciple is asked whether his teacher Confucius is a sage. The answer suggests that from the disciple's point of view Confucius is close to being a sage, for this is what Heaven intended for him. He has, however, yet to reach the state. Book VII: 25 finds Confucius lamenting that he can find no sage in his own generation. He states in fact that he would be fortunate indeed even to find a *chün-tzu,* a gentleman or nobleman or "lordling." In book XVI:8, the nobleman is said to stand in awe of three things: the Mandate of Heaven, great men, and the words of the sages. In book XIX:12, the sage is said to possess the beginnings and endings; that is, he possesses an ability to penetrate or understand all things and is suggestive of the *Shuo-wen*'s definition of sage as *t'ung,* penetrating.

Who, then, are the sages in the context of the Confucian *Analects*? It appears that only the sage kings of antiquity achieve the status of sage. Yao and Shun are described in the *Analects,* for example, as the highest standard of men (VI:28; XIV:45). Yao is described as equal to Heaven (VIII:19). Yü is described as sublime (VIII:18) and yet humble (VIII:21). What, then, of the Duke of Chou, the constant paradigm of virtue from the Confucian perspective? Even given the extraordinary status assigned to the Duke of Chou by Confucius, he is never spoken of as a sage. The same might be said for King Wu. Though a paradigm of virtue, King Wu needed ten ministers to govern, whereas the sage Shun needed only five (VIII:20). The category of sage seems thus to be limited to the figures Yao, Shun, and Yü for Confucius. The paradigms of virtuous rule, Kings Wen and Wu, as well as the Duke of Chou, by not being given the designation "sage" serve only to indicate the extraordinary level of achievement intended by the term "sage." What is particularly apparent in the context of the *Analects* is the separation of the sage from the capacities of normal men. There is no attempt to suggest that one can reach the state of sagehood. There is no reason to believe that another sage might not appear, but there have been none since the sage kings of antiquity, and for Confucius at least the sage is identified with this period of antiquity. They remain as figures removed from ordinary time and place. Centered in antiquity, they were thought to have acted on the basis of their direct apprehension of Heaven's ways, disclosing the patterns of Heaven's ways to men.

MENCIUS ON MAN AND SAGE

The term "sage" plays a far more prominent role in the writings of Mencius than the Confucian *Analects*. There are forty-seven occurrences of the word "sage" in the Mencius text and these can be summarized under several general themes. First, the sage for Mencius seems again for the most part to be represented best by the sage kings of antiquity. Mencius comments in several passages that Yao and Shun were of the age of sages and after them the way of sages fell into decline. Thus even Confucius himself cannot without difficulty measure up to the sages of the past (*Mencius* IIA.1; IIB.9). Second, there is a hope expressed by Mencius that sages will once again appear, presumably with the object of guiding man's ways in accordance with the ways of Heaven (*Mencius* IIA.2; IIIB.9). Third, a number of passages give characteristics of the sage, suggesting the possibility of a definition and characterization of the sage's role and nature. For example, Mencius says of the sage that he exhibits perfect human relations (*Mencius* IVA.2), he employs instruments with perfection—that is, he has practical skills (*Mencius* IVA.1)—he has a "transforming" influence upon others (*Mencius* VIIB.25), and there is a sense of wonder when in the presence of a sage (*Mencius* VIIA.24). Fourth, although there is an idealization of the sage kings of antiquity, there is also for Mencius a movement of the figure of the sage out of the context of antiquity. Unlike Confucius's view, the Duke of Chou is for Mencius a sage (*Mencius* IIB.9). Thus the concept has broken out of its time referent. Although the age of Yao and Shun is still the preferred context, the sage can now be found in different periods. This seems to have its effect in the interpretation of Confucius himself. From Mencius's point of view, Confucius himself is a sage (*Mencius* VB.1; IIA.2).

Finally, for Mencius there is a very different relation established between the sage and the capacity of ordinary man than seems suggested by Confucius. As the ideal of the sage breaks free of its sacred time referent in antiquity, the issue of the relation of the nature of the sage and the nature of ordinary or normal human capacities becomes more and more relevant. No longer is it possible to distinguish the ordinary man and the sage solely on the basis of a temporal context. How, then, does one adjudicate the nature of the sage and the nature of man? Mencius first argues that the sages of the past and those of the present have the same nature (*Mencius* IVB.1), an important premise to indicate that there is no difference in the use of the term "sage." Thus whether referring to Yao and Shun or to the Duke of Chou and Confucius, to call them sages is to say the same thing about each and thus to point to the same phenomenon. In another passage Mencius argues that sages are the same in kind with others but stand out through their capacity to manifest their character (*Mencius* IIA.7). For example, the sage realizes and thus manifests his nature of righteousness *before* normal men (Mencius VIA.7). The critical argument states that sages and ordinary men are by nature, *hsing,* the same (*Mencius* VIA.7). Its appropriate and significant conclusion follows—that any man might become a Yao or Shun (*Mencius* VIB.2).[8] Thus simply in the development of Confucian thought from Confucius to Mencius, the notion of the sage has transformed from one historically locked in antiquity to a potentially realizable goal. This transformation is predicated upon the articulation of man's nature, suggesting that all men, including the sages, possess the same basic nature of goodness that has been instilled in each by Heaven.

When put within the context of Denny's study of the saint in the Islamic tradition (chapter 3), the distinction drawn between a quality or state earned and a title bestowed is a useful one. Whereas for Confucius it would appear that Heaven has bestowed the title "sage" upon the sage kings of antiquity and has at least given Confucius himself some sense of his own destiny, for Mencius the situation seems very different. Mencius, in suggesting that anyone can become a Yao or Shun, leaves open the possibility that through rigorous learning and self-cultivation one can in fact become a sage. Thus the title is one that is earned through one's own effort. The ability of man to perfect himself specifically in terms of realizing the goal of sagehood becomes as well a basic part of the later Confucian tradition, what is known as Neo-Confucianism.

THE NEO-CONFUCIAN QUEST FOR SAGEHOOD

For the Neo-Confucian, sagehood was no longer an ideal of the past. Rather, it had become an ideal that stood as the end point of the cultivation and learning process.[9] Fundamentally it was thought to be realizable within the context of one's own lifetime. The *Chin-ssu lu* (*Reflections on Things at Hand*), a collection of sayings of prominent Neo-Confucians compiled in part by Chu Hsi (1130–1200), represents a kind of guidebook to the learning necessary for the realization of the goal of sagehood.[10] It was a work oriented not to the Confucian state orthodoxy and examination system but, rather, to the individual's own search for sagehood. Thus we find the second chapter beginning with the phrase, "The sage aspires to become Heaven, the worthy aspires to become a sage and the gentlemen aspires to become a worthy."[11] Sagehood thus stood as the goal of the learning process, and for many Neo-Confucians the focus of their lives remained the quest for sagehood. Chang Tsai (1021–1077), for example, often told his students "the way to understand the rules of propriety, to fulfill one's nature and to transform one's physical nature, and told them not to stop learning until they were equal to the sage."[12] According to the *Chin-ssu lu,* Ch'eng I (1033–1107) and Ch'eng Hao (1032–1085) even in their early teen years possessed the desire to pursue the goal of sagehood.[13] Kao P'an-lung (1562–1626), in the introduction to his autobiography, *K'un-hsüeh chi* (*Recollections on the Toils of Learning*), says, "At the age of twenty-five when I heard Magistrate Li Yüan-chung and Ku Ching-yang discuss learning, I resolved to pursue the quest of sagehood. [I considered] that there must be a way of becoming a sage, though I was yet unacquainted with the methods."[14] There is general agreement as to the relevancy of the goal. At the same time, however, there are different ways of structuring the learning and cultivation process for the realization of the goal.

The Ways of Neo-Confucian Learning

The Neo-Confucian movement is divided into two broadly based schools, the *Li-hsüeh,* or School of Principle, and the *Hsin-hsüeh,* or School of Mind. They differ from each other in terms of certain metaphysical assumptions, which in turn create differences in the pedagogical method for the realization of sagehood. For the School of Principle the focus is upon the uncovering of the basic moral structure thought to lie at the base of all phenomena and predicated upon a primarily monistic view of the presence or immanence of what for the Classical Confucian was referred to as the ways of Heaven. For the Neo-Confucian this approaches the idea of what Streng has referred to as cosmic law[15]—that is, an underlying moral order to be found in all things. Such an underlying moral structure is called Principle, *li.* It is within all things, including as well the nature of man. The task of the learning process is then the gradual realization of this Principle in one's nature through the understanding of Principle in other phenomena. The text known as the *Ta-hsüeh,* Great Learning, serves as a focal point of the Confucian method of learning and was of extreme importance to the Neo-Confucians.[16]

The method of learning outlined in the Great Learning suggests a series of stages. Learning begins with *ko-wu,* the investigation of things, and proceeds with the following steps; *chih-chih,* the extension of knowledge; *ch'eng-i,* sincerity of intention; *cheng-hsin,* rectification of mind; *hsiu-shen,* cultivation of self; *ch'i-chia,* regulation of the family; *chih-kuo,* ordering of the state; and *p'ing t'ien-hsia,* bringing peace to the world. The focus for the School of Principle is primarily upon the external rather than internal search for Principle. Thus tremendous importance is attached to the first two stages of the learning process—the investigation of things and the extension of knowledge. One is to investigate things, primarily understood to refer to classical literature and in particular the so-called Five Classics,[17] and through this process unlock or ferret out the underlying Principle. If we understand the role the Five Classics have played historically as templates of Heaven's ways,[18] the Neo-Confucian is simply suggesting a metaphysical basis for the examination of this material. Things thus investigated, this knowledge is extended to a broader sphere. In this manner one continues to build up a wider and wider knowledge of the Principle of things. At the third stage, the sincerity of intention, and the fourth stage, the rectification of the mind, the knowledge is returned to the individual with the purpose of exploring the inner dimensions of Principle within the individual in light of what has been learned of Principle from the external context. From the perspective of the School of Principle it is imperative to exercise the mind fully in pursuit of the knowledge of Principle. This involves not only the use of the mind but a correct attitudinal component as well. For Ch'eng I as well as Chu Hsi it was essential to have a mind of *ching,* a word that can be translated as either seriousness or reverence, and suggests the potential religious dimension of the learning.[19] For the School of Principle the emphasis remains upon the necessity of effort and discipline in order to acquire the knowledge of Principle necessary to realize the potential for sagehood within one's nature.

The School of Mind begins from the metaphysical premise that Principle is the substance of the mind, rather than the nature. This results in a very different focus in the method of learning, for the issue need no longer be seen in terms of the necessity of an external process of investigation. Instead the full potential for the realization of Principle lies within the individual himself. It is for this reason, for example, that Ch'eng Hao can focus upon the necessity of sincerity in the process of learning rather than the outward process of investigation.

> The student must first of all understand the nature of humanity (*jen*). . . . [One's duty] is to understand this truth and preserve humanity with sincerity (*ch'eng*) and seriousness (*ching*), that is all. There is no need to avoid things or restrict oneself. Nor is there any need for exhaustive search. . . . Exhaustive search is necessary when one has not found the truth, but if one preserves humanity long enough, the truth will automatically dawn on him. Why should we have to wait for exhaustive search?[20]

For Ch'eng Hao it is enough to preserve the potential one has through *ch'eng,* sincerity, and *ching,* seriousness-reverence. There is nothing to be added to this from external sources, and for this reason a process of investigation of things and extension of knowledge becomes not only secondary but simply quite irrelevant.

Wang Yang-ming (1472–1529), the great exponent of the School of Mind during the Ming dynasty, wrote a commentary to the Great Learning suggesting the ways in which the School of Principle had misinterpreted the true meaning of the text.[21] In this commentary we see perhaps the clearest formulations of the School of Mind approach to learning and in turn the differences between the School of Mind and the School of Principle. As Tu Wei-ming has argued in his study of the early and formative years of Wang Yang-ming's life, at issue in Wang Yang-ming's attitude toward the School of Principle is not a rejection of the method of investigation of things, but instead a radical reformulation of the process.[22] The example is frequently cited of Wang Yang-ming attempting to investigate the Principle of bamboo and after a period of days of concentrated investigation becoming ill rather than discovering anything about the underlying nature of the bamboo. This is often thought to be the basis of the rejection of the process of investigation of things by Wang Yang-ming; however, it is actually the basis for a reformulation of the understanding of the investigation process. The reformulation is predicated upon the necessity of realizing the full capability of one's own innate knowledge, *liang-chih.* "People fail to realize that the highest good is in their minds and seek it outside. As they believe that everything or every event has its own definite principle, they search for the highest good in individual things"[23]—thus the necessity to reformulate the meaning of the phrases *ko-wu* and *chih-*

chih. "Extension of knowledge is not what later scholars understand as enriching and widening knowledge. It is simply extending one's innate knowledge of the good to the utmost."[24] The extension of knowledge then points directly to the innate knowledge, *liang-chih,* and the process of *ko-wu,* investigation of things, becomes a substantive component of the claim for innate knowledge. For both processes the direction is inward. "To investigate is to rectify. It is to rectify that which is incorrect so it can return to its original correctness."[25] The investigation process is thus made an internal process of rectifying and realizing that which is already there, essentially what Mencius had spoken of as the sense of right and wrong common to all men (*Mencius* VIA.6). As Ch'eng Hao warns, referring again to Mencius, there should be no artificial effort to help it grow (*Mencius* IIA.2)[26]—that is, without effort exerted, the innate goodness will be preserved. Thus instead of an attitude stressing the importance of effort and discipline to investigate Principle which characterizes the School of Principle, the School of Mind emphasizes that the full potential of our goodness is innate and need only be preserved and brought to fruition. The goal for each school remains the same—sagehood—and to a large degree the characteristics attributed to sagehood remain the same, although differences in pedagogy and praxis persist.

The Nature of Sagehood

What, then, is meant by the realization of sagehood? It is obvious that it is a realizable goal for the Neo-Confucian whether of the School of Principle or the School of Mind. It is also clear that each school has its particular focus as well as methods for the actual cultivation and learning essential for the realization of the state of sagehood. Let us try initially to get some sense of what sagehood means for the Neo-Confucian.

First, the state of sagehood refers to the full realization of the potential of man's nature or mind. Man's nature or his mind, *hsin,* is thought to share in the basic moral nature of the universe. In many ways this is simply a development of the Mencian point of view, for Mencius had said that by coming to understand one's own nature, one came to understand the ways of Heaven (*Mencius* VIIA.1). This might be described as correlative thinking in which man's moral nature is seen as a microcosm of the ways of Heaven, the macrocosm. Within the framework of Neo-Confucianism this relationship is spoken of in terms of Principle, or the Principle of Heaven, *T'ien-li.* Thus the Neo-Confucian has raised the ways of Heaven to a conscious metaphysical structure and in so doing has laid the groundwork for the philosophical relation of man and the phenomena of the world. Chou Tun-i (1017–1073) says, for example, in response to a question on how one ought to become a sage,

> The essential way is to attain oneness [of mind]. By oneness is meant having no desire. Having no desire one is "empty" [absolutely pure and peaceful] while tranquil, and straightforward while in action. Being "empty" while tranquil, one becomes intelligent and hence penetrating. Being straightforward while active, one becomes impartial and hence all-embracing. Being intelligent, penetrating, impartial, and all-embracing, one is almost a sage.[27]

Emptiness for a Neo-Confucian suggests a mind free of pettiness and selfishness and the limitations such attitudes cause.[28] It is not a state of nothingness. It is rather that state in which one's mind is filled with the mind of the Way or the Tao and is thus descriptive of the sage.

Second, the state of sagehood is spoken of in terms of a sense of "oneness" with all things. Specifically this involves the manifestation of man's moral nature and in turn the realization that the basic nature of goodness found in man's nature or mind is shared with all things. It is in this sense that we can talk about the commonality of the microcosm, the individual in this case, and the macrocosm, all other things, for they share in the same underlying moral nature of the universe. Thus Ch'eng Hao speaks in terms of the essential unity between himself and the larger context. "The humane man forms one body with all things comprehensively."[29] Chang Tsai suggests that the sage is capable of entering into all things. "By enlarging one's mind, one can enter into all things in the world. As long as anything is not yet entered into, there is still something outside of the mind. . . . The sage . . . fully develops his nature and does not allow what is seen or heard to fetter his mind."[30] Another passage in the *Chin-ssu lu* focuses upon the basic feature of unity: "Combine the internal and the external into one and regard things and the self as equal. This is the way to see the fundamental point of the Way."[31] The basis of this unity, whether spoken of in terms of the transcendence of the dichotomy of internal and external or the ability of the sage to penetrate into all things, remains the common moral nature shared by all things. It is precisely this shared moral nature that Wang Yang-ming has called the innate good knowledge. It is that which at the metaphysical level unites the microcosm and the macrocosm. The sage is he who has fully penetrated his own nature or his own mind and thus directly comprehends the correlative nature of reality.

The Life of the Sage

With the relevance of the ideal of sagehood it certainly appears that there would be those who would claim of some the achievement of the goal. In a few cases such a claim might even be made of oneself, although this was a minority position[32] and for the vast majority the very ideal of sagehood precluded self-affirmation of such magnitude.[33] It is something imitable and yet its realization remains in the realm of the inimitable. However, it was certainly not beyond the capacity of Neo-Confucians to assign at least a near status to former and major figures of the tradition.

How does one determine sagehood in someone? As deBary has pointed out in his seminal study of spiritual practice in Neo-Confucianism, by far the greatest number of characteristics seem to be rendered as personality traits.[34] Thus the life of the individual is the telling comment upon realization of the goal. With that in mind, it is surely no coincidence that the final chapter of the *Chin-ssu lu* called "On the Dispositions of Sages and Worthies" contains biographies of Classical Confucian as well as Neo-Confucian figures. This is the subject matter of Confucian hagiography. One of the most famous of Neo-Confucian writings, the *Western Inscription* (*Hsi-ming*) of Chang Tsai,[35] is also an account of the ideal life, of how the sage would live and how he would perceive the world. From Chang Tsai's perspective the sage would see himself in fundamental unity with all other things. "Therefore that which extends throughout the universe I regard as my body and that which directs the universe I consider as my nature."[36] The practical ramifications become the basis of the life of the sage. "Even those who are tired and infirm, crippled or sick, those who have no brothers or children, wives or husbands, are all my brothers who are in distress and have no one to turn to."[37] The sage is thus one who feels commiseration with all living things.

The sense of commiseration on the part of the sage is a salient feature of the biographies of sages and worthies contained in the *Chin-ssu lu*. Of Ch'eng I it is said, for example,

> The master not only possessed an unusual nature by endowment, but his own nourishment of it was in accordance with

> the Way. . . . His conscientiousness and sincerity penetrated metal and stone, and his filial piety and brotherly respect influenced spiritual beings. As one looked at his countenance, one found that in dealing with people he was as warm as the spring sun. . . . He saw penetratingly and made no discrimination between himself and others. As one tried to fathom his depth, one realized that it was as great as a boundless ocean.[38]

Of Ch'eng Hao it was said,

> His self-cultivation was so complete that he was thoroughly imbued with the spirit of peacefulness, which was revealed in his voice and countenance. However, as one looked at him, he was so lofty and deep that none could treat him with disrespect. When he came upon things to do, he did them with ease and leisure, and no sense of urgency. But at the same time he was sincere and earnest, and did not treat them carelessly.[39]

And finally of Chou Tun-i, Ch'eng Hao himself wrote; Chou Tun-i "did not cut the grass growing outside his window. When asked about it, he said, '[The feeling of the grass] and mine are the same.' "[40] Chu Hsi says of this passage: "You can realize the matter yourself. You must see wherein one's feelings and that of the grass are the same."[41]

In these and other passages the sage is portrayed as penetrating in his knowledge; he understands his own nature as well as the nature of the macrocosm. The depth of his understanding seems obvious in his countenance as well as his actions. He is described as peaceful, warm, caring, utterly sincere and honest, serious and reverent, and displaying an extraordinary compassion for the life of others. In many respects such images differ little from the earliest image of the term "sage," although it is now accompanied by a metaphysical sophistication and a relevancy to the individual seeking his own self-understanding. The sages of antiquity, though primarily if not exclusively sage kings, have in a sense become relevant and intimate for the Neo-Confucian, and the *santus* of their presence is a model to all who seek to emulate the ideal.

THE SAGE AS SAINT?

What, then, is the relevance of the category "sainthood" to the Confucian sage? On the surface there appear to be a number of substantial differences between sage and saint, differences of a magnitude that might well raise the question of any attempt to establish commonality between the two. Let us begin by examining some of these differences. First, certainly any technical definition of saint from within the context of the Christian tradition either as one of the blessed dead in Heaven or as one who has received formal recognition by the Church as having exceptional holiness of life and thereby achieved an exalted station in Heaven is of little or no relevance to the Confucian context.[42] Second, van der Leeuw's sense of the saint as a person whose body possesses divinely potent attributes and is primarily a sacred—that is, powerful—object or, perhaps more important, a relic,[43] seems little connected to the Confucian notion of the sage. Van der Leeuw in fact emphasizes the obvious importance of the grave of the saint. "The world has no use for living saints; they are dead persons, or better still: the potency of the dead."[44] While it might be argued that the "historical mindedness"[45] of the Confucian lends an additional air of admiration if not veneration to the sage, there is little or no sense of the potency of power associated with the sage.

More might be said in this respect. One of the least-known and understood features of the Confucian tradition is the existence of the Confucian temple,[46] an official institution that allowed for the ritual veneration of Confucius, selected disciples, and various outstanding Confucians throughout the generations. In A.D. 59 the Han dynasty emperor Ming-ti officially recognized Confucius as the patron of *wen,*[47] literature in its broadest sense as the humane letters. Confucius thus became what I hardly dare describe as the "patron saint" of the community of scholars. Sacrifice was carried out to Confucius and the other assembled representatives of the tradition. Such practices have continued until comparatively recent times within the temple more recently called the *Wen-miao,* Temple of Literature or Temple of Learning. In many respects this seems (at least on the surface) little different from patron deities of various trades and activities that people the world of Chinese popular religion. The only obvious difference between popular religious expressions and the cult of Confucius is the connection of the Confucian temple to the official and orthodox state religion. In this respect it would only seem to substantiate van der Leeuw's interpretation—that is, that there is a potency about the person himself, particularly his body. Again, however, the Confucian tradition seems to provide a distinctive twist, for Confucius as the "patron saint" of scholars is indeed different from the vast realm of patron deities.

The history of the institution of the Confucian temple indicates that there was no special status assigned to the figures housed in the temple in terms of their persons—that is, their bodies and any potential for power associated with their bodies.[48] They were not venerated with the hope of sharing in their power, to put it in van der Leeuw's terms. Rather, it was the memory of the specific teaching associated with the individual that formed the focal point of veneration. This is further illustrated by the changing lineup of figures housed in the temple. Confucians were officially recognized by being placed in the temple, and this seems in large part to be a product of a commonality between their particular teachings and Confucian orthodoxy, in itself a fluid sea of ideas and practices. The Confucian temple clearly illustrates the Confucian tradition's ability to avoid either euhemerization of its heroes or apotheosization of its founders or later exemplars. The paradigms of the tradition remain free of deification. Remaining free of deification, the Confucian sages remain free of the dispensation of power. There is little or no indication of miraculous or supernatural activity. To a large extent this may be accounted for on the basis that there is no structure of belief to assign ontological status to the source of such power—that is, the continued existence of the sage in a state appropriate to appropriation of power.

Third, in much the same way W. Brede Kristensen's sense of the saint seems also of little relevance to the Confucian mode of expression for the sage. For Kristensen, "the saint knows that struggle between man and god, between finite and infinite, but from the very beginning he has denied and surrendered his humanity."[49] In this passage Kristensen is particularly concerned to isolate the saint from the Greek tragic hero. Thus the matrix of defining characteristics is centered in a specifically Western context of devotion and surrender to God as the salient image of the saint. Such an image has little relevance for the Confucian sage; however, its relative lack of usefulness to the Confucian tradition may be more its predilection to a theistic presupposition rather than the attitudinal component defined in terms of surrender itself. From Kristensen's point of view what makes a saint a saint is his or her utter self-surrender to God. If we substitute for God the category the Principle of Heaven, there is nothing that necessarily precludes the Confucian case, for the Confucian sage is precisely that individual who has brought the ways of Heaven or the Principle of Heaven into his life. That is, he has established his own self-identity in terms of what he takes to be the Absolute. This in turn involves "surrender," if by surrender is meant orienting oneself entirely by that which is regarded as the Absolute.

Where Kristensen's characterization suggests limitations for the Confucian tradition is in the degree to which one's humanity is viewed as diametrically opposed to the attitude of surrender to God. As portrayed by Kristensen, God is removed from man, and man seems necessitated to surrender his humanity in the act of surrender to God. From the Confucian point of view it would seem to be precisely man's humanity that defines man's relation to the Absolute. The Confucian tradition sees man's nature as an expression of the Absolute, tending toward a monistic rather than theistic worldview. It is thus the sphere of human relations and "ordinariness" that become the basis for the Confucian religious life. At least on the surface, Kristensen's model of the saint seems only with some difficulty viewed outside of a strictly theistic structure, and little is suggested in terms of the ramifications of such a model of sainthood for its appearance in a radically different religious model.

Were we to limit ourselves to these particular characterizations of the saint there would be little relation with the Confucian sage. However, other characterizations and descriptions of the saint are not entirely irrelevant to the sage. First, although the technical definition of saint in a strictly Christian context has little or no meaning whatsoever in the Confucian tradition, the derivation of the word "saint" in terms of the Latin *sanctus,* Greek *hagios,* and Hebrew *qadosh* suggests that which is set apart and thus that which is thereby sacred.[50] In this broadest context the saint is simply the holy person of a given tradition. Even the Arabic for saint, *walī,* meaning a friend of God, if viewed in terms of the relationship established between finite and infinite is suggestive of the role played by the Confucian sage. The sage in this sense is the holy person of the Confucian tradition. Referring again to the basic philological structure of the word "sage," the sage is the one who penetrates the ways of Heaven and discloses them to man. The saint as the holy person of a given tradition, and the Confucian sage would thus appear to share a common nomenclature. This is, of course, assuming that the Confucian tradition does indeed have a religious dimension that is central to its core and thus may not be described in either secular humanistic terms or the language of ethics. However, the derivation of the term "saint" in terms of sacred and thus holy person only points to the broader category of holy person in general. As the epitome of the religious dimension of the Confucian tradition, the sage is the full embodiment of sacredness and thus the holy person of the Confucian tradition. Is the commonality at this level significant? The question that remains, of course, is whether by establishing the category "holy person" we have sufficiently weakened the category "saint" to no longer articulate its distinctiveness. If the term "saint" is to be employed and not simply "holy person," something more must be intended. It is one thing to refer to the Confucian sage as a holy person, but it seems quite another to call the Confucian sage a saint.

Second, let us return to a further point made by van der Leeuw concerning the character of the saint. While van der Leeuw's sense of the potency of power associated with the saint, particularly his corpse, seems of little relevance to the Confucian sage, van der Leeuw also emphasizes the activity of the saint on behalf of man.[51] In this sense the saint is he who takes on the trials and tribulations of mankind, working for the betterment of man and the elimination of suffering. This is a characteristic of the saint that would not apply to all religious functionaries who might otherwise be spoken of as holy persons. When we observe the role of the Confucian sage we find the sage's commitment to benefiting man one of the primary characteristics emphasized. The sage is the epitome of such concern for the feeling of man. We have seen this in terms of the images associated with the sage kings of antiquity for Confucius and Mencius. In turn such concern finds its quintessential reiteration in the Neo-Confucian tradition in the *Western Inscription* of Chang Tsai in which the sage is depicted as a brother to all living things. Fan Chung-yen (989–1052), a Sung dynasty Neo-Confucian, summed up the characteristic by saying that the ideal of the Confucian was to be the first to take on the troubles of the world and the last in enjoying its pleasures.

What is particularly helpful about van der Leeuw's characterization is the degree to which a central feature of the Confucian sage can be focused upon. In this sense it is possible not only to see the sage as the epitome of the tradition's religious depth and thus a holy person but in addition to suggest that the sage shares a critical feature with the category "saint" as that category itself would be differentiated from the larger context of "holy person."

Third, the work of Joachim Wach permits us to explore further the common ground of sage and saint. For Wach the distinguishing characteristic of the saint is his or her personal character.[52] The influence of the saint, according to Wach, is a quiet and gentle one. This is to distinguish the saint from the prophet whose role by definition is one of activity. The influence of the saint is by the exemplary character of his life, his imitable facet, and thus his role as a model to the community.

For Wach the saint's prestige and influence are not measured by achievements, by professional associations, or by excelling in intellectual or even practical talents.[53] It simply returns time and time again to the quiet and exemplary life. The driving force in this life is the basic religious experience that has formed the foundation upon which the life is built.

In his classic exploration of the psychological dimension of religious experience, William James has suggested similar characteristics of the saint.[54] For James the saint is one who feels himself part of a "wider life," has a sense of "friendly continuity of the Ideal Power with his own life," has an immense elation and sense of freedom as well as the "shifting of the emotional center towards loving."[55] The practical consequences for James in terms of the life lived are asceticism, strength of the soul, purity, and charity. Obviously such categories are very broad. To avoid a broader context of "holy person" such characteristics can be placed within the framework of Wach's sense of the personal character of the saint. James has said of saints: "Yet they are impregnators of the world, vivifiers and animators of potentialities of goodness which but for them would lie forever dormant."[56]

It is within this context of the exemplary life that the Confucian model of the sage seems most relevant. The Confucian sage lives his life within the framework of the ways of Heaven or the Principle of Heaven. The sage is he who is aware of the relation of his own nature with that of Heaven, and it is the concreteness of the life lived that serves as the exemplification of the sage's understanding and religious depth. Such a figure serves as an exemplar and his life itself is the measure of his understanding. The sage is both imitable and inimitable; imitable as a model and inimitable in terms of the depth of his understanding. The biographies of the sages and worthies found in the *Chin-ssu lu* serve to illustrate the importance placed upon the imitability of the sage yet recognizing always an inimitable dimension. Such biographies point to the features Wach and James discuss. The sage is quiet, at ease, serene, compassionate, and committed to serving fellow beings. The degree to which such features stand out as prominent features of the saint is the degree to which the sage and the saint share common ground.

Fourth, a corollary to the exemplary life may at first appear to differentiate sage and saint. The saint seems to be known primarily for his humbleness, his gentleness, and his self-effacement, according to Wach.[57] He is not known for intellectual prowess. The term "sage," however, as we have already seen, seems to be easily extendable to intellectual ability from its basic meaning "to penetrate." To penetrate things is to understand them, and it was the sage who was regarded as the quintessential expression of such understanding. For the Classical Confucian the sages were primarily if not exclusively the sage kings of antiquity. That they are sage kings rather than simply sages is of importance. In this capacity as ruler the sheer exercise of the position involves more than humbleness, gentleness, and self-effacement. The definition of sage in the *Shuo-wen* is appropriate. The sage king is he who can rule because he possesses the penetration or understanding of the ways of Heaven. It is important to remember, however, that while the sage has a high degree of intelligence, the primary motivation and intentionality of the sage is to bring the ways of man into accord with the ways of Heaven. Cleverness or adroitness are not ends in themselves but only by-products of the penetration or understanding the sage has acquired. In this sense the sage even of the Classical Confucian may be a humble and gentle person, not in terms of the role and function he occupies but in terms of his attitude within such a role. The obvious difference between sage and saint is the difference in external role and thus capacity for manifesting humbleness, gentleness, and self-effacement. As an internal attitude the difference is potentially far less obvious.

The situation with the Neo-Confucians' view of the sage suggests a far stronger sense of commonality between sage and saint. For the Classical Confucian the sage remained a sage king; both time referent and role model were established. For the Neo-Confucian, conversely, the goal of sagehood was seen as something realizable within one's lifetime. This did not mean that one would become a sage king. Rather, it suggested simply the perfection of one's nature. Such perfection of the nature involves an introspective process of penetrating the roots of the nature, and, as we have seen, this may be accomplished in either internal or external modes. With the traditional Confucian focus upon learning and thus the role of learning in the goal of sagehood, those who pursued the path developed intellectual ability. Again, however, such intellectual ability is not an end in itself. The goal remains sagehood, and sagehood was viewed as a point of understanding in which the relation of one's nature and the nature of the macrocosm would be seen in unity. Often such a point of understanding was spoken of in experiential terms, and for those who had such experiences it was spoken of in a humble and self-effacing manner. The experience itself was often the occasion for the direct realization of the ubiquitous ways of Heaven or the Principle of Heaven. Although spoken of in terms of penetration and understanding, the personalities revealed in the *Chin-ssu lu* display humbleness, gentleness, and self-effacement. Thus what appears to differentiate sage and saint is simply one further indication of the potential commonality to be found.

Fifth, to focus only upon the gentleness and humbleness of the saint may present only one dimension of a complex figure. Is it not the case that saints are also frequently associated with processes of change and transformation?[58] A saint may act as a key component if not the focus of a revitalization movement and as such is a symbol of change as well as involvement and activity. This does not make the saint a prophet, as Wach might suggest, but simply broadens the role played by the saint. Saint and prophet remain separate, not in terms of quietude and activity but rather in terms of what one might call the style of pronouncement of knowledge. Thus to describe fully the phenomenon of sainthood, it seems necessary to point to salient characteristics that include an active capacity as well as the contemplative and quiet modes, bearing in mind that there is nothing necessarily inimical about the relationship between humbleness and activity.

The capacities of quietude and activity can serve as useful referents to the Confucian tradition as well. The Confucian sage can be portrayed in both active and passive contexts. Central always to the makeup of the sage is his ability to correct the ills of the world. This is reflected in the sage kings of antiquity who through their rule were able to bring harmony into the world. It is also reflected in the Neo-Confucian tradition in the unceasing notion that it was the responsibility of the Confucian to serve in government to attempt to correct or rectify the ways of man. Confucius himself is a good example in his seemingly unceasing attempt to reinstate the ways of the ancients that the world might thereby be rectified.

There is perhaps a certain amount of tension between modes expressive of quietude and those focused upon activity. The dominant image of the sage in Classical Confucianism is primarily activity. He is first and foremost a sage king. For the Neo-Confucian, conversely, dimensions of quietude as well as activity are explored. In fact the difference between the two major schools of Neo-Confucianism, the School of Principle and the School of Mind, may revolve in large part around the dominance of either quietude or activity within the forms of learning and praxis. In both schools the focus remained the rectification of the ways of the world. As the Great Learning suggested, however, the rectification of the world begins with self-rectification. In the eight stages of learning reiterated in the Great Learning, one through five concerns various aspects of inward self-cultivation. To a certain degree at least the School of Principle focused upon a methodical procedure that gradually accumulated knowledge and often included contemplative means. The School of Mind, however, tended to focus upon the immediate realization of the substance of the mind and ironically tended to avoid contemplative forms of praxis. For the School of Mind the focus of the praxis was within the context of activity itself, *kung-fu*. Thus the image of the Confucian sage has a broader dimension than the focus upon quietude alone would suggest. In the larger context the ideal of sagehood has for the Neo-Confucian images of activity as well as contemplation. In this respect sage and saint continue to complement each other.

What we have thus far seen would suggest a certain commonality of characteristics between sage and saint clustered primarily around the sense of exemplariness or imitability of the character of each. The saint seems, however, to hold together a delicate balance of exemplariness or imitability and "otherness" or inimitability. If the saint is he whose distinctive status is related to this balance of imitability and inimitability, can any common ground be maintained with the Confucian sage? After all, the Confucian tradition, as we have seen in a variety of ways in the present chapter, has consciously minimized the expression of "otherness" through miraculous or supernatural means. This, however, does not necessarily preclude the category "otherness" from appropriate application to what at first appears to be other than otherness—that is, ordinariness. In other words, is not the notion of otherness itself perhaps applied with an already established theological framework suggesting a transcendent rather than immanent referent? The Confucian sage is indeed an exemplar of the perfection of man's nature of goodness, and such an accomplishment is held in high esteem by the broader cultural context. The records of the sage's deeds suggest an ordinariness in their focus, yet the ordinariness itself has the character of the religious when seen within the soteriological context of the tradition, what Fingarette has referred to as the secular as sacred.[59] To develop man's moral nature from the Confucian perspective is not only to realize man's full potential but to establish the essential relation between man and the ways of Heaven or the Principle of Heaven from the Neo-Confucian perspective. As such, precisely those activities centered upon the development of man's nature have for the Confucian the character of otherness, if by "otherness" is meant not exclusively transcendence but simply establishment of the relationship between the finite and the infinite whether in transcendent or immanent modes. Otherness as a recognition of the imminence of the Absolute articulates the structure of the Confucian tradition. As such the sage represents a capacity for otherness. On the one hand, then, the sage is characterized by an imitability, yet his nature seems to possess an otherness. Anyone can become a sage; the path of learning and self-cultivation is long and arduous but remains a realizable goal. And yet the status of sage is distinctive, perhaps even uniquc, and while the path is imitable the goal itself retains a dimension of inimitability. The sage and the saint remain within a common mode of expression: the foci for both is found in the balance of imitability and inimitability.

Sage and saint have, then, the capacity to broaden each other. The focus of the Confucian sage upon the perfection of man's nature and the sage's fundamental humanism lends new breadth to the term "saint." We have the possibility of the saint's religious dimension revealed in his own humanity. At the same time, the possible application of the term "saint" to the Confucian context reaffirms the still often overlooked religious dimension of the Confucian tradition; and although any wholesale adoption of the term "saint" for sage should certainly be qualified, the sheer possibility of commonality at least partially adumbrates the religious potential found within the Confucian sage.

NOTES

1. James Hastings, *Encyclopaedia of Religion and Ethics* (New York: Charles Scribner's Sons, 1921), 11: 51.

2. Those who have examined the sage as a religious figure include Wm. Theodore deBary, "Neo-Confucian Cultivation and the Seventeenth-Century 'Enlightenment,'" in *The Unfolding of Neo-Confucianism,* ed. W. T. deBary (New York: Columbia University Press, 1975), pp. 141–216; R. L. Taylor, *The Cultivation of Sagehood as a Religious Goal in Neo-Confucianism: A Study of Selected Writings of Kao P'an-lung (1562–1626)* (Missoula, Mont.: American Academy of Religion/Scholar's Press, 1978) and R. L. Taylor, "Neo-Confucianism, Sagehood and the Religious Dimension," *Journal of Chinese Philosophy* 2, no. 4 (September 1975): 389–415.

3. *Shuo-wen chieh-tzu ku-lin* (Taipei: Ting-chih shu-chü, 1977), 9: 1086.

4. Edward H. Schafer, *Combined Supplements to Mathews* (Berkeley: Department of Oriental Languages, 1978), p. 36.

5. Bernhard Karlgren, *Grammata Serica Recensa* (Stockholm: Museum of Far Eastern Antiquities, 1964), p. 222.

6. Ibid.

7. Contained in the *Hsi-ch'uan t'ung-lun* commentary, *Shuo-wen chieh-tzu ku-lin,* 9: 1086.

8. As the passage explores the point, Mencius argues that nothing separates the ordinary man from the sages. If he wants to be a sage he should simply act as one.

9. A thorough discussion of the relevance of the goal of sagehood to the Neo-Confucian may be found in both deBary, "Neo-Confucian Cultivation," and Taylor, *Cultivation of Sagehood.*

10. See deBary, "Neo-Confucian Cultivation," pp. 153–160 for a discussion of the *Chin-ssu lu.* For a translation of the *Chin-ssu lu,* see W. T. Chan, trans., *Reflections on Things at Hand: The Neo-Confucian Anthology Compiled by Chu Hsi and Lü Tsu-ch'ien* (New York: Columbia University Press, 1967).

11. Chan, *Reflections,* p. 35.

12. Ibid., p. 307.

13. Ibid., p. 308.

14. Taylor, *Cultivation of Sagehood,* p. 121.

15. Frederick Streng, *Understanding Religious Life* (Belmont, Calif.: Wadsworth Publishing Company, 1976), pp. 99–110.

16. *Ta-hsüeh,* or Great Learning, was originally a chapter in the ritual classic *Li-chi,* Book of Rites. It became an important separate work and was elevated to the Confucian canon by Chu Hsi (1130–1200) when he included it as one of the four major Confucian writings in the collection called the Four Books, which is composed of the Great Learning, the Chung-yung, or Doctrine of the Mean, the Confucian Analects, and the Mencius.

17. The Five Classics include the *Shu-ching,* or Book of History; the *Shih-ching,* or Book of Poetry; the *I-ching,* or Book of Changes; the *Ch'un-ch'iu,* or Spring and Autumn; as well as several works dealing with rites spoken of as the *Li-ching,* or Books of Rites.

18. The word for "classic" is an interesting one. It originally means "warp" and presumably from the sense of warp as the continuity of a piece of woven material, the term comes to mean "classic"—that is, that which provides continuity to a cultural matrix. In terms of the various glosses of the word see Karlgren, *Grammata Serica Recensa,* p. 219.

19. See deBary, "Neo-Confucian Cultivation," p. 166, for an examination of the dimensions of the term *ching.*

20. W. T. deBary, Wing-tsit Chan, and Burton Watson, *Sources of Chinese Tradition* (New York: Columbia University Press, 1960), pp. 559–560.

21. For Wang Yang-ming's commentary on the Great Learning, see W. T. Chan, trans., *Instructions for Practical Living and Other Neo-Confucian Writings by Wang Yang-ming* (New York: Columbia University Press), pp. 271–280.

22. The specific issue of *ko-wu* is discussed in Tu Wei-ming, *Neo-Confucian Thought in Action: Wang Yang-ming's Youth (1472–1509)* (Berkeley, Los Angeles, London: University of California Press, 1976), pp. 163–167.

23. Chan, *Instructions,* p. 275.

24. Ibid., p. 278.

25. Ibid., p. 279.
26. DeBary et al., *Sources of Chinese Tradition,* p. 560.
27. Ibid., p. 515.
28. DeBary, "Neo-Confucian Cultivation," pp. 184–188.
29. DeBary et al., *Sources of Chinese Tradition,* p. 559.
30. Chan, *Reflections,* pp. 74–75.
31. Ibid., p. 85.
32. One finds such expressions in the T'ai-chou School, perhaps the most radical of the followers of Wang Yang-ming. See, for example, W. T. deBary, "Individualism and Humanitarianism in Late Ming Thought," in *Self and Society in Ming Thought,* ed. W. T. deBary (New York: Columbia University Press, 1970), pp. 171–188.
33. My own research with Neo-Confucian religious autobiography has indicated that in the assessment process of the autobiography the individual concludes that the goal of sagehood is still far in the distance. Such autobiographies tend to end with some statement indicating not what has been accomplished but the distance that still separates the individual from his goal. See, for example R. L. Taylor, "The Centered Self: Religious Autobiography in the Neo-Confucian Tradition," *History of Religions* 17, nos. 3 & 4 (February & May 1978): 266–283; idem, "Acquiring a Point of View: Confucian Dimensions of Self-Reflection," *Monumenta Serica* 34 (1982): 145–170; "Journey into Self: The Autobiographical Reflections of Hu Chih," *History of Religions* 21, no. 4 (May 1982): 321–338.
34. DeBary, "Neo-Confucian Cultivation," pp. 156–157.
35. DeBary et al., *Sources of Chinese Tradition,* pp. 524–525.
36. Ibid., p. 524.
37. Ibid.
38. Chan, *Reflections,* p. 299.
39. Ibid., pp. 305–306.
40. Ibid., p. 302.
41. Ibid., p. 303.
42. *The Compact Edition of the Oxford English Dictionary* (New York: Oxford University Press, 1971), 2: 2623.
43. G. van der Leeuw, *Religion in Essence and Manifestation* (New York: Harper & Row, 1963), pp. 236–237.
44. Ibid., p. 238.
45. W. T. deBary, "Some Common Tendencies in Neo-Confucianism," in *Confucianism in Action,* ed. David Nivison and Arthur Wright (Stanford: Stanford University Press, 1959), pp. 42–43.
46. Though an old work, one of the few studies that exists on the Confucian temple is John K. Shryock, *The Origin and Development of the State Cult of Confucius* (New York: Paragon Book Reprint Corp., 1966; American Historical Association, 1932). See also R. L. Taylor, *The Way of Heaven: An Introduction to the Confucian Religious Life* (Leiden: E. J. Brill, 1986).
47. Shryock, *State Cult,* p. 103.
48. Shryock's conclusions are interesting in terms of the difficulty of discussing an institution that almost by its definition is religious, and yet the charac-

teristics assigned to Confucius and his disciple appear to preclude dimensions of religion that focus upon any form of transcendent referent. Shryock, *State Cult,* pp. 223–233.

49. W. Brede Kristensen, *The Meaning of Religion: Lectures in the Phenomenology of Religion* (The Hague: Martinus Nijhoff, 1960), p. 259.

50. Donald Attwater, *The Penguin Dictionary of Saints* (Baltimore, Md.: Penguin Books, 1965), p. 7.

51. Van der Leeuw, *Religion in Essence and Manifestation,* p. 236.

52. Joachim Wach, *Sociology of Religion* (Chicago: University of Chicago Press, 1971), p. 358.

53. Ibid.

54. William James, *The Varieties of Religious Experience, A Study in Human Nature* (New York: Modern Library, 1929), pp. 254–369.

55. Ibid., pp. 266–267.

56. Ibid., p. 350.

57. Wach, *Sociology of Religion,* p. 358.

58. I am indebted to the fellow contributor to this volume Charles White, who in his capacity as the discussant on a panel where this paper was first presented at the American Academy of Religion meeting (San Francisco, December 1981) suggested that traditional models of the saint as he who is only quiet and passive limits the dimensions of sainthood.

59. Herbert Fingarette, *Confucius—The Secular as Sacred* (New York: Harper & Row, 1972).

Afterword: Toward a Comparative Study of Sainthood

In the foreword we suggested that there are two major problems in the notion of sainthood: the student's problem of whether the term applies univocally across the various world religions, and the adherent's problem of how to combine saintly imitability with the distinctive status of the saint. We suggested that the first of these problems might be solved by consideration of the second, if the term "saint" could be taken to mean a figure who gives rise to the tension between religious imitability and otherness. Although the second problem thus proves useful, it is not itself subject to any final solution, either by the scholar or by the adherent; the tension between imitability and otherness remains ever central to religion, and it would be naive to expect its resolution. What we can do, as students of religion, is examine the ways in which this tension is dealt with in different religious and cultural milieus. Having seen the essential features of sanctity in several of the world's major religions, we may now set our findings into a comparative framework. Detailed and definitive comparison is obviously beyond our ambitions, but some possible leads emerge as starting points for further inquiry.

Definition of "sainthood" is easiest when there is institutional authority to determine and apply criteria of sanctity. Christianity, with more strictly established institutions than other religious traditions, has a concept of sainthood that is sharply delineated; Judaism, with its lack of institutional hierarchy, has no official notion of sainthood whatsoever. To be sure, the phenomenon of sainthood may exist in a tradition without official recognition, but when this phenomenon is defined merely through popular cult the definition is not likely to be conceptually tidy.

Even within Christianity popular veneration and official canonization have at times betrayed very different notions of saintly character and function. There has been popular veneration of individuals of dubious morality, in cases in which such individuals have suffered sudden, brutal, and apparently unjust death, and in particular when such individuals could be represented as patron saints for an oppressed populace. On the level of official interpretation, however, it is possible to be much more precise: morally, a saint is an individual of heroic virtue; theologically, he or she is a person blessed with the rewards of heaven; liturgically, he or she is a fitting object of public cult. Only the last of these definitions becomes officially clarified in the ceremonial act of canonization. Yet the individuals thus declared saints qualify as such in all three senses, so that in them one can see concrete examples of saintliness in all its fullness. Officially defined saints, like those with merely popular following, fulfill the roles of patron, protector, intercessor, and wonder-worker, but in addition they serve as examples of a rigorously articulated moral code. Popular and ecclesiastical notions of sainthood are held together within the structure of the saints' cults: the popular tendency may be to seek miracles through the saints' intercession, but churchmen are on hand to remind the supplicants, in sermons as in hagiographic literature, that it is because of their exemplary virtue that the saints hold such marvelous powers.

Not surprisingly, the popular and official elements are less interwoven in a tradition such as Judaism, where sainthood from the outset is more strictly a popular phenomenon without official sanction. This is not to say that the mystical leaders venerated as saints do not attain that status through the exercise of spiritual gifts; clearly they do. The case of Shabbatai Zevi is an extreme instance, though, of the differentiation that can arise between popular and official notions: even his defection from Judaism did not disqualify him from the kind of unofficial veneration accorded Jewish saints. As Robert Cohn makes clear, there are numerous problems with the notion of a Jewish "saint"; the emphasis on holy individuals that is so strong in Christianity is incompatible with the Jewish focus on the people as collectivity, as well as with other central features of Judaism. It is among the leaders—the rabbis—however, that these problems have been most clearly discerned.

In this as in other areas Islam represents an interesting midpoint between Judaism and Christianity. The walīs are not so central to Islam as are the saints of Catholic and Orthodox Christianity, and the popular veneration accorded them outdistances the respect paid them by sophisticated Muslims. Yet their role within Islam is recognized by the leadership and reinforces the official faith and practice of the tradition. Quranic Islam does not admit the possibility of intercessors, yet later development gives that role to the *walīs*. Unlike Judaism, Islam has the specific term *walī*, which has come to mean something similar to the Christian "saint," although it refers more to an active relationship than to specific quality or status.

In his chapter on the Hindu saint Charles White shows that the notion of sainthood is central to Hinduism given that Hinduism believes that all beings participate in the divine nature. Hinduism depicts the deities anthropomorphically, symbolizing the closeness of the divine and human realms. The history of Hinduism abounds with *avatars* and saints, frequently with no clear line of demarcation between them. Indeed, as White observes, "one of the difficulties in coming to a clear understanding of what the concepts of saint and sanctity might mean in India is that there are few persons of any consequence in the intellectual life of the Indian people who were connected with religion who did not also acquire some of the patina of the saintly individual."

In the Theravāda Buddhist tradition the *arahant* represented the ideal of sainthood, whereas for the Mahāyāna Buddhist tradition the Bodhisattva superseded the *arahant*. Thus Donald Lopez has analyzed the Mahāyāna conception of this Bodhisattva, the "one who is heroic in his intention to achieve enlightenment." The Bodhisattva can be considered under the heading of "saint" because he manifests doctrinal purity, heroic virtue, and miraculous intercession—from life to life, if not after death, as is the case with Western saints. The Bodhisattva's path comprises stages that perfect the two aims of attaining his own enlightenment and securing enlightenment for all beings.

Does Confucianism have saints? Rodney Taylor has demonstrated that although Confucianism has minimized the emphasis on the supernatural, the Confucian sage can usefully be compared with and considered to be a saint. The sage represents "the epitome of the religious dimension of the Confucian tradition" and "the full embodiment of sacredness." The sage identifies with and finds his identity in terms of the ways of Heaven, which represents the Confucian equivalent of deity. Thus we find a sainthood without theism similar to that of the Buddhist tradition. Like the arahant and the Bodhisattva, the sage works for the improvement of humanity and the elimination of suffering.

To say that the term "saint" has *some* meaning in each tradition, however, is not to say that it has the *same* meaning in each tradition. Whether there is a common denominator or essence of sainthood that can be found in each religion remains a major question. One might suggest that the model proposed for Christianity applies *mutatis mutandis* to the other traditions as well—that the Sufi becomes recognized as *walī* because of his combination of asceticism and contemplation, that some form of service to humanity is vital in all the various Jewish manifestations of sainthood, and that saints of whatever tradition tend to display miraculous or other supernormal abilities. Whether one wishes to pursue such a hypothesis or not will depend in part on whether one is analyzing the phenomenon of saintly behavior in itself or the explicit formulations of saintly behavior held within the various traditions. If one is engaged in the former enterprise, it may be useful to say and then demonstrate that in all the world's religions saints tend to fuse asceticism, contemplation, and active service in some permutation or other. But if one is interested instead in the explicit conceptions of sainthood maintained by adherents of the various traditions, one is likely to find fundamentally different emphases. Asceticism, contemplation, and active service are categories operative and significant within Christianity; scholarship, righteousness, and devotion may be terms suited to isolation of those factors that determine Jewish saintliness.

In many ways the Theravāda Buddhist notion of the arahant seems to support the idea that there is an essence of sainthood continuous throughout religious culture. As they are depicted in the texts, the arahants resemble the virtuous, wise, holy individuals in all traditions. Yet we must recognize that the virtue and wisdom of the arahant are understood in the context of the Indian and Buddhist tradition. The arahant has perfected the three stages of the Buddhist path: *sīla* or ethics, *samādhi* or meditative concentration, and *paññā* or wisdom. Each of these qualities has a distinctively Buddhist flavor. Although the ethical virtues, for example, can be found in other traditions of sainthood, the Buddhist legends give them a particularly Indian flavor of asceticism. It is stressed also that the arahants had been perfecting these qualities for countless lifetimes in the cycles of rebirth. These outward moral virtues are but preparation in the Buddhist view for the higher inward virtues, such as restraint of the senses and of the mind.

The distinctively Indian character of the qualities of the arahant also appears clearly in the descriptions of the attainment of wisdom through meditation. In this process the arahant is, on the one hand, comparable to Western mystics; yet distinctively Indian in the nature of his path, when the arahant proclaims his conquest of the spiritual hindrances and his liberation from both ignorance and the cycle of rebirth, he seems distinctively Indian and Buddhist. When he is said to possess miraculous powers as a result of this attainment, however, the arahant seems comparable to the saints of other traditions.

The Bodhisattva ideal serves to expand our cross-cultural understanding of sainthood for he is clearly comparable to Western saints in many attributes and yet at the same time represents a distinctively Indian form of sainthood compatible with the Hindu and Theravāda ideals. We see the Indian flavor of this ideal of sanctification, first of all, in its orientation toward wisdom. The Bodhisattva's path of perfection leads to wisdom, salvific wisdom that liberates one from suffering and ignorance. The Indian-ness of the ideal also is evident in the extent to which transmigration serves as a presupposition for the conception of the Bodhisattva's path. The Bodhisattva requires countless lifetimes to attain perfection. During these lifetimes the perfections that the Bodhisattva pursues have to do with improving one's *karma,* the force that governs one's status in the process of transmigration. The perfections of giving (*dāṇa*), virtue (*sīla*), and compassion (*karuṇā*), for example, have their roots in the Indian tradition as actions that generate positive *karma.* Thus whereas the virtues cultivated may be similar to the virtues of the saints in other religions, the rationale behind the Bodhisattva's virtues is distinctively Indian.

It is always tempting for Westerners to try to adjudicate the intro-Buddhist dispute concerning the superiority of the Bodhisattva to the arahant. Instead of doing that, however, we shall simply observe that the similarities between the arahant and the Bodhisattva are greater than the differences. Both pursue essentially the same wisdom and moral perfections. The differences between them have more to do with the evolution of the Buddhist tradition and the elevation of compassion to the status of the supreme virtue. Philosophical developments also played a part in this process, allowing Mahāyāna to posit the possibility and even the desirability of having "as many Buddhas as possible and as quickly as possible" (see Lopez's chapter).

Despite distinctively Confucian qualities of the sage, Taylor demonstrates that the Confucianists attribute many of the typical saintly virtues and accomplishments to the sage. These can be summarized by noting that the sage exemplifies both quietude and activity. The sage is passive, having achieved oneness of mind and penetration of reality. Hence the sage is a wise teacher. But activity also characterizes the sage, who has boundless concern for all beings. Like the saints of all traditions and especially the Indian and Buddhist saints, the sage has become selfless, uniting with all. Thus the sage is humble and commiserates with the problems that people have in life. The sage's compassion indeed sounds very Buddhist when Ch'eng Hao refuses to cut his grass because he feels sympathy for it.

The problem of imitability versus otherness is, as we have seen, a central one in the notion of sainthood. As we suggested in the foreword, saints may be defined as religious individuals who, while serving as models for imitation by virtue of their moral and religious qualities, become elevated to a status that makes them inaccessible for this role. Yet the tension between imitability and otherness manifests itself somewhat differently in each of the traditions.

In Christianity the tension is quite clear. One can find statements in the Christian literature to the effect that all Christians are called to saintliness, and the saints' vitae often encourage emulation of their virtues. Yet there is also a clear sense that the saints have a distinctive vocation to exceptional rigor, and that imitation of their extremes is unwise, if not indeed dangerous. Certain of the favors bestowed on them are de facto inimitable (working miracles, seeing visions); even certain actions that might be imitated (rigorous fasting and mortification, separation from spouse and family, labor on the mission field) are *de jure* unacceptable for those who do not have the appropriate vocation. What one can see in this kind of distinction is the effort of ecclesiastical leaders to reconcile opposing tendencies within Christianity: the rigorist drive toward the fullness of commonly accepted Christian ideals, and the moderate force that recognizes realistically that most Christians cannot adopt extreme forms of behavior without great peril. The saints are accommodated as exemplars of virtue but with qualifications and as intercessors before God's throne because of their own exemption from these qualifications.

Similar problems arise in Judaism, as Cohn's discussion of saintly ideals makes clear, even though nothing quite corresponds to the Christian ecclesiastical supervision of conflicting ideals and their resolution. The basic ideals of scholarship, righteousness, and devotional fervor are accessible to all, yet in various ways the highest representatives of these ideals tend to become inimitable. Although anyone may attain the righteousness of the *tsaddiq,* there is a mystical strain within Judaism whose members see the *tsaddiqim* as supernormal individuals who serve as a "foundation" for the world; the normal righteous person possesses more or less of the moral quality for righteousness, but the *tsaddiq* possesses special cosmic significance. So also, the exceptional fervor of the *hasid* leader is something reserved for the few, and medieval *ḥasidim* conceived themselves as a select minority within Judaism—but in modern times the tension between imitability and otherness shows itself in the continuity between the exceptional devotion of the master and the tempered piety of the disciple. The absence of an institutional hierarchy to coordinate these tendencies makes for disunity: whereas Christian saints are uniformly accepted and diversely interpreted among Catholics or Orthodox, Jewish *ḥasidim* have evoked severe resistance from many fellow Jews.

In Islam the problem takes on different dimensions, mainly because of the disparity between the role of prophet and that of *walī.* As Denny points out, the prophet is altogether inimitable, whereas the *walī* is only partly so. Even the prophet's miracles are on a different level, which the saints cannot attain. According to al-Hujwiri, "The prophets are constantly exempt from the attributes of humanity, while the saints are so only temporarily." Yet the saints too are decidedly inimitable, as is suggested by the notion that they constitute a special and fixed class of 4,000 hidden within humanity and 355 arranged hierarchically in God's court. For Islam as for Judaism (and, in occasional texts, Christianity as well), saints have a special cosmic role even while still on earth—and when they die they, like their counterparts in other religions, have glorious intercessory powers which they exercise on behalf of the devotees who go on pilgrimage to their tombs. The distinction between the imitable and inimitable properties of the *walī* is clear especially from those titles that Denny marshalls forth: the earned titles, which the *walīs* share with other Moslems, and the bestowed or attributed titles, which they alone possess. If even the *walī* is thus in a certain measure inimitable, it is no less true that the prophet is in some degree imitable: devout Moslems follow the *Sunnah* (custom) of Muhammad, even through the symbolic gesture of adopting his names. (One might suggest a parallel, though not identical, phenomenon in Christianity: the inimitability of Christ is greater than that of the saints, yet he remains in important ways imitable, and indeed imitation of Christ has long been central to Christian piety.)

The Hindu saints, numerous as they are, demonstrate the same tension between the characteristics of imitability and otherness. Moral and spiritual perfection, the qualities that the saints personify, represent the goals of the tradition for all people. The saints not only embody the norm but most have preached the path to that norm and pointed the way to liberation. For ordinary people, however, the saint represents a "wholly other" plane of existence that more readily inspires veneration than imitation. Hinduism can account for such differences in the spiritual capabilities and attainments of persons by referring to the concept of transmigration. Given that saints have reached perfection over many lifetimes, householders need not feel that perfection must be attained in this life.

We have seen in chapter 5 that the Theravāda Buddhist tradition has a conception of the arahant that can properly be compared with Western notions of sainthood. The arahant represents the goal of the tradition, the ideal of wisdom and perfection. As such he necessarily stands as both a model for imitation and an object of veneration. This dual nature of the arahant reflects the Theravāda worldview, which can be symbolized by pairs of contrary but linked concepts such as *saṃsāra* and *nibbāna*. In this view the arahant is linked with the ordinary person via a dynamic of transformation: the arahant represents what the ordinary person can become by transforming himself from a state of ignorance to one of truth. As in Hinduism, the notion of transmigration provides the framework that makes both veneration and imitation of the arahant possible. The ordinary people understand that arahants should be venerated as beings that stand on a much higher spiritual plane because of lifetimes of perfection. Although the ordinary person cannot at present imitate the perfected arahant, he can imitate the arahant's path of perfection, which begins precisely with venerating the arahant and gaining merit or good *karma*. Therefore the Theravāda scriptures set out detailed descriptions of the gradual path to perfections that a person can pursue over many lifetimes.

On the question of the Bodhisattva's imitability and otherness, Lopez has observed that the Mahāyāna distinction between celestial Bodhisattvas, who function as gods, and common Bodhisattvas, who are historical persons treading the path, serves to mitigate the tension here. The celestial Bodhisattvas deserve veneration; the common Bodhisattvas, imitation. As Lopez notes, however, the tension is not entirely resolved, for the common Bodhisattvas, because of the magnitude of their undertaking, serve as objects of veneration as well. Here again, as in other Indian religions, transmigration enters in as one way of reconciling the tension between venerating and imitating the "common Bodhisattva." The ordinary person, accepting transmigration, can both imitate the Bodhisattva in his aspiration and venerate him for his fortitude.

The Confucian sage clearly exhibits the tension between imitability and otherness characteristic of sainthood generally. As a person who fulfills the moral virtues and the ways of Heaven, the sage represents the chief exemplar for all people, but it is precisely the depth of his perfection that renders the sage inimitable and a representative of otherness. Otherness, Taylor points out, however, symbolized for the Confucian tradition the immanence of the infinite rather than the transcendence. This notion that the realization of the human potential puts one in harmony with the ways of Heaven also closely resembles the Buddhist conception of the saint as one who fulfills *dharma,* the universal law.

The questions we have dealt with so far—the applicability of the concept of sainthood to various traditions and the problem of imitability versus otherness—are only some of the many points of comparison that might be used to analyze sainthood in world religions. One other question that deserves attention is the historical evolution of sainthood within each tradition. Does sainthood emerge fully developed in the earliest stages of a religion's history, or does it appear gradually and undergo its own transitions? Within Christianity the first step occurred in the second century, with the veneration of martyrs; when monks emerged as "successors to the martyrs" in the fourth century, basic concepts of Christian saintliness were fixed for the remainder of Christian history, and until very recent times the only real changes have been variations on the common theme of monastic sanctity. Different types of individuals have been conceived as vehicles of this tradition (bishops, monks, nuns, friars, laypeople, etc.), but the spirituality they have embodied has been essentially monastic. Perhaps because ideals of Judaism have been less the result of official (and thus conservative) propaganda, there has been more variation among Jewish saints; the features that a first-century rabbi and an eighteenth-century *ḥasid* have in common are less marked than those that link the Desert Fathers with the later saints of Christendom. The lack of an institution to impress a common monastic mold has likewise made for greater diversity within Islam, in which sainthood is construed broadly enough to include female scholars as well as those who die in religious warfare. What Islam has in common with Christianity is a common term that applied at first to a broad variety of ordinary as well as extraordinary devotees (*hagios* = holy person or saint, *walī* = friend or patron) and came to have more specific reference in the early history of the tradition.

By providing a diachronic view of the development of Hinduism, White has shown that the essence of Hindu sainthood developed quite early. The Vedas, Upaniṣhads and early Buddhist texts established the model of the Rsï and the monk or ascetic. This model of sainthood emphasized asceticism, renunciation, paranormal powers, and mystic wisdom or insight. These qualities resemble those attributed to saints in other traditions and cultures; albeit Indian culture gave a distinctive Hindu meaning to these characteristics. Although the norm of the Hindu saint developed early in the tradition, it also continued to evolve with the tradition. White shows that Sankara could be said to represent the beginning of the history of the Hindu saint, since he gave it a new definition in response to the Buddhists. Similarly, later figures, such as the poet saints or the Vaiṣṇava "Sants" of Mararashtra, continued to refine and recast the Hindu concept of human perfection and liberation. Sainthood in Hinduism was not limited to the ancient period or to any single period, for saints abound in Hinduism to the present day, when, as White observes, the saints have been called to meet a new crisis—the challenge of secularism and modernism.

In the Theravāda Buddhist tradition the notion of the arahant changed very little over time because the arahant represented the goal of the path of perfection. This path was delineated early and the outlines of the arahant's character were set. What did change, however, was Theravāda's beliefs concerning the plausibility of arahantship. As the Theravāda tradition developed, the path to arahantship became less and less plausible until the present day, when many orthodox Theravādins believe that no arahants have appeared for centuries.[1]

As to whether the Bodhisattva ideal develops, Lopez indicates that it developed along with the Buddhist tradition. Beginning with the Hināyāna notion of a Bodhisattva as a future, supreme Buddha, the notion underwent a radical transformation in the Mahāyāna sutras, followed by a clarification and expansion in the Mahāyāna Sastras.

In the Confucian development of sagehood we see that the notion of the sage developed from Confucius to the Neo-Confucians. The development was from sagehood as an implausible ideal to a plausible ideal. This represents somewhat the same pattern of development that we have seen in the development of the arahant ideal, although in Theravāda the pendulum once again swung back toward implausibility and it was believed that no arahants could be found. For Confucianism it appears that if the sage was not a "saint" in the early formulations, he became more saintly as the ideal developed and came to be regarded as a plausible goal. The Confucian sage provides important insights into the cross-cultural conception of the saint.

NOTE

1. See G. Bond, "The Development and Elaboration of the Arahant Ideal," *J.A.A.R.* (June 1984).

Contributors

George D. Bond, Associate Professor of the History and Literature of Religions, Northwestern University. He is a specialist in Theravāda Buddhism and is the author of *The Word of the Buddha: The Tipiṭaka and Its Interpretation in Theravāda Buddhism* (1982). His forthcoming book on the Theravāda revival, entitled *The Buddhist Revival in Sri Lanka: Religious Tradition, Reinterpretation and Response,* will be published in 1988.

Richard Keickhefer, Professor of the History and Literature of Religions, Northwestern University. His work is mainly in late medieval Christianity. He has published *European Witch Trials: Their Foundations in Popular and Learned Culture, 1300–1500* (1976), *Repression of Heresy in Medieval Germany* (1979), *Unquiet Souls: Fourteenth-Century Saints and Their Religious Milieu* (1984), and articles on Meister Eckhart and John Tauler.

Robert L. Cohn, Philip and Muriel Berman Scholar in Jewish Studies, Department of Religion, Lafayette College. He has done work on Jewish sacred geography and on biblical narrative. His book is *The Shape of Sacred Space: Four Biblical Studies* (1981). In addition, he is coauthor of *Exploring the Hebrew Bible* (1988).

Frederick M. Denny, Associate Professor of Religious Studies, University of Colorado, Boulder. His books include *An Introduction to Islam* (1985), *Islamic Ritual Practices* (coauthored), and *The Holy Book in Comparative Perspective* (coedited with R. Taylor).

Donald Lopez, Jr., Associate Professor of Religion, Middlebury College. He is the author of *A Study of Svatantrika* and *The Heart Sutra Explained: Indian and Tibetan Commentaries* (1987).

Rodney L. Taylor, Associate Professor of Religious Studies, University of Colorado, Boulder. He is a specialist in Chinese religions and is the author of *The Cultivation of Sagehood as a Religious Goal in Neo-Confucianism (1978), The Way of Heaven: An Introduction to the Confucian Religious Life* (1985), and *The Holy Book in Comparative Perspective* (coedited with F. Denny, 1985).

Charles S. J. White, Professor of Religion and Philosophy, The American University. His published work includes articles on Swami Muktananda, the Sai Baba movement, Sufism in Hindi literature, and Krishna.

Index

Designer: U.C. Press Staff
Compositor: Prestige Typography
Text: 10/13 Sabon
Display: Sabon